An Introduction to Personalism

Juan Manuel Burgos

An Introduction to Personalism

Foreword by John F. Crosby
Translated by R. T. Allen

The Catholic University of America Press
Washington, D.C.

Originally published in Spanish as *Introducción al Personalismo*
(Madrid: Palabra, 2012).

English translation copyright © 2018
The Catholic University of America Press
All rights reserved
The paper used in this publication meets the minimum
requirements of American National Standards for Information
Science—Permanence of Paper for Printed Library Materials,
ANSI Z39.48-1984.
∞

Library of Congress Cataloging-in-Publication Data
Names: Burgos, Juan Manuel, 1961– author.
Title: An introduction to personalism / Juan Manuel Burgos ;
foreword by John F. Crosby ; translated by R. T. Allen.
Other titles: Introduccion al personalismo. English
Description: Washington, D.C. : The Catholic University of
America Press, 2018. | Includes bibliographical references
and index.
Identifiers: LCCN 2017033724 | ISBN 9780813229874
(pbk. : alk. paper)
Subjects: LCSH: Personalism.
Classification: LCC B828.5 .B8513 2018 | DDC 141/.5—dc23
LC record available at https://lccn.loc.gov/2017033724

To my mother,
that the invisible may
become visible.

Contents

Foreword by John F. Crosby   ix
Preface   xiii

CHAPTER ONE **Origins**   1

    Europe in the First Half of the Twentieth Century: Change and Crisis   1

    Positivism and Scientism   5

    The Ascendancy of Individualism and the Collectivisms   8

    Philosophical Influences   17

    Crisis and the Cultural Renewal of Catholicism   25

    The Personalist Awakening   30

CHAPTER TWO **French Personalism**   35

    Jacques Maritain (1882–1973): Thomistic Personalism   39

    Gabriel Marcel (1889–1973): Existentialist Personalism   55

    Emmanuel Mounier (1905–50): Communitarian Personalism   64

    Maurice Nédoncelle (1905–76): Metaphysical Personalism   85

CHAPTER THREE **Other Personalist Currents** 91
    Italian Personalism 91
    Polish Personalism 100
    Personalism in German 119
    Personalism in Spain 142
    British and American Personalism 163

CHAPTER FOUR **Personalist Philosophy: A Proposal** 178
    Is Personalism a Philosophy? 180
    Concepts, Definitions, and Classifications 194
    Structural Features of Personalism 203
    Personalism as a Realist Philosophy 215
    Personalism as a New Philosophy 222

Bibliography 235
Index 255

Foreword

John F. Crosby

I have learned from this admirable book of Juan Manuel Burgos much about myself as a personalist philosopher. I have for years been thinking and writing about the personalist issues that he identifies in his chapter 4. But Burgos helps me to understand better the place of personalism within twentieth-century thought and within the whole of Western philosophy. He helps me to understand better who my intellectual ancestors are and what they were reacting to. He helps me to understand better the respects in which personalist thought has had to break with the legacy of Greek philosophy. And this is not just historical information that I add to my personalist views; it is historical understanding that enables me to bring my personalist views into clearer focus.

But most of all, I have come through his book to understand better how the personalists saw the encounter between Christianity and modernity. We cannot even begin to understand the rise of personalism, Burgos says, if we do not understand the concern that drove some deeply committed Catholic thinkers who wanted to engage modern thought and to be full participants in the philosophical debates of our time. These philosophers did not think that this aspiration for engagement and participation could be fulfilled simply by reviving Thomistic philosophy. While they did not want to abandon Thomism altogether, while they were in fact in many ways nourished by it, and especially by the philosophical realism that it represents, they could not be entirely satisfied with a philosophy that was developed before the "turn to the subject" and that does not approach man primarily as person. They could not help seeing in Thomism a vision of man that Karol Wojtyła called "cosmological" as distinct from "personalist." They felt that as Thomists they would not be able to make the originality of Christian revelation fully felt by their contemporaries. They wanted to speak to the deepest aspirations of the modern world, and did not see how they could accomplish this by trying to restore Christian philosophy as it was in the thirteenth century. They wanted to speak not only to "the theological intellect," but also to "the religious imagination," to use the language of John Henry Newman. But this required them to draw on the resources provided by existentialism and phenomenology. They wanted to give just as creative a response to the philosophical ferment in the contemporary world as St. Thomas had given to the Aristotelian ferment in the thirteenth century; but this required them to become, not just Thomists, but personalists (or personalistic Thomists). For the challenge today is not to receive the Aristotelian philosophy into the Christian intellectual tradition, but to receive the "turn to the subject." Burgos studies those twentieth-century Christian philosophers who saw in the concept of "person," which arises in the Trinitarian and Christological debates of the fourth and fifth centuries, the most fruitful point of contact between the contemporary world and the Christian intellectual tradition. These philosophers regret that the concept of person remained confined for so many centuries to the treatises on the Trinity; they are eager to bring it into our treatises on man.

The title of Burgos's book, though accurate, could be deceptive. It makes us expect a study of one relatively minor movement of thought in contemporary philosophy. And indeed another author might have written a study of personalism that treats it as minor. But Burgos understands well what is really at issue for Christian philosophers. He inserts his study within the struggle of Christian thinkers to find the right philosophical key in which to conduct the encounter between Christianity and the modern world. It is a struggle that must continue into the twenty-first century.

Preface

Personalism is a philosophy that was born in Europe during the first half of the twentieth century. It is characterized by placing the person at the center of its reflection and of its conceptual structure. It arises from multiple sources, but was consolidated in France in the 1930s. Since then it has acquired a notable importance in the whole of Europe, influencing such relevant events as the UN Declaration of Human Rights, the constitutions of European states after the Second World War, and the Second Vatican Council. Nevertheless, during the sixties it lost relevance because of the combined influences of Marxism, structuralism, the crises after Vatican II, and the ideologies linked to the events of May 1968, among other factors.

Today, however, that situation has changed, and personalism is in a period of expansion: publications by and about personalist philosophers are constantly appearing; the number of doctoral theses and conferences is increasing; its application to new areas, such as psychology and personalist bioethics, is being investigated; new institutions which are inspired by personalism or promote it are being founded, and so on. In addition, its growth is not confined to the academic world but also affects the general public. In our epoch, characterized by a crisis of ideologies, the post-modern prohibition of grand narratives, and social media which are as rich in information as they are lacking in reference points, the need for an anthropology[1] that offers an integral, harmonic, and profound vision of the human being becomes ever more urgent. Personalism appears to be able to offer this necessary vision.

The aim of this book is to introduce this philosophy to the reader via a survey of its authors and a description of its fundamental concepts, in the hope that the reader will discover its grandeur, beauty, and potential, and in doing so he can rediscover too the dignity and richness of the human person.

This text is the result of a long reflection of the author, the first fruit of which came in 2000 with the book titled *El personalismo*, which was followed by many others, and in particular a revision of the first one, titled, *Introducción al personalismo* (2012). The current text is largely based on this work of 2012, but has been expanded, updated, and revised thoroughly to fit in as much as possible with English-speaking readers.

The publication would not have been possible without the collaboration of many friends. First of all, I want to mention Richard Allen, who took the initiative in translating the text of 2012 and did the bulk of the work, and second, Fr. Benjamin Wilkinson, who revised the entirety of the translation, improving and perfecting it, thanks to his excellent knowledge of Spanish and, of course, of English. I also wish to express my gratitude for the collaboration of my friend Jim Beauregard, who has also worked on some aspects of the translation. I should also thank many professors for their support, who, with their positive evaluations, have facilitated the English edition of this book, such as Josef Seifert, Randall E. Auxier, Adrian Reimers, Grzegorz Holub, Miguel Acosta, Simon Smith, and Denis Larriveé, in addition to others already

---

1. By "anthropology," throughout this book, the author means "philosophical anthropology," a branch of philosophy familiar in many universities in Continental Europe, which deals with all aspects of human being in a comprehensive manner. It does not refer to the comparative study of human cultures and their development, which is the subject matter of anthropology departments in the United States and Great Britain.—Trans.

mentioned. And, last but not least, I would like to thank the editor of the Catholic University of America Press, John Martino, for his enthusiasm, support, and competence—without him this book would never have been published; and Louise A. Mitchell, for her splendid work of copyediting.

An Introduction to Personalism

CHAPTER ONE | **Origins**

1 | Europe in the First Half of the Twentieth Century: Change and Crisis

Personalism arose in Europe during the first half of the twentieth century as a movement of collective response to a complex combination of social, cultural, and philosophical questions. World War I led to a great crisis of values, perceived by some as a global crisis of Western civilization and connected to a growing de-Christianization. This ideological decline in the optimism surrounding "modern" civilization gave a space for the growth of individualism, but also collectivisms of the right (fascism and Nazism) and of the left (Marxism). Among scholars, the previously dominant idealistical philosophy (Immanuel Kant, Georg Hegel) was giving way in multiple directions: towards existentialism of the self by readers of Søren Kierkegaard; towards an increasingly arrogant scientistic materialism; which denied the truth-value of any non-experimental affirmation; and towards a greater focus on specific "themes," including woman, interpersonal relations, and community, that had to be elucidated critically. Among Catholics of this era, there was ineluctable need to face modernity in a critical way, following the "modernist crisis" centered in France in the first two decades of the century, even as it was recognized that "modern" ideology was in retreat. The Wall Street crash of 1929 generated a further economic and ideological crisis, and the political instability caused by the debility of the parliamentary democracies (especially Weimar Germany) did not seem able to stem the rising tide of collectivist sentiment.

This whole complex combination of problems merged slowly and in very diverse ways into what has been called "the personalist awakening." Personalists became aware that, to face these questions and, above all, to surpass them, it was necessary to have recourse to the concept of person and to construct, from there, a new philosophical project, a new anthropology.

This reconstruction followed many varied paths, frequently interrelated and, at times, relatively independent: from the proposals of the personalist ethics of Max Scheler, through the Thomistic personalism of Jacques Maritain, the communitarian personalism of Emmanuel Mounier, the philosophies of dialogue of Jewish thinkers such as Martin Buber and Emmanuel Levinas, and the personalist existentialism of Gabriel Marcel. They all recognized similar problems and aimed to resolve them within a common philosophical matrix, personalism. These philosophical proposals will be set forth in the following chapters. In preparation for this, the complex framework which made space for all these philosophies will be clarified, because it will provide some magnificent and indispensable hermeneutic keys for understanding them in depth.

Probably the most adequate and definitive word to express the general sentiment that originated the personalist awakening is "crisis": the existence of a very profound social, moral, and intellectual crisis which demanded an adequate response. This crisis became especially acute between the First and Second World Wars. Just as Europe was coming out of one terrible catastrophe, it appeared to be inevitably heading toward another one of even greater dimensions.

This crisis was also perceived by personalist thinkers who intended to respond from different angles, both theoretical and practical. Scheler had already anticipated it with clarity in a series of lectures given in 1927 (later published as *Man's Place in the Cosmos*), in which he affirmed that modern man had lost his orientation, becoming an enigma for himself. Still earlier, Kierkegaard had intuited that the collectivist systems of the Hegelian variety could lead only to the crushing of man, and therefore they must be left behind. By the 1930s, the conviction became acute that a solution to the cultural and ideological challenges from collectivism and individualism was ever more urgent; a crisis of civilization, not a simply intellectual problem.

Catholics in particular conceived this crisis as a change of epoch in which a civilization that for two thousand years had been based on Christianity, fed by its sap, and inspired, more or less explicitly, by its ethics and dogmas, had decided to expressly cease being Christian and to follow other paths—other paths which seemed to lead to a precipice. Pierre van der Meer, a Dutch intellectual close to Maritain and the French novelist Léon Bloy, stated during this period of time:

> Enormous events have taken place in these last twenty-five years (1914–39). The face of the world has been totally changed. All the values in force before 1914 have been displaced. The tablets of the old law of Christian civilization have been broken, and our civilization has lost its unity, and is not even Christian any more, however much, old and tired, we nurtured the illusion of living eternally under its shadow. We believed that at least it would endure as long as us. We didn't suspect the possibility of a mutation.[1]

The young, French scholar Mounier shared the same perception, but his perspective was more comprehensive. The problem was not to be found only in Catholicism: it was more complex, and had to be faced globally and radically with a spiritual revolution, which was the only way of dealing thoroughly with it. For this reason and to this end, he founded the review *Esprit*, as his wife, Paulette Leclercq, explained.

> There appeared, before his eyes, an extreme human emergency. The civilizational crisis had wreaked havoc on all sides and dangerously shook existing structures. In the entire world, the economic crisis on Wall Street

---

1. Pieter van der Meer, *Hombres y Dios*, trans. W. de Ulupe (Buenos Aires: Desclée de Brower, 1949), 9–10.

in 1929, the social crisis with millions unemployed everywhere. In France, a political and cultural crisis, since, beneath the apparent economic and capitalist security, the climate of traditional and stereotyped humanism would be swiftly swept away by the Popular Front and by sinister rustlings in its colonial empire. On our borders, in Germany and also in Italy the individual is threatened at every turn by the collectivist pressure of the Nazi and Fascist regimes. Not to mention the regime in Russia, of which little was known in 1932, but enough to understand that it would crush the dignity of the human person. On all sides man's profound liberty of expression and action was threatened.[2]

Nevertheless, not all personalist thinkers judged the crisis to be so extreme. In this respect, Mounier was special—perhaps because of his youth—and he probably overestimated its importance and gravity. Even if Western society had grave internal and external problems, it still had sufficient resources for subsistence, as history seems reliably to have demonstrated. In any case, both the real crisis and the perception—more or less accurate—of that crisis is an essential frame of reference for understanding the personalist movement. There was consciousness, beyond all doubt, of a very serious problem that could not be left without an answer. And this pressing stimulus was a decisive motive as much in the creation of personalist thinking as in its diffusion and consolidation.

The complexity of the crisis and, more generally, of the European situation in the first half of the twentieth century, does not allow us to review it in detail. It is necessary to limit the scope of the analysis. Therefore, we shall examine only some of the more relevant factors which shaped that *pathos* and *ethos* from which personalism arose: the atmosphere of scientism which influenced, by way of reaction, many personalists, driving them to proclaim the primacy of the spiritual; the dominance of the opposing movements of individualism and collectiv-

---

2. Paulette Mounier, "Cristiani e non credenti nell'ambito del personalismo," in *Mounier trent'anni dopo. Atti del Convergo di studio dell'università cattolica* (Milan: Vita e Pensiero, 1981), 17.

ism, which were key in the determination of the concept of person both because personalists reacted to these two movements but also assumed of some of their theses; some philosophical presuppositions and problems (Kant, Kierkegaard, etc.) which foreshadowed personalism and, finally, the specific perception of this problem in Catholicism, since the vast majority of personalists were Catholics who lived their convictions profoundly.[3]

2 | Positivism and Scientism

One of the most characteristic features of the beginning of the twentieth century in Europe was the positivistic and scientistic mentality, driven by the tremendous success attained by experimental science and by a parallel rise of atheism and agnosticism. The numerous achievements of science, in fields such as physics, medicine, and biology, led to an increasing valuation of the experimental method and of scientific knowledge which, certainly, was nothing new. This trend had already begun much earlier, to the point that the philosophies of René Descartes or Kant could not be understood without taking it into account; but the exponential progress of scientific knowledge led not only to an exaggeration of the importance of its method, but also to its self-declaration as the *only* method of valid knowledge.[4] To some extent, it was an understandable attitude. In face of the obscurities, imprecision, and contradictions of the human sciences such as sociology and psychology and the esoteric reasoning of the idealism then dominant in philosophy, the scientific method stood out as the standard of knowledge and reason. The application of this method brought secure, certain, verifiable,

---

3. In fact many of them were converts, including Maritain, Marcel, Dietrich Von Hildebrand, and Edith Stein.

4. Edmund Husserl denounced this in *The Crisis of the European Sciences* (1936), but he did not manage to avoid falling under its spell, since one way of understanding the phenomenology that he pioneered is as the elaboration of a method competing with experimental science *on its own territory*, that is, as an attempt to reach an absolute semantic univocity of concepts, which is completely impossible.

and progressive knowledge. It was not necessary to return again and again to the same ideas, to discuss what had already been established, to question what had already been surpassed. Knowledge advanced, progressed, and produced, as a result of these efforts, marvelous inventions (the telephone, electric lighting, automobiles, airplanes, and so on) which, if necessary, confirmed in practice the validity of its approach. The inevitable counterpart was the progressive discrediting of the human sciences, since only a science which could submit to the experimental method could be considered truly science; otherwise its epistemological status was automatically limited to that of the Aristotelian *doxa*, mere opinion or popular belief.

The distance from positivistic scientism to exacerbated materialism was a very small step, a step which was taken by many intellectuals, especially when the nineteenth century appeared to have demonstrated that many religious beliefs either "explained" only what man, *up until that moment*, had not managed to explain by science, or simply were false: projections of the human spirit which denied itself in order to construct realities which alienated it.[5]

Charles Darwin's evolutionism—along with many other influences, such as the works of Freud, Nietzsche, Auguste Comte, and John Watson—had a particular impact because they appeared to scientifically demonstrate that man was no more than mere evolved matter, certainly very complex and sophisticated, perhaps even indescribable and incomprehensible, but in the end, matter.[6] So, on the one hand, the scientific method seemed to be the only truly valid method in the ambit of knowledge—in the area of hard epistemology. On the other hand, science progressively unseated religion, seeming to show that the pillars of religion

---

5. "What is positive in the conception of the divine being can only be human, the conception of man, as an object of consciousness, can only be negative. To enrich God, man must become poor; that God may be all, man must be nothing." Ludwig Feuerbach, *The Essence of Christianity*, trans. George Eliot (1841; Amherst, NY: Prometheus, 1989).

6. As is known, in his first and most famous work, *The Origin of Species* (1859), Darwin limited his theory to the animal kingdom, but later he applied it also to man in *The Descent of Man, and Selection in Relation to Sex* (1871).

either were false (for example, the theory of fixed species) or could be explained scientifically (man had not been created by God, but rather was the result of evolution from apes). The conclusions which necessarily followed were: (1) man was only a complex combination of cells; (2) the positive sciences which studied experimental data were the only valid sciences, and the rest of the disciplines, including all philosophy except philosophy of science, was either a delightful entertainment or a refuge for weak or old-fashioned souls, incapable of facing reality.

This framework explains numerous intellectual projects of the era marked by the predominance of this mentality: the rise of logic among the positivists of the Vienna Circle, the search for a universal language of one single semantic, similar to mathematics, the turn to behaviorism in psychology thanks to John Watson, etc. Conversely, we see the decline of the human sciences (accompanied by frequent, and rather pathetic, attempts to convert them into experimental sciences), of philosophical anthropology, and, even more so, of metaphysics.

Raïssa Maritain was perhaps one of those who best described this atmosphere. As is known, she (a Russian Jew) and Jacques Maritain, her future husband (at the time an agnostic Protestant), met at the Sorbonne at the beginning of the twentieth century and shared from the start the intellectual and spiritual need to find a global explanation of reality. "Our perfect interpenetration," wrote Raïssa,

> our happiness, all the sweetness of the world, all the art of humanity could not lead us to admit without reason—in whatever sense in which this expression could be understood—the misery, unhappiness, the malice of man. Either it was possible to justify the world, and in that case it could not exist without a knowledge that led to the truth, or life was not worth another instant of attention.[7]

They both hoped to find a response to these questions at university, but what they actually found was a closed positivistic and scien-

---

7. Raïssa Maritain, *Les grandes amitiés* (Paris: Desclée de Brower, 1949), 87.

tistic environment in which those questions had no place, an environment which led, inescapably, to relativism and intellectual skepticism. "Young people who finished their philosophical studies were learned and intelligent, but lacking confidence in ideas except as instruments of rhetoric, and completely disarmed for spiritual struggles and for the conflicts of the world."[8]

The scientist mentality continues to have great weight in European culture, though moderated by revisions regarding the epistemological grounding of science as formulated by Thomas Kuhn and Karl Popper, among others.[9] But, at that moment, it constituted a detonator which led a group of intellectuals, including the personalists, to recognize the need to articulate a consistent response, since the predominance of scientist thought not only hampered the progress of the human sciences, but also threw into a squalid ghetto anyone who attempted to think in terms of transcendence, not merely in the religious sense, but even in the simply meta-material sense. One of the keys to understanding the origin and meaning of transcendence is found in the slogan "primacy of the spiritual," coined by Maritain but used profusely by Mounier and others.[10]

3 | The Ascendancy of Individualism and the Collectivisms

Other important factors that converged in the formation of personalism were individualism and collectivism, which, as Paul Landsberg affirmed in the 1930s, are the "two forms of thinking and feeling which dominate spirits and form public and private opinions in the Western

---

8. Ibid., 79–80. Gilson and Mounier suffered very similar experiences at the Sorbonne.

9. See Thomas Kuhn, *The Structure of Scientific Revolutions*, 3rd ed. (Chicago: University of Chicago Press, 1996).

10. See Jacques Maritain, *Primauté du spirituel* (Paris: Plon, 1927).

world today."[11] They were profoundly antithetic currents, but they met at the extremes, forming a powerful pincer that made the search for an alternative inevitable.

3.1 | Individualism

Individualism is a difficult attitude or mentality to define, since its ideological characteristics are diffuse. It is not a theoretical current like Marxism or fascism, nor does it have any thinker who would be its essential point of reference. We shall offer a very schematic characterization through three traits: utilitarian ethics, the defense of the rights of the individual, and capitalism.[12]

Utilitarian ethics makes its appearance in the English-speaking world and is represented by figures of the stature of Thomas Hobbes, David Hume, Jeremy Bentham and John Stuart Mill. Its fundamental postulate is the maximization of pleasure and the minimization of pain: an action is valid if it maximizes the pleasure or minimizes the pain in the world. This maxim has in its favor that, from within, it presents a social principle, but it possesses a fundamental weakness: it admits no absolute rule. Everything is subject to calculation, including the person. If eliminating a human being would maximize the pleasure or minimize the pain in the world, it would, according to utilitarian ethics, have to be carried out. But this, in Kant's terms, is a pure instrumen-

---

11. Paul Landsberg, *Problemas del personalismo* (1937; repr., Salamanca: Mounier, 2006), 106. Landsberg, a Christian Jew born in Germany, was a disciple of Scheler, but with the advance of Nazism he had to escape to Spain, which he finally left at the end of the civil war and went to France, where he joined the *Esprit* movement. Finally he was detained by the Gestapo in Pau and sent to the concentration camp at Oranienburg, where he died.

12. This presentation is very limited and succinct and aims to reflect the characteristics of this ideology or current of thought in the period dominated by a capitalism with very few social controls. In particular, utilitarian ethics is presented here in its most radical form; there are also more moderate versions, such as that of John Locke or Adam Smith in *The Theory of Moral Sentiments*, despite the fact that to Smith is attributed the concept of "the invisible hand."

talization of the person, who does not constitute an absolute value in himself, but only a mere good, very important, but subject to the golden rule of utility.

Another characteristic of individualism, in a certain sense antithetic to utilitarian ethics, is the firm and determined *defense of the rights of the individual* above any collective. The individualists demanded that the State should not interfere in the private affairs of the individual and his ability to decide for himself regarding everything involving him. No one should intervene, unless harm would be caused to others. John Stuart Mill classically expounded this doctrine:

> The only purpose for which power can be rightfully exercised over any member of a civilized community, against his will, is to prevent harm to others. His own good, either physical or moral, is not a sufficient warrant. He cannot rightfully be compelled to do or forbear because it will be better for him to do so, because it will make him happier, because, in the opinions of others, to do so would be wise, or even right. These are good reasons for remonstrating with him, or reasoning with him, or persuading him, or entreating him, but not for compelling him, or visiting him with any evil in case he do otherwise. To justify that, the conduct from which it is desired to deter him, must be calculated to produce evil to some one else.... Over himself, over his own body and mind, the individual is sovereign.[13]

As we can see, Mill, and with him individualism, postulated a sovereign autonomy of the individual limited only by harm to others.

Capitalism, as it appears in the first years of the twentieth century, is the third leg of individualism. More concretely, it was a primitive and savage capitalism, a direct descendent of the Industrial Revolution, which had not yet been controlled, understood, or checked. Although, strictly speaking, capitalism had emerged long before the end of the nineteenth century,[14] the structures of capitalist production accelerated

---

13. John Stuart Mill, *On Liberty* (New Haven: Yale University Press, 2003), 80–81.
14. See Max Weber, *The Protestant Ethic and the Spirit of Capitalism*, trans. Talcott Parsons (New York: Scribner, 1958).

exponentially with the appearance of mechanization. The problems accelerated too. The massive migration from rural areas to the city by those who wanted to work in the factories generated enormous urban problems, simultaneously creating an oversupply of labor that employers used to their own benefit, severely exploiting the workers. It was a period of ever lower wages, longer working hours, the suppression of breaks and holidays, and the employment of women and children in jobs which caused very severe physical exhaustion, and other hardships.

And, as the workers became poorer, the bourgeoisie became richer and stronger. European markets boiled over with activity under the rule of *laissez faire, laissez passer*, which, founded on neoclassical economic theory, postulated the non-intervention of the State in the markets. The markets were thought to be capable of self-regulation through the "invisible hand" which acted secretly but effectively in the mechanics of the system. The theory maintained, furthermore, that the search for the good of the individual generated, via these invisible mechanisms, the good of the collective. In this way, the wealthy class, sustained by its exponential gains and the endorsement of a supposedly social economic theory, either completely disregarded the disfavored classes, or even directly caused their poverty. Thus, the discontent, hostility, and rancor of the proletarian masses were forged, feeding and justifying Marxism. And thus did the crash of 1929 arrive with its disastrous consequences.

This is the individualism that Mounier implacably criticized.[15] But, despite all the reasons why Mounier doubtless had to take this position, it does not seem problematic to state that he overstretched his limits when he made the bourgeois individual into the paradigm of *all* the evils of the era, even though that bourgeois also stood up for the individual before the State, petitioning for the individual an independence and autonomy that all the collectivist regimes denied. So then, individ-

---

15. See Emmanuel Mounier, *Manifeste au service du personnalisme* (1936), in *Oeuvres*, vol. 1, *Révolution personnaliste et communautaire (1932–1935)* (Paris: Éditions du Seuil, 1961), 497. Translated by Monks of St. John's Abbey as *A Personalist Manifesto* (New York: Longman, Green, 1938).

ualism, with all its dark points, also had a positive aspect, Kierkegaardian and personalist in tone: it defended the primacy of the subject over the society. The major problem, of course, is that this subject was an individual who was exclusively preoccupied with himself and his welfare, not a person determined to place his talents at the service of the community and society.[16]

3.2 | The Collectivisms

3.2.1 | Marxism

The collectivisms are situated at the opposite extreme: against the individual, the collective; against individualism, collectivism. The isolated individual was nothing. He was nothing even if he was gathered in a bourgeois society which, without values or points of reference, seemed headed toward a catastrophe even greater than the one it had just left behind. The individual, therefore, must forget his rights, prerogatives, and pride, and unite himself with other forces in order to save his class or his country; moreover, he must dedicate himself completely to this task, surrender himself with all his energy to a destiny that lay beyond him, but which, precisely for this reason, filled him with meaning in a much more complete way than the mere search for increased wealth which occupied and preoccupied the individualistic and avid bourgeoisie.

Collectivism was not merely a visceral reaction. It could—and did—find solid reasons in Hegelian idealism, which inspired Marxism (Left Hegelianism) as much as it did Nazism and fascism (Right Hegelianism). Hegel had theorized about the priority of the system over the individual, and, within the system, the pre-eminence of the State as the

---

16. This is the context in which the individual-person dialectic, present in many personalists, such as Maritain, Mounier, or Buber, should be situated. It is not a question of two metaphysical principles for understanding the subject, but rather of two *ways* of understanding man. In other words, it is an *ethical question*. The only man who exists, if he wants to live adequately, must abandon the attitude of an individual and transform himself ethically into a person.

perfect, modern form of political organization. The various collectivisms were theoretically rooted in these ideas, although radicalizing the Hegelian positions, since Hegel had postulated a State under the rule of law, whereas, in the collectivisms of the time, the rights of individuals were totally subject to the power of collectivity, in whatever form it was adopted: race, people, nation, etc.

Marxism was aimed at the proletariat, the displaced masses oppressed and exploited by capitalism, proposing to them salvation through class struggle. Its starting point was a radical injustice which demanded a solution, but it was not alone in its preoccupation with the problems of workers. The socialist movement, anarchism, labor unions, the "social question" as it was raised in Catholicism, were other attempts to solve a very serious problem. Marxism distinguished itself by its radicalism, its efficacious joining of theory and praxis,[17] and by having sophisticated theoretical groundings founded on the social analyses of Marx and on his revision and adaptation of the theories of Ludwig Feuerbach and Hegel. The resulting central nucleus is well-known: class-war as the means for solving the workers' problem, that is, the destruction of the capitalist class as the only way to construct the new man and achieve the dictatorship of the proletariat, the communist paradise. Marxism subordinates everything to this objective, including persons. The ultimate goal was decisive. This goal justified the means, impressing into revolutionary praxis a completely instrumental ethics: what served the interests of the party and the revolution was ethical. It was a position that the Communist parties executed, both before and after attaining power, with a rigor and efficacy worthy of a greater cause.

And so, although the Marxist movement was inspired by a violent injustice, and was capable of mobilizing the noble energies of countless men and women who gave their lives for it, it did so, far too often,

---

17. "The philosophers have only interpreted the world, in various ways. The point, however, is to *change* it." Karl Marx and Friedrich Engels, *The Communist Manifesto* (New York: Pocket Books, 1964). See also Gavin Kitching, *Karl Marx and the Philosophy of Praxis* (London: Routledge, 1988).

not just at the cost of their own lives but also of their spirits, since its intrinsically erroneous anthropology vitiated the structures of the Communist parties and states, and led to injustices and crimes much greater that those it was supposed to resolve.[18]

3.2.2 | Fascism and Nazism

In contraposition to individualism, and also to Marxism (although sharing sociological presuppositions with the latter) collectivisms of the Right emerged: fascism and Nazism. These reacted against the absence of values in individualism and against a feeble parliamentarianism which appeared incapable of governing society. They appointed themselves champions of the struggle against a communism prepared to flood Europe with its revolution. They presented, therefore, a certain degree of "spirituality" because they postulated not only economic or individualist values—more benefits, more power—but also, just like Marxism, they proposed a collective ideal to which individuals could subscribe in order to confer meaning to their frayed and disoriented existence. The major problem, similar to what occurred in Marxism, is that this collective ideal turned into the ultimate source of meaning.

Italian fascism concretized the State as its source of meaning, practically deifying it. Benito Mussolini came to affirm that "the State is the true reality of the individual" and that "everything is in the State and nothing human exists nor *a fortiori* has value outside the State." And Gino Arias, one of the theorists of the fascist regime, established in unequivocal terms the relation between the individual and the collective: "The individual lives in the Nation of which he is an *infinitesimal and*

---

18. Maritain gives a very detailed criticism of Marxism, attending also to his aspirations for justice, in the second chapter of *Humanisme intégral* (1936). See *Integral Humanism: Temporal and Spiritual Problems of a New Christendom*, trans. Joseph Evans, in *Integral Humanism, Freedom in the Modern World, and A Letter on Independence*, trans. Otto Bird, Joseph Evans, and Richard O'Sullivan (Notre Dame, Ind.: University of Notre Dame Press, 1996), 141–345.

transient element, and of whose ends he must be considered an *organ and instrument*." In Nazism, the source of meaning was not the State, but instead the German people itself, "the community of the people," the *Volkstum* or the *Volksgemeinschaft*, which could present a very attractive face with its return to what is natural, the land, camaraderie, national roots. But, as Mounier warned, "the *Volkstum* calls its members to fidelity in joy. But anyone who resists is driven from the community with a brutality which one would not imagine when people focus only on the smile of the regime. The greatness of the German nation still has the supreme value of all the efforts."[19]

The historical consequences of both positions, Nazism and fascism, are well known. The basic anthropological error dominated the positive factors latent in the projects of social construction, and the human being was transformed into a mere disposable tool, subject to the interests of the "State" or "People," represented by charismatic leaders who had received the gift of guiding and directing the destinies of the collectives. They constituted the total authority, political and moral. They had been predestined to represent and direct the collectivity, and in consequence their word was automatically transformed into law, not only positive but also moral law.[20]

There is no need to insist on this. We know what happened afterwards but, in the interwar period, when these collectivisms were still being formed, everything was not so clear. Many crimes had yet to be committed, and one could only intuit, with greater or less lucidity, what would follow from certain assumptions and actions. And those who intuited it were not always capable of taking the consequent step of working to counteract this trajectory.

---

19. Mounier, *Manifeste au service du personnalisme*, 504, 506–7.
20. Romano Guardini analyzed the ideological process which occurred in Germany in the 1930s by which the figure of the *Führer* was collectively accepted as "the one to whose indications one could and must surrender himself with total confidence and who would lead them to the greatest imaginable destination." See "El salvador en el mito, la religión y la política," in Romano Guardini, *Escritos políticos* (Palabra: Madrid, 2010), 27–88.

Personalism was born largely in reaction to these antithetical positions, as an absolutely indispensable alternative to present in the face of this panorama. "Life and thought," Buber affirmed, "are here placed in the same problematic situation. As life erroneously supposes that it has to choose between individualism and collectivism, so erroneously supposes that it has to choose between an individualistic anthropology and a collectivistic sociology. The genuine third alternative, when it is found, will point the way."[21]

Personalism aimed to be that excluded alternative, an option in favor of the person that took from individualism its defense of the rights of the subject and from the collectivisms their ethical tension towards the construction of a common project, but both framed and integrated into its own presuppositions: the primacy of the person before society balanced by the correlative obligation to serve this same society through a commitment that could demand serious sacrifices. The personalist, therefore, could be differentiated both from the comfortable individualist bourgeois and from the collectivist fanatic. He sought to develop a balanced middle way whose axis was the dignity of the person, but without implying the renunciation of serious and difficult commitments or decisions.[22]

---

21. Martin Buber, "What Is Man?" in *Between Man and Man*, trans. Ronald Gregor-Smith (New York: Routledge, 2002), 240.

22. This conceptual framework is what would allow Landsberg to justify, in the environment immediately previous to World War II, his possible armed intervention in the conflict which appeared to be approaching inevitably. "If I properly understand our common personalist position," he affirms, "we are neither war-mongers like the National Socialists, nor pacifists, like some individualists. We see that there is a peace that is nothing but an incipient war and which cannot cease to lead to an open war. We see that there are values worthy of being defended with every sacrifice. We affirm that there should exist in them a spirit of true peace which can and must continue to exist even in the cruelest war, and that they will never renounce the effort towards a more positive peace in the world, never, until the end of history," Landsberg, *Problemas del personalismo*, 117.

4 | Philosophical Influences

We now turn to an analysis of the philosophical genealogy of personalism in a precise sense: that of the influences which brought about the emergence of personalist thought. In this sense, and in spite of the relative diversity of these authors, a guiding thread may be woven which, in our judgment, runs through Kant, Kierkegaard, and existentialism, Edmund Husserl's phenomenology, and Thomism (particularly in its neo-Thomistic version).[23]

4.1 | Immanuel Kant and the Dignity of the Person

Immanuel Kant influences personalism above all by way of his philosophical formulation of the dignity of the person, in particular, in the *Groundwork of the Metaphysics of Morals*. In this text we find affirmations of a clearly personalist flavor: for example, a sharp distinction between things and persons:

> Beings whose existence depends, not on our will, but on nature, have none the less, if they are non-rational beings, only a relative value, as means, and are consequently called *things*. Rational beings, on the other hand, are called *persons* because their nature already marks them out as ends in themselves—that is, as something which ought not merely to be used as a means—and consequently imposes to that extent a limit on all arbitrary treatment of them (and is an object of reverence).[24]

---

23. The philosophy of dialogue we take to be integrated into personalism (see chap. 3, sec. 3.2, below). Some authors also give relevance to John Henry Newman. "The effort to analyze the concrete real acts with which consciousness judges and with which it accepts the faith were going to serve as the source of inspiration of some French philosophers of the spirit (such as Blondel, Bergson, and much later, Nédoncelle) and German phenomenologists, such as Max Scheler." Juan Luis Lorda, *Antropología cristiana: Del Concilio Vaticano II a Juan Pablo II* (Madrid: Palabra, 1996), 30–31. See also John F. Crosby, *The Personalism of John Henry Newman* (Washington, D.C.: The Catholic University of America Press, 2015).

24. Immanuel Kant, *The Moral Law: Kant's Groundwork of the Metaphysics of Morals*, trans. H. J. Paton (London: Hutchinson, 1948), 90–91 (2nd German ed., 65; Royal Prussian Academy ed., 428).

A thesis deduced from this is the famous categorical imperative, which prohibits the instrumentalization of the person. This philosophical principle is assumed in one way or another by all personalists: "Act in such a way that you always treat humanity, whether in your own person or in the person of any other, never simply as a means, but always at the same time as an end."[25]

To this Kant adds one of the first explicit formulations, in a modern philosophical framework, of the dignity of the person understood as "the *dignity* of a rational being who obeys no law other than that which he at the same time enacts himself. In the kingdom of ends everything has either a *price* or a *dignity*. If it has a price, something else can be put in its place as an *equivalent*; if it is exalted above all price and so admits of no equivalent, then it has a dignity."[26] And the list could continue with concepts such as autonomy and the critique of Aristotelian *eudaimonia* (happiness).[27]

Kant's influence is explicitly present, for example, in Karol Wojtyła's formulation of the personalist norm directly inspired by the categorical imperative even though built upon different anthropological presuppositions: "This norm," Wojtyła explains, "in its negative aspect, states that the person is the kind of good which does not admit of use and cannot be treated as an object of use and as such the means to an end. In its positive form the personalistic norm confirms this: the person is a good towards which the only proper and adequate attitude is love. This positive content of the personalistic norm is precisely what the commandment to love teaches."[28]

Kant's influence on personalism, however, should not be overstat-

---

25. Ibid., 91 (2nd German ed., 66–67; Royal Prussian Academy ed., 429).
26. Ibid., 96 (2nd German ed., 77; Royal Prussian Academy ed., 435).
27. "Kant could be said to have laid the foundations of modern personalist ethics. From the point of view of the development of ethical reflection, this is a very important stage." John Paul II, *Memory and Identity: Conversations at the Dawn of a Millennium* (New York: Rizzoli, 2005), 36.
28. Karol Wojtyła, *Love and Responsibility*, trans. H. T. Willetts (New York: Farrar, Straus and Giroux, 1981), 41.

ed. Even in those philosophers such as Wojtyła, in whom it is explicit, it is collateral and not structural. Wojtyła is neither a Kantian nor a neo-Kantian; his basic premises are Thomistic and phenomenological, not Kantian, the formalism of which, furthermore, he criticized forcefully. Similarly, although Dietrich von Hildebrand adopted Kant's criticism of eudaimonism in ethics, he did so from very different anthropological premises. In many other personalists Kant's presence goes unnoticed beyond his inevitable influence as a central figure in philosophy. Because of this one may conclude that the influence of Kant in personalism is limited: some authors are inspired by him, but none of them appropriate his fundamental premises, be they epistemological, anthropological, or ethical.[29]

4.2 | Søren Kierkegaard and Existentialism

A much greater factor in the rise of personalism is, without a doubt, existentialism, initiated by Søren Kierkegaard (1813–55) with the vindication of the importance of the *singular individual*, the direct precedent of the modern concept of the person.[30] In opposition to Hegel's system which privileged the abstract and collective, the impersonal and absolute, and which thus contributed to the rise of the collectivisms, Kierkegaard appears as the prophet of the singular man, of the individual, of the one who really exists, valuable in himself, unique and unrepeatable, immersed in a singular existence in which he must decide his destiny before men and before God.

With this battle, with this rebellion, Kierkegaard laid the foundations for the defeat of idealism and initiated the great themes that

---

29. In a similar sense, Carlos Díaz put Kant in the trunk of his "tree of personalism" but accompanied by Husserl's phenomenology and Scheler's axiology, and fed by Christianity as its roots. Carlos Díaz, *¿Qué es el personalismo communitario?* (Salamanca: Mounier, 2002), 42.

30. Mounier, in his tree of existentialisms, situates Kierkegaard as the trunk from which all the existentialisms proceed, and of which personalism would be a branch. *Introduction to the Existentialisms*, trans. Philip Mairet (London: Methuen, 1948), 3.

would mark existentialist philosophy and, in a more indirect way, personalism. The primacy of the individual is most significant. Contrary to any non-existent abstraction, the unique individual is presented as the primary and absolute value *par excellence*, up to the point where he is capable of rising above his own genus: humanity. "In every animal genus the species is the highest thing, is the ideal form; the changing individual is a precarious reality that continually arises and disappears.... Only in the human genus, the situation, because of Christianity, is inverted and the individual is higher than the genus."[31]

Kierkegaard contributed, in addition, concepts of great transcendence, such as the anthropological relevance of *interpersonality* and, in particular, of the relation of man with a God-Person. Later, the philosophy of dialogue would forcefully insist upon this point, but Kierkegaard before them was already proclaiming with intensity the decisive character which the relation with others and with God had for the individual.

> Until then the human spirit was defined by its relation with objects: the relation of knowledge (the object before consciousness), and of will (the object as a good to be wanted). Kierkegaard's contribution places in first place the relationship with a personal being, God. The human spirit is defined much more by its personal relations than by its relation with objects. After the immense Hegelian monologue of the Absolute Spirit, the philosophies of dialogue were going to appear.[32]

Kierkegaard also opened a path in ethics by insisting on the dramatic and anguished character of life and on the capacity of man to make himself. Again in opposition to Hegel, and perhaps in an excessively tormented tone which came in part from his peculiar and extreme personality, he insisted that man finds himself alone before his decisions, and that they and they alone determine his destiny. The good and the bad are the elements of a drama that man cannot avoid even if he want-

---

31. Søren Kierkegaard, *Diary*, ed. Cornelio Fabro (1854; Brescia: Morcelliana, 1982), vol. 11, 86.
32. Lorda, *Antropología cristiana*, 30.

ed to, because the moral choice is ineluctable, and the individuality and unrepeatability of personal experience limit the points of reference that help him to make his decision, and at bottom these points of reference are different in each concrete case.

In this way Kierkegaard opened the door to existentialism: man, finite and limited, depends on his liberty and finds himself immersed in the dramatic currents of existence. This new philosophical approach allowed for diverse expressions. One of them was formulated by Jean-Paul Sartre when he affirmed the pre-eminence of existence over essence.[33] Much more in harmony with Kierkegaard's perspective is the other possible existentialism, developed by Gabriel Marcel, which, fully conscious that the interior moral experience of each man is unique and unrepeatable, finds itself capable of integrating it into the common human condition. This is an existentialism that accepts a persistent nucleus of humanity, although it insists that man is devoted to his freedom and is thus an open project which depends on each individual. When Kierkegaard was rediscovered in the twentieth century, personalism would take up these themes as a source of inspiration, although with a less dramatic and anguished perspective.[34] Man is free, but his freedom does not necessarily give rise to an anguished or tormented tension; it is possible to cope with it.

4.3 | Edmund Husserl and Phenomenology

It is common knowledge that Edmund Husserl (1859–1938) began his philosophical journey under the mark of positivism, which denied any scientific validity to humanistic and philosophical knowledge, and of the epigones of idealism, with Hegel as the great point of reference. In this context, a philosophy with a realist orientation and a treatment

---

33. See Jean-Paul Sartre, *Existentialism and Humanism*, trans. Philip Mairet (London: Methuen, 1949).

34. "Existentialism presents, in general, the image of a personalism somewhat on edge." Mounier, *Introduction to the Existentialisms*.

of realities transcending matter was practically impossible. Husserl's well-known reaction was his philosophical proclamation that brought a notable success: "To the things themselves!" Returning to the classical notion of intentionality, which Franz Brentano had recovered from oblivion, Husserl proposed that the philosopher should concern himself not with ideal constructions but with what he sees, pure and simple, what his mind presents to him as given, to things just as they are effectively present before the intelligence in the world. This return to things themselves should overcome not only the idealist tradition in which what is perceived is, in one way or another, the fruit of consciousness or, at least, does not exist independently of it. It should also overcome the challenge of positivism and the scientism that accused any philosophical knowledge of being subjective and thus irrelevant. It was necessary to prove that philosophical statements possessed scientific value and were free from prejudice and misunderstandings. But, how to prove this?

Husserl's great intuition consisted in developing a new philosophical mode of approaching reality: the phenomenological method,[35] which fundamentally consisted in placing oneself before reality while eliminating all pre-judgments and preconceived views in order to attempt *to see* what reality presented and nothing more. To capture essences in all their epistemological purity would thus eliminate the positivist imputations. Against the given in the pure intuition of essences, in effect, there would then be no possible objection: if what intelligence presented with clarity were doubted, what hope or possibility would there be for knowledge?

Husserl powerfully developed the elements of his method and the phenomenological theory which little by little began to proceed from the former. The two are, to a certain extent, separable elements, although it is a complex question.[36] The method as such, as a pure methodolo-

---

35. See Bernhard Waldenfels, *Einführung in die Phänomenologie* (Munich: Fink, 1992). On the method, see Edmund Husserl, *Logical Investigations*, trans. J. N. Findlay (London: Routledge, 1973); idem, *Ideas Pertaining to a Pure Phenomenology and to a Phenomenological Philosophy, Book I*, trans. Fred Kersten (The Hague: Nijhoff, 1989).

36. For Adolf von Reinach, for example, "This is the essential point: phenomenology

gy, was very attractive to realist philosophers because it propounded a modern philosophical path that was compatible with the basic premises of realism. Furthermore, it enriched realism with subjectivity, which is very present in the phenomenological perspective but practically absent in scholasticism and the classical tradition. Because of this, Husserl soon developed a group of disciples who enthusiastically followed his proposals: Max Scheler, Edith Stein, Adolf von Reinach, the married couple Theodor Conrad and Hedwig Martius, Alexander Koyré, Roman Ingarden, and others. They were called "the Göttingen group."

Subsequently, the situation became more complicated. Husserl in his later work *Ideas* made an unexpected turn toward idealism, renouncing to some extent the realist proposition on which he had based his first great work, *Logical Investigations*.[37] The Göttingen group could not follow him in this turn, because their attachment to realism was more decisive than the attachment they may have had to Husserl. They continued on a separate path, led more or less clearly by Scheler and constituting what has often been called realist phenomenology.

Husserl's influence on personalism comes via two paths: the phenomenological method and the constitution of the Göttingen group. The phenomenological method has been used, more or less strictly, by the ma-

---

is not a system of propositions and philosophical truths ... but only a method of philosophy which is necessary for treating philosophical problems." Von Reinach, "Concerning Phenomenology," *The Personalist* 50, no. 2 (1969): 194. However, the question is not so evident, for in fact Husserl ended up tying it to a transcendental conception of reality; more precisely, the method is so important that it ends up becoming a philosophy in itself, but a transcendental one.

37. There has been and continues to be much discussion about whether this change was sudden or only a smooth turn which intensified tendencies already present in *Logical Investigations*. Currently, there is a tendency to postulate continuity and not rupture between the two Husserls (the "realist" and the "idealist," to put it simply). Be that as it may, the fact is that the Göttingen group saw it as a very significant change to the extent that they separated from Husserl. Paul Ricoeur was also of this opinion, and added that hermeneutics put an end to the second Husserl: "What hermeneutics destroyed was not phenomenology but the idealistic interpretation that Husserl offered of it in his *Ideas I* and *Cartesian Meditations*." Ricoeur, "Intellectual Autobiography," in *The Philosophy of Paul Ricoeur*, ed. L. E. Hahn (Chicago: Open Court Publishing Co., 1995), 34.

jority of personalists (although stripped of its idealist components such as the *epoché*) since it supplies a procedure for a careful and respectful analysis of reality which at the same time permits the comprehension of subjectivity. And, with respect of the Göttingen group, its relation with personalism is so tight that many of them can simply be considered personalist philosophers: von Hildebrand, Stein, and so on.[38]

4.4 | Thomism

The influence of Thomism can be detected among personalists, in the first place, through its presence in almost all the Catholic philosophers of the age. The re-proposal of the doctrine of Thomas Aquinas that Pope Leo XIII had brought about in 1879 transformed Thomism into the quasi-official doctrine of Catholicism and, thus, into the doctrine that was taught in the principal Catholic institutions. It was inevitable, therefore, that any Catholic philosopher knew Thomism with sufficient depth.[39]

A different question is the attitude of the personalists to Thomism. Maritain is the paradigm of one of these attitudes, because he always considered himself to be a Thomist, as he repeatedly stated. Aquinas's thought constituted for him the basic structure of his philosophy which he never renounced.[40] But his was a rather isolated position. In general, personalists maintained a more distant attitude because they considered that Thomistic philosophy as such could not be re-proposed as such in the contemporary world. Certainly, it was regarded as one of the principal philosophies in the history of ideas, and for its own merits, not because it was endorsed by the popes. In addition, its affinity with Catholicism conferred on it a privileged place within Catholic thought. But, all things considered, it was understood that St. Thomas was too

---

38. See chap. 3, sec. 3.1, below.

39. The philosophers of dialogue, on the contrary, are, in general, quite distant from Thomistic philosophy because of the dialogical character of their thinking and the Jewish background of the majority of them.

40. See chap. 2, sec. 1, below.

distant from the contemporary world; his world was different, from an age past, the medieval. And, genius that he was, his philosophy could not resolve the problems of the present.

This conviction unfolded in two modalities. One group aimed at a profound reformulation of Thomas's thought, understanding this as the construction of a personalist philosophy which included Thomistic elements, and not a simple adaptation.[41] No personalism is a mere modified Thomism, the differences between the two are too great. Karol Wojtyła and Edith Stein are two examples of this: their proposal is an original synthesis of Thomism and phenomenology.

Other philosophers, more simply, received Thomism as a foundation present in their philosophy which supplied, among other things, one of the best possible formulations of philosophical realism, a point on which all were in agreement. But they did not use the basic concepts of Thomism for their particular formulations of personalism. Mounier is an example of this last position.[42]

5 | Crisis and the Cultural Renewal of Catholicism

The cultural situation of Catholicism was essential both to the rise of personalism and to the configuration of its features, since the greater part of personalists were fervent Catholics, in such a way that their religious experience was interwoven with their thinking. Not being merely nominal Catholics, their Christianity necessarily had to be integrated or confronted with their perception of the world. And so, the values and disvalues of Catholicism appealed to them directly either as a source of inspiration or as a problem to be solved.

---

41. The attempts at adaptation should be considered internal to Thomism, as, for example, those of Désiré Mercier or Joseph Maréchal. On this topic, see Gerard A. McCool, *From Unity to Pluralism: The Internal Evolution of Thomism* (New York: Fordham University Press, 1992).

42. According to Ricoeur, Mounier would be "in the line of an essential Thomism." Paul Ricoeur, "Une philosophie personnaliste," *Esprit* 174, no. 12 (1950): 868–69.

The crisis of Christianity is probably the aspect which presented itself to them as their highest priority. Although crisis literature is frequent in Christianity (perhaps because Christians too often expect the same perfection of their earthly society as is found in the heavenly one), in the first decades of the twentieth century and especially in the interwar period, the conviction that society in general and Christianity in particular were in the midst of a historic crisis was common. Christian elites detected a global and explicit rejection of Christianity by European culture, which had never occurred before. Étienne Gilson wrote:

> Our times witness one of the most important historical events, and even the most important which has happened since the conversion of Europe to Christianity: the abandonment of Christianity proclaimed for the first time by Europe, the conscious decision made by the modern world not only to not adhere to the Christian faith, but to not even live by the moral wealth that Christianity bequeathed it and to organize itself on new foundations that owed nothing to it.[43]

This decision had a long history that went back to the Renaissance and later disaffections and disagreements. But it was necessary to honestly recognize that Christians also formed part of this phenomenon because of their lack of attention to and coherence with the revealed message. Christianity had become institutionalized, clericalized, and lazy. Ceding the initiative in the development of history, it had allied itself, in Mounier's terms, with the "established disorder." And, in consequence, from many points of view, especially the cultural, it found itself in retreat. Not only were the avant-gardes not led by Christians, but, on the contrary, they were nearly always hostile to Christianity, which, in the best of cases, was considered inoffensive. Evolutionism, Marxism, psychoanalysis, Nietzsche, and the artistic and poetic avant-gardes, are good examples of this.

The acute realization of this fact—the conviction that Christianity

---

43. Étienne Gilson, *Por un orden católico*, trans. J. A. Maravall (Madrid: Cruz y Raya, 1936), 15–16.

was not being faithful to the potentialities of its own charism—generated a cultural reaction of enormous depth. The list of names is truly impressive.

In the novel, with figures such as the Norwegian Sigrid Unset, the German Getrud von Le Fort, the Frenchmen Georges Bernanos and François Mauriac; in essays, the Italian Giovanni Papini and the Englishmen G.K. Chesterton, Hilaire Belloc, and Christopher Dawson; in political thought with the founder of the Italian Popular Party, Luigi Sturzo; in spirituality with Columba Marmion, Ronald Knox, and Robert Hugh Benson in England. In philosophy one can point to Romano Guardini, Edith Stein, and Peter Wust in Germany, and Jacques Maritain, Étienne Gilson, Gabriel Marcel, and Emmanuel Mounier in France; in poetry, with Paul Claudel and T. S. Eliot.[44]

To them can be added Nikolai Berdyaev, J. R. R. Tolkien,[45] Miguel de Unamuno, José Martínez Ruiz "Azorín," Gregorio Marañón, Ramón Menéndez Pidal, Charles Péguy, Léon Bloy, Landsberg, and the list could go on.

In the philosophical sphere, the one which especially interests us, the reaction took shape as an imperious need to confront modern philosophy. There was an urgency to awake from the comfortable nap of a worn-out philosophy which subsisted thanks only to the protection of the ecclesiastical umbrella, because it was evident that philosophy inspired by Catholicism, or, more simply, by Christianity, had lost the battle. And it was equally clear that Christianity, as an intellectual religion, needed a philosophy. What should, or more simply, what could this philosophy be?

Leo XIII, in his famous encyclical *Aeterni Patris* (1879), had already given a reply by proclaiming a return to scholasticism and especially to St. Thomas. Rediscovering in a certain sense the importance and utility of Thomistic philosophy, as much for itself as for theology and Chris-

---

44. Mariano Fazio, *Cristianos en la encrucijada: Los intelectuales cristianos en el período de entreguerras* (Madrid: Rialp, 2008), 13.
45. See Joseph Pearce, *Literary Converts: Spiritual Inspiration in an Age of Unbelief* (London: Harper Collins, 1999).

tianity in general, he had proposed the return to Aquinas—to the authentic Aquinas, not to distorted and inferior interpretations and commentaries—as the sure means for recuperating an orthodox philosophy capable of confronting the intellectual challenges of modernity.

> Let carefully selected teachers endeavor to implant the doctrine of Thomas Aquinas in the minds of students, and set forth clearly his solidity and excellence over others. Let the universities already founded or to be founded by you [the bishops] illustrate and defend this doctrine, and use it for the refutation of prevailing errors. But, lest the false for the true or the corrupt for the pure be drunk in, be ye watchful that the doctrine of Thomas be drawn from his own fountains, or at least from those rivulets which, derived from the very fount, have thus far flowed, according to the established agreement of learned men, pure and clear; be careful to guard the minds of youth from those which are said to flow thence, but in reality are gathered from strange and unwholesome streams.[46]

This appeal by Leo XIII brought rich results. It led to a renewal of Thomistic studies with meticulous editions of the original texts, a discovery of the philosophical pluralism of the Middle Ages (above all, through the investigations of Étienne Gilson) and a relaunching of neo-Thomism which produced such relevant figures as Gilson and Maritain. It also generated problems, but in any case, it was unable to achieve the much desired reunification between Christianity and culture.[47] Although these philosophers received ample recognition, the

---

46. Leo XIII, encyclical letter *Aeterni Patris* (August 4, 1879), no. 31, https://w2.vatican.va/content/leo-xiii/en/encyclicals/documents/hf_l-xiii_enc_04081879_aeterni-patris.html.

47. "Exaggeration should be avoided. Official approval of a certain line of thought could and did produce a party-spirit which was narrow and polemical. At no time was Thomism as such imposed on Catholic philosophers in a way which it would imply that it was a part of the Catholic faith. In theory the autonomy of philosophy was upheld. It is however undeniable that in some circles there was a marked tendency to depict Thomism as the only line of thought which really fitted in with Catholic theology. The theory was of course that it fitted in because it was true rather than it must be true because it fitted in. But one can hardly shut one's eyes to the fact that in many ecclesiastical institutions, Thomism, or what was considered such, came to be taught in a dogmatic manner analogous to that in which Marxism-Leninism is taught in Communist-dominated educa-

general tendency of European culture maintained its course of alienation from Christianity.

This solution was insufficient. The path taken by modern philosophy since Descartes was too long and too deep for one single philosopher, even if it was a genius, such as Aquinas, to suffice in order to achieve a convergence. A much greater effort was needed, and it was necessary to run more risks. It was impossible to turn back as if time had not passed. The dominant philosophy could not simply be ignored or repudiated. But, in addition to this, was everything in it negative? Did it not have elements which could or even should be integrated into the new philosophy which should be forged for the future? Personalist thinkers understood, without a doubt, that this was the adequate attitude. Only a slow and arduous labor of integration of modern philosophy could give philosophy inspired by Christianity not only the philosophical legitimacy to take its place in the contemporary debate of ideas, but also adequate height and depth.[48]

But personalism took still another step. It understood that *a renewed philosophical inspiration in Christianity* was possible, supported by the conviction that it still had resources which had been ignored and not sufficiently explored. Gilson had brilliantly shown everything that Christianity had contributed to philosophy,[49] but there was an intuition that there was yet more, that the source had not run dry; it had only been blocked by the debris of Greek rationalism. Thomas Aquinas, in a titanic

---

tion. At the same time the 'back to Aquinas's movement could obviously stimulate more able minds to endeavor to recapture the spirit of Aquinas and to create a synthesis in the light of the contemporary cultural situation. And there have certainly been Thomist philosophers who have embraced Thomist principles not because they were taught to do so, but because they came to believe in their validity, and who have tried to apply these principles in a constructive way to modern problems." Frederick Copleston, *A History of Philosophy*, vol. 9, *Modern Philosophy* (London: Search Press, 1975), 250–51.

48. This movement was not always well received. On the contrary, there were frequent problems, misunderstandings, risks of ecclesiastical condemnation or, more frequently, the risk of being put aside. But, in time, this direction was officially taken by the Church at Vatican II. See Philip Trower, *Turmoil and Truth: The Historical Roots of the Modern Crisis in the Catholic Church* (Oxford: Family Press, 2003).

49. See Étienne Gilson, *History of Christian Philosophy in the Middle Ages* (London: Sheed and Ward, 1955).

and memorable effort, had done Christian thought the great service of baptizing Aristotle, but at the price of an excessive dependency which had ended up sealing off some philosophical paths that were not only adaptable by Christianity, but even manifested in a more adequate way its own true essence. It was necessary to unload this Greek ballast,[50] which hindered progress, and to explore those paths, to open the sealed sources so that a spring to feed Christian philosophy might gush forth once again. The combined work done by the personalists allowed the water from this spring to run again, making room for new or profoundly renewed concepts: person, corporeality, love, heart, interpersonal relations, etc.[51]

6 | The Personalist Awakening

Let us recapitulate. The early twentieth century presented two great movements, both mutually opposed to one another and both hostile to the person: individualism and collectivism. It was not a matter of simple theoretical or academic proposals, but rather of influential social movements capable of mobilizing millions of persons, and whose combined action constituted a pincer which appeared to leave no alternative. One would have to be either with individualism and against collectivism, or with collectivism and against individualism.

This enormous social tension was framed, in addition, in the context of an intellectual crisis and a situation of international convulsion. The intellectual crisis did not exactly consist of a total obfuscation of intellect, since in this period there were spectacular scientific and technical

---

50. See Juan Manuel Burgos, *Repensar la naturaleza humana* (Pamplona: EUNSA, 2007), esp. 58–64. The overcoming of the Greek ballast on personalism does not proceed by way of forgetting or debilitating rationality, as, for example, postulated by postmodernity and which has been denounced repeatedly by Joseph Ratzinger (Pope Benedict XVI), but only by a recovery of specifically Christian elements for philosophy.

51. See Emmanuel Mounier, *Personnalisme et Christianisme*, in idem, *Oeuvres*, vol. 1, *Révolution personnaliste et communautaire (1932–1935)*, 841–70. Translated as "Personalism and Christianity," in *Race, Nation, Person*, ed. Joseph T. Delos et al. (New York: Barnes and Noble, 1944), 323–80.

advances; instead, it consisted of a rejection of transcendence, a loss of cultural premises rooted in Christianity and an impressive advance of scientist, nihilist, and relativist positions. The social and international crisis, fed by this intellectual deterioration, the opposing ideologies, the excesses of capitalism, aggressive collectivism, nationalisms, and concomitant factors, was especially dramatic and led to events as unfortunate as the two world wars.

In the face of this anguishing situation, several thinkers felt the need to work out an intellectual response which would contribute to resolving the serious matters in play. This response would have to have, in the first place, a strong weight of newness because, although it could not pretend to reject the legacy of tradition, it was evident that propounding old notions was insufficient to mend the split between culture and Christianity or to launch an alternative cultural or philosophical project. Something more was necessary: an original and audacious construction capable of opening a space in the vortex of European culture.

On the other hand, this response, although it was theoretical in origin, would have to be structured in such a way as would allow social mediation in order to facilitate the elaboration of proposals for action. The pressure of individualism and the collectivisms left no room for a merely speculative theory. Society needed a theory with an internal structure that would allow for the elaboration of a social project that was a viable alternative to individualism and collectivism. Little by little it became clear, although confused and indefinite at the beginning, that this alternative could be found in the notion of person.

"Person" is an ancient notion, of Christian origin. It was, therefore, sufficiently familiar, but it had seldom been utilized. Scholasticism did not make much use of it, although it certainly took the notion into account. And modern thought turned to other concepts to express the human condition: consciousness, subject, the "I."[52] So, to return to the person, to the experience of being a person and of encountering other

---

52. See Juan Manuel Burgos, *Antropología: una guía para la existencia*, 6th ed. (Madrid: Palabra, 2017), 26–38, "La noción de persona a través de la historia."

persons as the point of departure for thinking, was a new path that had not yet been taken. It was a path, furthermore, that appeared to offer the answers that were being sought.

On one hand, the concept of person, such as it was beginning to be used at that time (thanks to the combined efforts of Scheler, Maritain, Mounier, Maurice Nédoncelle, Maurice Blondel and many others), was modern and thus able to integrate specifically modern themes, such as the "I," experience, or subjectivity. Moreover, understood as a subsistent and autonomous but essentially social being, it presented itself as, in Buber's words, the "excluded alternative" to individualism and collectivism. It was distinguished and separated from the egocentric individual by stressing the moral obligation to serve others and the community, but it did not fall into the collectivist orbit because, due to his intrinsic dignity, the person possesses an absolute and noninterchangeable value and a series of inalienable rights. Furthermore, the transition from these approaches to a social or political theory was relatively immediate.

Thus was the *personalist awakening* configured, to use an expression from Nunzio Bombacci.[53] This awakening consisted of the continuous and recurrent recourse to the concept of the person within social, philosophical, or theological spheres, motivated by the intuition that this was the key term for the resolution of the great problems which were in play. And this personalist awakening is what made room, in various but interrelated ways, for personalism in its several forms.

---

53. "In these years not a few authors center their own reflection on the person and his relations with the community, drawing upon the riches of the perennial personalism of Christian thought. Thus in the Lutheran world, at the start of the 1930s, Dietrich Bonhöffer sought in *Sanctorum Communio*, exactly in the person-community relation, a solid basis for his investigations into the renewal of ecclesiology. In Catholic theology the research of the Dominicans of *Le Saulchoir* stands out. In the small Belgian center [at Kain]—where the Dominicans' school has been transferred because of the Combres laws (1905), which strongly rejected the activities of the religious orders in France— Marie-Dominique Chenu [1895–1990] and others devoted themselves to the study of personalist themes with a strong sense of community which was deepened by the study of St. Thomas." Nunzio Bombaci, *Emmanuel Mounier: Una vida, un testimonio*, trans. Carlos Diaz (Salamanca: Mounier, 2002), 114.

In the following chapters I will expound on the life and, above all, the thought of the principal personalists who have emerged from the complex socio-cultural context which I have just described. For my presentation, I have chosen a classification that combines cultural areas and groups of thought. The cultural areas are linguistic and basically correspond with nations: France, Italy, Poland, Spain, Germany and Austria, Britain, and the United States. When possible, I have isolated within them the currents of personalism that have their own identity, such as realist phenomenology or dialogical philosophy. Although other perspectives are possible, I think that this approach allows for a sufficiently structured and complete comprehension of the whole personalist phenomenon since it lets the reader focus both on the currents, which in the majority of cases are in the context of a common language, and on the individual thinkers.

We will begin with French personalism which, historically speaking, is the most important, above all because of the presence of Mounier. His prominence in the formation of personalism, and, in particular, in its consolidation as a visible movement, is decisive. After that we will analyze the rest of the cultural areas. We will explain the thought of all the truly great personalists, although with more or less detail according to each case and our knowledge. From the start, we alert the reader that we do not intend to compose a complete history of personalism or mention every possible personalist. That would require much more space and, above all, much more wisdom. Our objective is simpler: to introduce personalism by way of its principal authors and to provide an overview of the movement.

With respect to the names, to the list of personalist philosophers, the consensus is sufficiently general. There are some discussions, both internal to personalism as a philosophical school and external, about the figures of greatest importance, but the disagreements are minor and, in good measure, inevitable, given the complex and multilateral nature of personalist philosophy.[54] Something similar occurs with the lists of

---

54. See Battista Mondin, *Storia dell'Antropologia Filosofica*, vol. 2 (Bologna: Edizioni

existentialists, communitarians, or phenomenologists; they do not exactly coincide either, but, in the end, the lists have, more or less, the same names with some small divergences. A different question regards the issue of doctrinal unity; how alike or different are the various personalisms? But we shall come to that later.

Studio Domenicano, 2002), 514–660, "Le antropologie personaliste"; Thomas Rourke and Rosita C. Rourke, *A Theory of Personalism* (Lanham, Md., Lexington Books, 2005); Vittorio Possenti, *Il principio persona* (Rome: Armando Editore, 2006), Agustín Domingo Moratalla, *Un humanismo del siglo XX: el personalismo* (Madrid: Pedagógicas, 1985); Armando Rigobello, *Il personalismo*, 2nd ed. (Rome: Città Nuova, 1978); Czeslaw Bartnik, *Studies in Personalist System* (Lublin: KUL, 2006); Jonas Norgaard Mortensen, *The Common Good: An Introduction to Personalism* (Wilmington, Del.: Vernon Press, 2017).

CHAPTER TWO | **French Personalism**

French personalism in addition to the common influences mentioned in the previous chapter, was born under other specific impulses, among them, Henri-Louis Bergson, the philosophy of spirit, Charles Péguy, and Léon Bloy.[1] The impact of each is, however, very different. Bergson influenced the rise of personalism as a philosopher able to confront the dominant scientism. His theory of intuition, in effect, postulated the validity of a type of knowledge distinct from the merely experimental, and for this reason, he constituted an important point of reference for the young philosophers who aspired to be something more than philosophers of science. In particular, Bergson's influence was important in the intellectual evolution of Jacques Maritain, as Raïssa recalled, speaking of her husband:

> Someone I know well wrote much later that "man is an animal who feeds on transcendentals." In different terms, Bergson assured us that such food was within our reach, that we are capable of truly knowing reality, that through intuition we may attain to the absolute; and we interpreted as saying that we could truly, absolutely *know what is*. It mattered little to us whether this might come through intuition which transcends concepts or

---

[1]. Nikolai Berdyaev was also influential, as was Maurice Blondel with his theory of action.

through intelligence which forms them; the important, the essential thing was the possible result: to attain the absolute.[2]

French philosophy of the spirit, represented by René Le Senne (1882–1954) and Louis Lavelle (1883–1951),[3] was also influential in the birth of personalism, and in a more direct manner since its theoretical and anthropological presuppositions were much closer.[4] The foe which they tried to combat was, again, scientism; and, to that end, they founded in 1934 a philosophical book series with the publisher Aubier, titled *Philosophie de l'esprit*, which gained much renown. The object of this collection was to create room for philosophy that vindicated transcendence in an age in which it had been practically eradicated from the cultural atmosphere. These philosophers had several points in common with Bergson, for example, a certain spiritualism which had points of contact with that developed by Bergson in *L'evolution créatrice*, but the differences were important, since their perspective was more classical, and perhaps, above all, they intended to reach a greater objectivity. They started with the subject, and in this they were modern, but they did not trust Bergsonian intuition. Rather they sought an analysis of consciousness in its objective aspects which intended to include the problematic or negative elements present in existentialism: including temporality, limit situations, finitude, evil, and error. This philosophy of spirit presented, furthermore, a strong dose of metaphysics joined with a marked emphasis on the idea of destiny and the spiritual vocation of the human

---

2. Raïssa Maritain, *We Have Been Friends Together: Memoirs*, trans. Julie Kernan (New York: Longmans, Green and Co., 1942), 83–84. Originally published as *Les grandes amitiés* (Paris: Desclée de Brower, 1949), 94–95. Maritain, after his encounter with Thomism, revised his position on Bergson, see *La philosophie bergsonienne* (Paris: Rivière, 1914).

3. See Battista Mondin, *Storia dell'Antropologia Filosofica*, vol. 2 (Bologna: Edizioni Studio Domenicano, 2002), 471–513.

4. There is also an Italian version of the philosophy of spirit, developed as a "filosofia dell'integralità" by Michele Federico Sciacca (1908–75). Some of its main works are *L'uomo, questo* squilibrato (1956); *Atto ed Essere* (1956); *Morte ed immortalità* (1959); *La libertà e il tempo* (1965); *L'oscuramento dell'intelligenza* (1970); and *Ontologia triadica e trinitaria* (1972).

person. It was, without a doubt, one of the currents that contributed to the personalist awakening that took place in France during the 1930s.

Charles Péguy (1873–1914) and Léon Bloy (1846–1917) were atypical persons with an atypical influence on the personalists, although this influence was not less intense because of it. Their Catholicism was profound but very far from traditional forms, marked by a radical criticism of any kind of idleness, abuse, or conformism, all of which influenced persons as significant as Emmanuel Mounier and Maritain. In particular, Bloy was the principal agent in the conversion of Maritain and other intellectuals to Catholicism, and Péguy decisively influenced the intellectual and personal itinerary of Mounier. Neither Péguy nor Bloy can be considered a philosopher in the strict sense. Péguy wrote poetry and plays; Bloy was a novelist. Both wrote numerous essays and were well-versed in controversy. In a manner similar to Kierkegaard, they were radical, peculiar, and profound characters, incorruptibly faithful to a dramatically colored vocation and with paradoxical personalities that separated them from the modern world but, at the same time, allowed them to intuit the new needs of anthropology. They were living models and intellectual points of reference for the French personalists, encouraging them to follow their path in search of a renewed, profound, and dynamic anthropology from the perspective of a Catholicism that wished to break its links with a well-off bourgeoisie.

From these specific sources French personalism was born, a personalism which boasts of a wide spectrum of representatives. For our survey we have selected four of them, Maritain, Gabriel Marcel, Mounier, and Maurice Nédoncelle, whom we consider to be the most important. Some followers of Mounier, such as Jean-Marie Doménach or, especially, Jean Lacroix, should also have a privileged place, but space limits our possibilities, and we will defer our analysis of Lacroix's conception of personalism to chapter 4.[5] Regarding Paul Ricoeur, we do not con-

---

5. Jean Lacroix (1900–1986) was much influenced by Blondel and was a disciple- companion of Mounier. Together they founded *Esprit*, although the indisputable leadership

sider him to be a personalist, even though his teachers were Marcel, Mounier, Edmund Husserl, and Karl Jaspers; for this reason, he is not included in our survey, although we will consider his vision of personalism in chapter 4.[6]

We shall present the four great French personalists in chronological order, which coincides with the internal theoretical influences among them. Maritain, the first of them, developed a specific personalism with Thomistic roots. Marcel established the connection between personalism and existentialism. Both Maritain and Marcel belonged to the generation previous to Mounier, whom they significantly influenced. Maritain, in particular, played a relevant part in the first years of the journal *Esprit*,[7] as adviser and counselor to Mounier, who had previously attended the meetings that the Maritains organized in Meudon. Nédoncelle, on the contrary, although a contemporary of Mounier, is, in a certain sense, dependent on him, since his principal works appeared

---

was assumed by Mounier. Some of Lacroix's best known works are: *Personne et amour* (1942); *Force et faiblesse de la famille* (1948); *Marxisme, existentialisme, personnalisme: Présence de l'éternité dans le temps* (1949); *L'échec* (1964); *Le désir et les désirs* (1975); *Philosophie de la culpabilité* (1977). We treat his vision of personalism in "Personalism as Anti-ideology" in chap. 4, sec. 1.2, below.

6. Some authors include Paul Ricoeur within personalism—I also have done so on occasion—but a more attentive analysis of his thought shows that this opinion might not be correct; and not so much (or not only) because Ricoeur announced the death of personalism, but also because his theoretical bases are substantially divergent from those characteristic of this group of thinkers (see chap. 4 below), beginning with the fact that he does not employ the concept of person but rather that of subject. This is no obstacle to finding in Ricoeur a solid affinity with personalism based on the fact that his three great, recognized teachers are Marcel, Jaspers, and Husserl, in addition to a certain influence from Mounier. He also constitutes an ideal reference for a connection or amplification of personalism with the hermeneutics of symbols and texts and provides an exceptional platform for the analysis of personal identity in works such as *Oneself as Another* (1990) among many other contributions. But we understand that his not-specifically-personalist character can easily be deduced from his own intellectual biography in which there is only one very limited allusion to Mounier and none to the concept of person. See Ricoeur, "Intellectual Autobiography," in *The Philosophy of Paul Ricoeur*, ed. L. E. Hahn (Chicago: Open Court Pubishing Co., 1995), 3–53; and also Johann Michel, *Paul Ricoeur, un philosophie de l'agir humain* (Paris: Cerf, 2006).

7. Marcel was also present at the birth of *Esprit*.

when Mounier's explicit personalism had already been presented forcefully in the French cultural panorama.

1 | Jacques Maritain (1882–1973): Thomistic Personalism
1.1 | Life and Works

Jacques Maritain was born in Paris on November 18, 1882, into a Protestant family. His father Paul was a lawyer, and his mother, Geneviève Fabre, was the daughter of a Republican deputy in the National Assembly.[8] He studied at the Sorbonne, where he obtained a degree in philosophy and another in natural sciences. During his youth he showed great sympathy for humanitarian socialism, and it was precisely in a demonstration on behalf of Russian socialist students persecuted by the tsar where he met Raïssa Oumansoff, a Russian Jew who became his wife and companion for the rest of her life. These two young people profoundly suffered the impact of education at the Sorbonne, which was characterized by materialism, pragmatism, scientism, and relativism, to the point that they contemplated the possibility of suicide if they did not find sure and profound truths to which they could cling. At that moment Henri Bergson opened a door to hope, and their friendships with Charles Péguy and Léon Bloy opened a the way to Christianity. They were both baptized into the Catholic Church in 1906.

After a two-year stay in Heidelberg where they studied biology, the Maritains returned to Paris. Here the key event in their philosophical

---

8. For the biography of Maritain, see Jean Luc Barré, *Jacques et Raïssa Maritain: Les mendiantes du ciel* (Paris: Stock, 1995), translated by Bernard Doering as *Jacques and Raïssa Maritain: Beggars for Heaven* (Notre Dame, Ind.: University of Notre Dame Press, 2005); Juan Manuel Burgos, *Para comprender a Jacques Maritain* (Salamanca: Fundación Emmanuel Mounier, 2005); William J. Notthingham, *Christian Faith and Secular Action: An Introduction to the Life and Thought of Jacques Maritain* (St. Louis, Mo.: The Bethany Press, 1968); and Jacques Maritain, *Oeuvres complètes, vol. 12, Carnet de notes* (Paris: Ed. Saint-Paul, 1992), translated by Joseph W. Evans as *Notebooks* (Albany, N.Y.: Magi Books, 1984). See also Antonio Pavan, *La formazione del pensiero di J. Maritain*, 2nd ed. (Padova: Libreria Gregoriana Editrice, 1985).

journey occurred: the encounter with St. Thomas Aquinas. Maritain perceived Thomas as an illumination of his intellect and remained faithful to him for all his life. The Thomism of Maritain's first works was very combative and orthodox, and his attitude toward modernity was quite critical. From these years, of importance are his first book, *La philosophie bergsonienne* (1913), in which he marked his distance from Bergson; *Trois réformateurs: Luther, Descartes, Rousseau* (1925), in which he analyzed the process of the secularization of Christian truths in these authors; *Antimoderne* (1922); and his first book on aesthetics, *Art et scolastique* (1920).

Maritain collaborated in this period with the journal *La revue universelle*, associated with the problematic movement *Action française*, which was nationalist, monarchist, and conservative in its outlook. The condemnation of the group by Pope Pius XI in 1926, by which he forbade Catholics to participate in this movement, hit Maritain hard and caused a profound inner commotion. He was moved to revise the ideological position that had led him to collaborate in journals ideologically aligned with *Action française*. During these years, the Maritains made their house in Meudon, on the outskirts of Paris, an important center of meetings and discussions attended by philosophers (such as Mounier), theologians, and intellectuals of very diverse types, especially artists: writers such as Jean Cocteau, François Mauriac, Julien Green, and Paul Claudel, painters such as Georges Rouault, Gino Severini, and Marc Chagall, musicians such as Erik Satie, Arthur Lourié, and Igor Stravinsky, to mention just some of the most important names.

In 1932 he published his first great work, *Distinguer pour unir, ou les degrés du savoir*, in which he made a profound analysis of the different levels of knowledge from the perspective of critical realism (similar to Étienne Gilson's).[9] That same year he met Mounier and collaborated with him on the review *Esprit*. Within a general framework of understanding, they maintained different intellectual and political positions

---

9. See Étienne Gilson, *Le réalisme méthodique* (Paris: Pierre Téqui, 1935). Translated by Philip Trower as *Methodical Realism* (Front Royal, Va.: Christendom Press, 1990).

which gave rise to debates and controversies.[10] Mounier was in favor of a more active intervention in social debates and advocated a more radical change in relation to traditional philosophical positions. Maritain also desired to intervene in the course of society, but without moving away from his stance as an intellectual and without entering directly into the political struggle. Also, although he was an innovator, he was a declared Thomist, and some of his studies were notably technical and erudite, while Mounier from the start opted for an open personalism and for writings of a more cultural character.

In 1936 Maritain published his best known work, *Integral Humanism*, which provoked harsh polemical responses throughout the world and was translated into numerous languages. It was his first great work of political philosophy in which he analyzed the European cultural and political tradition, setting forth both an interpretation of medieval Christendom and a new model of Christendom which accommodated some principles of modernity. This book had spectacular repercussions, ranging from the most acerbic criticisms to a fervent reception among some Christian Democrat political movements which took it as a guide for the analysis of European history and as a model for social action. In *Integral Humanism* Maritain also proposed for the first time in a systematic way his vision of communitarian personalism based on the three-term formula individual-person-common good.

In 1940, when he was away in Toronto, at the Institute of Mediaeval Studies founded by Gilson, the Nazi police went to look for Maritain at his house in Meudon. The Maritains then decided not to return to France, which would mean the beginning of a long stay in the United States. His experiences in the United States would notably influence his perception of politics. From this first period came *The Rights of Man and Natural Law* (1943) and *Christianity and Democracy* (1943). At the end of World War II, Charles de Gaulle proposed him as French ambassador to the Holy See. Maritain accepted reluctantly, although he carried out

---

10. See Sylvain Guena, *Correspondence Jacques Maritain et Emmanuel Mounier (1929–49)* (Paris: Desclée de Brouwer, 2016).

his duties for three years. As head of the French delegation he played an important role in the development of the Universal Declaration of Human Rights which the UN adopted in 1948. He returned to the United States where he wrote two other great works, *Man and the State* (1951), his second great work on political philosophy; and *Creative Intuition in Art and Poetry* (1953), the fruit of decades of reflection.

In 1960, during a trip to France, Raïssa died in Paris. The blow to Maritain, already nearly eighty, was very hard. He decided to retire from the world and to live in Toulouse. In spite of this, he continued to write and publish, among other works, *The Peasant of the Garonne* (1967), his view of the debates following Vatican Council II. This late work, too, had significant repercussions. For some it constituted a betrayal of progressive principles due to its affirmations in favor of the traditional doctrine of the Church and the papal Magisterium; others, on the contrary, considered it a return by Maritain to the classical and traditional approaches which, according to them, he had been progressively abandoning in his books on political philosophy, anthropology, and aesthetics. In reality, there was no essential change of orientation; he only insisted strongly on the key elements of Thomism and Christianity that he had always held but had been in the background in his work on other subjects.

He died in 1973. We can conclude this brief survey of his long and fruitful life with this beautiful autobiographical passage composed at Princeton University when he was seventy-two.

> Who am I? A professor? I don't believe so: I teach out of necessity. A writer? Perhaps. A philosopher? I hope so. But also a type of romantic of justice, ready to imagine, after each battle, that it and the truth will triumph among men. And also, perhaps, a type of water diviner with the head to the earth in order to hear the noise of the hidden sources and of the invisible germinations. And also, and like every Christian, despite and in the middle of miseries and failings, and of all the betrayed graces of which I become conscious in the evening of my life, a beggar of heaven, disguised as a man of the world, a type of secret agent of the King of Kings in the ter-

ritory of the prince of this world, who decides to risk himself like Kipling's cat, which walked alone.[11]

This summary of his life already provides a first idea of the magnitude and diversity of his work, but the books mentioned are only a small part of his output. In fact, this output is of such importance that it has come to be spoken of at times as the *Summa Maritainiana*, like a modern and updated version of the *Summa theologiae* of St. Thomas. His interests, in effect, covered almost every field and extended to questions as disparate as existentialism, Freud's psychoanalysis, the opinions of commentators on St. Thomas on practical reason, the aesthetics of Picasso, Dalí or Dante, democracy, religion, or culture, and logic and metaphysics, to name a few.

This diversity could suggest that he was an anarchic and unsystematic thinker, but that would be an erroneous assessment. He was, it is clear, creative, restless, and forceful, adhering to the culture of his time and attentive to the innovations and advances of philosophy and science, which, along with his longevity, permitted him to treat a great plurality of themes. But, within this great flow of thought, it is possible to delimit five specific areas to which he gave special attention over long periods and to which he returned once and again from different points of view. They are the following:

(1) Epistemology and logic: *L'ordre des concepts* (1923); *Distinguer pour unir ou les degrés du savoir* (1932); *De la philosophie chrétienne* (1933); *Science et sagesse* (1934).
(2) History of philosophy: *La philosophie bergsonienne* (1913); *Antimoderne* (1922); *Trois réformateurs* (1925); *La philosophie morale I: examen historique des grandes systèmes* (1960).
(3) Anthropology and morality: *Quatre essais sure l'esprit dans sa condition charnelle* (1939); *La personne et le bien commun* (1947); *La loi naturelle ou loi non écrite* (1950); *Neuf leçons sur les notions premières de la philosophie morale* (1951).

11. Maritain, *Carnet de notes*, 130.

(4) Aesthetics: *Art et scolastique* (1920); *Creative Intuition in Art and Poetry* (1953); *The Responsibility of the Artist* (1960).
(5) Political philosophy: *Du régime temporel et de la liberté* (1933); *Humanisme intégral* (1936); *Christianisme et démocratie* (1943); *Man and the State* (1951).[12]

We shall spend more time especially on anthropology and his social and political thought, because that is where we can find and elucidate his role and influence as a personalist philosopher.

1.2 | A Thomistic Personalism

Maritain's philosophy was, so to speak, one of the best achievements of the encyclical *Aeterni Patris*, that is, of the project of renewal of Thomism desired by Pope Leo XIII and, with him, an important part of the Church. After the convulsion of his intellectual and existential itinerary, it was precisely thanks to the Church that he encountered St. Thomas. Fr. Humbert Clérissac, a Dominican and Maritain's spiritual director, recommended that he read the *Summa theologiae*. The great work constituted for him an authentic intellectual revelation in a critical moment in which he was seeking his philosophical path after having resolved the spiritual one. "I experienced then," he affirmed, "an illumination of reason. My philosophical vocation had been restored to me in full."[13] From this moment on, the identification with Thomism was an essential and permanent feature of his entire philosophical work.[14]

---

12. Also to be noted are his investigations in metaphysics (*Sept leçons sur l'être*, 1933), on existentialism, on culture (*Réligion et culture*, 1930), his forays into education (*Pour une philosophie de l'éducation*, 1959), the philosophy of nature (*La philosophie de la nature*, 1936), the philosophy of history (*On the Philosophy of History*, 1957), or theology (*De la grâce et de la humanité du Jesús*, 1967, and *De l'Église du Christ*, 1970).
13. Jacques Maritain, *Oeuvres complètes*, vol. 11, *Le philosophe dans la cité* (Paris: Ed. Saint-Paul, 1992), 27–28.
14. Pope John Paul II referred to it in this way: "The 'illumination of reason' aroused in the young Maritain such a profound adhesion to the thought of St. Thomas that, by a spontaneous movement of his spirit, he became one of the principal creators of that

Initially, as has already been mentioned, Maritain's Thomism was closed and aggressive, a "convert's" Thomism, incapable of finding fissures in its own doctrine and of noticing good things in contrary positions. But this attitude was quickly superseded. On the one hand, his complex personal journey had made him familiar with many worlds before arriving at Thomism, in such a way that it was very difficult for him to remain in an excessively narrow path, limited and without perspectives. But, above all, his mentality was naturally open and integrated, and, little by little, he forged his own path in the middle of his initially grim Thomism until he was able to transform it, gradually, into an open, vibrant, and creative Thomism.

Maritain presented Aquinas's positions with a renewed vigor because he was able to perceive, beyond the Scholastic commentaries to which Thomism had frequently been reduced, the real intuition that had illuminated the Angelic Doctor's writings. In this way, the force of one of the great geniuses of philosophy reappeared in Maritain's writings, revitalized and updated, with a presentation that made it accessible and attractive to the man of the twentieth century. But Maritain did not stop there. Imitating his master, who synthesized all the knowledge of his time, he became aware with ever greater clarity that it was not sufficient to reproduce St. Thomas, however well this task might be done. If Thomism wanted to be at the level of the times, at the level of the mission which was expected of it, namely, to overcome the historic fracture between culture and Christianity, it had to integrate within itself all the valid contributions of philosophy and the sciences. Otherwise, it would fail, since it would limit itself to being a doctrine of the past.

'Thomistic renaissance' that the Magisterium of the Church, with Leo XIII, had desired and promoted as a response to the principle needs of modern culture, and as a way to overcome the divorce 'contra natura' between reason and faith (*Aeterni Patris*, 1879). To this vocation, which led him to suffer difficulties, incomprehension, and confrontations, he remained faithful until death." John Paul II, "Lettera al 'Convegno promosso nel centenario della nascita di Jacques Maritain,' 5-VIII-1982," in *Jacques Maritain oggi*, ed. V. Possenti (Milan: Vita e Pensiero, 1983), 18.

Maritain confronted this complex and difficult task in two directions: diachronic and synchronic. The diachronic was oriented toward a philosophy of history and, above all, a revision of the history of philosophy that would show what philosophical elements of the past should be integrated into Thomism. In other words, Maritain had to face the question of modernity. What should be taken up, if anything, from all the philosophy that had been written since St. Thomas?

Modern thought's starting point was an error: the *cogito* of Descartes. This fact could not be denied, and the consequences were readily visible: the development of all of the idealist philosophy with its atheist cadence, as Cornelio Fabro put it.[15] But for Maritain this did not imply that *all the philosophy* formulated from that perspective was necessarily erroneous and, even less, that some concrete and specific developments could not be rescued. On the contrary, it was evident that there were very valuable elements that it was urgent to recover. And not only for strategic reasons—since taking on some features of modern thought, due to its dominance, could facilitate the approach of contemporary thinkers—but also because of an issue of truth: this thought had produced incontestable philosophical advances which could not be dismissed. Maritain, then, like later personalists, adopted what he called the "judgment of ambiguity." He rejected a total condemnation of modern thought, presuming that it was necessary to discriminate among its theses; and he thus confronted the more closed Scholastic currents of Catholic philosophy, according to which right reason since Descartes had suffered damage so basic that the postulates of the philosophies which were inspired by or derived from it were radically vitiated. Maritain agreed that the *cogito* was not valid as a point of departure, but his general analysis was much more positive: the tree of modernity had also generated good fruit.

He applied the same approach, in the synchronic sense, to contem-

---

15. See Cornelio Fabro, *Introduzione all'ateismo moderno* (Roma: Studium,1969), 1:599–612; 2:1035–1036.

porary thought. Always from a decidedly Thomistic framework, he realized that it was necessary to respond to the innovations which were being presented by the sciences and, above all, by the new cultural and philosophical tendencies. He made an effort to integrate them, as far as possible, into Thomism. In this sense, one can indicate, for example, his effort to give a more existential character to metaphysics[16] and, especially, because it is the aspect which most interests us, his renewed perspectives on ethics and anthropology.

In ethics, especially to be stressed are, for example, his interest in practical reason,[17] his innovative studies of natural law which were aimed at moving away from its presentation as a legalistic formalism,[18] the importance he gives to experience as the starting point for ethics,[19] his moving from a syllogistic understanding of moral judgment to an emphasis on the unrepeatable individuality of each ethical decision because of its strictly singular character,[20] his attempt to integrate values into the classical system of ends, and so on.

In anthropology the first item to be emphasized is Maritain's reap-

---

16. See Jacques Maritain, *Sept leçons sur l'être* (Paris: Pierre Téqui, 1933). Translated as *A Preface to Metaphysics: Seven Lectures on Being* (New York: Sheed and Ward, 1939).

17. See Juan Manuel Burgos, *La inteligencia ética. La propuesta de Jacques Maritain* (Bern: Peter Lang, 1995).

18. See Jacques Maritain, *La loi naturelle ou loi non écrite: texte inédit*, ed. Georges Brazzola (Fribourg, Switzerlande: Éditions universitaires, 1986). Translated by William Sweet as "Lectures on Natural Law," in *The Collected Works of Jacques Maritain*, vol. 6 (Notre Dame, Ind.: University of Notre Dame Press, forthcoming).

19. "There is a distinction between a *philosophical* knowledge of moral values and a *natural, pre-philosophical knowledge* of these values. This distinction is not made because moral philosophy presupposes moral experience. There is a moral knowledge possessed by the ordinary man along with common experience, which precedes philosophical knowledge. Ordinary people are not expected to have philosophy in order to have morality." Jacques Maritain, *Neuf leçons sur les notions premières de la philosophie morale* (Paris: Pierre Téqui, 1951). Translated by Cornelia N. Borgerhoff as *An Introduction to Basic Problems of Moral Philosophy* (Albany, N.Y.: Magi Books, 1990). This was taken up again much later by Karol Wojtyła.

20. See Jacques Maritain, *Court traité de l'existence et de l'existant* (Paris: Hartmann, 1947). Translated by Lewis Galantière and Gerald B. Phelan as *Existence and the Existent* (New York: Pantheon Books, 1948).

praisal and use of the concept of person, which St. Thomas of course discussed but never used intensively. In Maritain, however, it became the starting point of his anthropology, formalized in his famous distinction between individual and person.

> The word "person" is reserved for substances which possess that divine thing, the spirit, and are in consequence, each by itself [*à elle seule*], a world above to the whole bodily order, a spiritual and moral world which, strictly speaking, is not *a part* of this universe....
>
> The word "individual," on the contrary, is common to man and beast, and to plant, microbe, and atom.... So that in so far as we are individuals we are only a fragment of matter, a part of this universe, distinct, no doubt, but a part, a point in that immense network of forces and influences, physical and cosmic, vegetative and animal, ethnic, atavistic, hereditary, economic, and historic, to whose laws we are subject. As individuals, we are subject to the stars. As persons, we rule them.[21]

To this may be added his attempt, perhaps somewhat clumsy, to integrate subjectivity into the Thomistic system.

It is possible, then, to conclude that in anthropology and ethics Maritain pointed to many of the great themes of personalism, but only in an inchoate form. In this area he did not produce any grandiose and complete synthesis, as he did in epistemology, political philosophy, and aesthetics. He remained in the domain of the sketch, the essay, and the

---

21. Jacques Maritain, *Three Reformers: Luther, Descartes, Rousseau* (New York: Charles Scribner's Sons, 1929), 20–21. Carlos Santamaría, *Jacques Maritain y la polémica del bien común* (Madrid: Asociación Católica Nacional de Propagandistas, 1955), 79–80, indicates that Maritain was inspired, in the elaboration of these concepts, by the thought of Réginald Garrigou-Lagrange (a French neo-Thomistic theologian), for example in his book, *Le Sens Commun*, 3rd ed. (1921). The problem of the relation between individual and person, as also that of its articulation with the common good, is complex in Maritain (see Burgos, *Para comprender a Jacques Maritain*, 149–60). See also Jacques Maritain, *The Person and the Common Good*, trans. John Fitzgerald (Notre Dame, Ind.: University of Notre Dame Press, 1966), 33: "the human being is caught between two poles; a material pole, which, in reality, does not concern the true person but rather the shadow of personality or what, in the strict sense, is called *individuality*, and a spiritual pole, which does concern *true personality*.... Thus, we are confronted with the distinction between *individuality* and *personality*."

proposal. The reasons for this limitation are not entirely clear, although we could suggest that the innovations which he contributed to personalism were not compatible with his structurally Thomistic foundation, and that, consciously or not, this prevented him from elaborating complex structures and obliged him to limit himself to sketching new paths. Whatever the case, and apart from possible interpretations, what should be recognized is that the lack of great works of synthesis in ethics and anthropology from Maritain is a fact.

1.3 | Political Philosophy

Social and political philosophy, to which Maritain dedicated himself after the condemnation of *Action française*, was another matter. Perhaps because the political philosophy of St. Thomas is more limited, and, besides, as much as Maritain attempted to count on it, the social context was so different that it could only be a distant source of inspiration, Maritain worked with greater freedom and his contributions were more original and creative. His work in this area, very complex and extensive and of great influence, can be described from the starting point of his two principal texts: *Integral Humanism* and *Man and the State.*

Integral Humanism was published in 1936 and had a tremendous impact, as we noted above.[22] It is not easy to summarize the essential facts about so dense a work, but it is certainly possible to indicate the essential point, the perspective which orients everything: the rejection of Catholic traditionalism at the political level, which implied a nuanced criticism of medieval Christianity and of its anthropological

---

22. There were three lines of interpretation. A large majority of Catholic intellectuals valued this work in a very positive way and took it as a source of inspiration for a way of being both Catholic and modern. Progressive thinkers, especially after Vatican Council II, considered that Maritain had not gone far enough. And the more traditionalist line confronted Maritain and accused him of being a secularist and betraying Christian principles. This line strongly opposed Maritain and caused him notable problems, but, from the ideological point of view, it ceased to have even a minimum of coherence after Vatican Council II which adopted the outlook of Maritain's theses.

vision. Maritain came to the conclusion that this model of society was finished; it belonged to the past.[23] He drew the consequences: it would have to be abandoned definitively, without any sterile nostalgia, and a different political and cultural perspective would have to be adopted: the acceptance and assimilation of values that modernity had contributed and which the present world lived. What were these values? The rehabilitation of what is human, proposed by the Reformation and the Renaissance; the licit petition for the autonomy of worldly things with respect to the sacred which carried with it a greater separation between Church and State; the emergence of plurality, about which political consequences had to be deduced; the realization that the level of Christianity in a society depended essentially on the attitude and *personal* quality of Christians and not on any institutional structure (however important it may be); and so on.

However, although these elements were valid, positive, and unrenounceable, they could not be accepted naively in an uncritical manner, because the price that European society had paid to acquire them had been far too high. In effect, although it could be said truthfully that post-medieval society had rediscovered man, it was equally true that it had done so while forgetting about God. Modernity had forged an exclusively anthropocentric humanism which, for that very reason, was destined to fail. And in order to radically resolve that situation it was necessary to adopt those conquests, completing them with the dimension that they had lost, transcendence. What was necessary, in other words, was a complete, integral humanism, that would not forget the human, but which would take account of the fact than man only realizes himself fully in God. "At this new moment of the history of Christian culture, the creature would not be belittled or annihilated before God; and neither would it be rehabilitated without God or against God; it would be rehabilitated *in* God." The key point is that, "the creature be truly respected

---

23. This does not imply a simply negative valuation of this epoch, but only the recognition that every model of society pertains to a determined historical period and cannot be proposed again as if utopian when that period has ended.

in its connection with God and *because* receiving everything from Him; humanism, but theocentric humanism, rooted where man has his roots, integral humanism, humanism of the Incarnation."[24] This integral humanism needed to be promoted, fundamentally, for lay people; and from it the "new Christendom" would arise, which would replace the medieval one on the basis of modern parameters. "Thus a vitally Christian social renewal will be a work of sanctity or it will be nothing; a sanctity, that is, turned toward the temporal, the secular, the profane. Has not the world known leaders of the people who were saints: If a new Christendom arises in history, it will be the work of such a kind of sanctity."[25]

Man and the State has a slightly distinct approach since it is a book of political philosophy—not of historical-cultural analysis—which, also, is situated in a different context, the United States, a society characterized by living in a stable democracy since the American Revolution and by possessing, at that time, a much more developed and balanced capitalism than Europe's. Such a different atmosphere notably influenced Maritain's thinking and led him to modify some of the theses and attitudes of *Integral Humanism*. In this latter work, for example, though the economic questions are generally treated tangentially, there is an attitude that is at bottom contrary to the capitalist world (quite similar to Mounier's) and considers it the fruit of a comfortable and egoistic bourgeois attitude which ends up transforming man into an object and elevating money as the supreme good. The American experience allowed him to recognize that not all capitalism necessarily fitted these parameters: there were more human versions, compatible with the dignity of the person and removed from the exploitative attitude of the industrial revolution. Because of this there are no criticisms of capitalism in *Man and the State*.[26]

---

24. Jacques Maritain, "Integral Humanism: Temporal and Spiritual Problems of a New Christendom," in *The Collected Works of Jacques Maritain*, vol. 11, *Integral Humanism, Freedom in the Modern World, and A Letter on Independence*, trans. Otto Bird, Joseph Evans, and Richard O'Sullivan (Notre Dame, Ind.: University of Notre Dame Press, 1966), 197.
25. Ibid., 229.
26. Maritain himself confirmed the existence of this change of perspective in *Reflec-*

But the principal contribution of this work is a political philosophy of democracy. Maritain found in America a democratic system that responded to his expectations of both the correct way in which government should be exercised and also the adequate structure of the social order. All of this caused a significant change of course in his thought. Above all, it confirmed for him the value of democracy as the most adequate system of government, an assertion that nowadays could only be surprising if one forgets that the generalized stabilization of democratic regimes in Continental Europe has only occurred with clarity since World War II.[27] The previous democratic systems had many limitations and, in some cases, were not far from revolutionary Jacobin stances which, in their time, caused the Reign of Terror and afterwards continued producing social instability. For this reason, it was not surprising that democracy was regarded with suspicion by some and with open hostility by others.[28] But Maritain encountered, in the United States, a secular and pacific democratic experience which not only was respectful of the social framework, but was also in itself the cause of the stability of its institutions. Thus his view of this subject was profoundly modified to the point that his principal objective turned to the attempt to understand, justify, and defend this system, as well as to study its relation to Christianity. This approach is inchoate in works such as *The Rights of Man and the Natural Law* (1943) or *Christianity and Democracy* (1945), and its definitive and complete formulation can be found in *Man and the State*.[29]

---

tions on America (New York: Scribner, 1958), where he affirms that he believed that he had found in this country a society close to his formulation of the new Christendom: "a secular society of religious inspiration."

27. Robert A. Dahl, *On Democracy* (New Haven, Conn.: Yale University Press, 2000).

28. Mounier exhibited a much more antagonistic attitude toward parliamentarianism than Maritain.

29. See Jacques Maritain, *The Rights of Man and the Natural Law*, trans. Doris C. Anson (New York: Charles Scribner's Sons, 1943); Maritain, *Christianity and Democracy*, trans. Doris C. Anson (London: Centenary Press, 1945). See also Maritain, *Man and the State* (Chicago: University of Chicago Press, 1951).

1.4 | Communitarian Personalism

At the meeting point between his vision of the person and his political philosophy we find one of Maritain's more important contributions to personalism: his theoretical elaboration of communitarian personalism, understood as the determination of the set of relationships, priorities, and dependencies which configure the person's relation with society from a personalist point of view. It is interesting to note that, although the expression "communitarian personalism" is automatically associated with Mounier, it was not he who coined it, but Maritain, as he himself relates:

> Thanks especially, I believe, to Emmanuel Mounier, the expression "personalist and communitarian" has become something of a catch phrase for French Catholic thought and rhetoric. I am not without some responsibility for this myself. At a time when it mattered very much to oppose to the totalitarian slogans a new—and true—one, I had gently solicited my grey cells, and finally, in one of my books of that period, advanced the phrase in question. It is from me, I believe, that Mounier got it.[30]

The question, in any case, is secondary. What is decisive is that, in Maritain's writings, we find the basic principles of communitarian personalism formulated, understanding those principles to be the personalist keys to the interrelation between person and society.

"The conception of the regime of civilization or of the temporal order which seems to me to be founded in reason," he affirms in *Integral Humanism*, under the heading *The Temporal City Abstractly Considered: Communal and Personalist Aspects*,

> has three typical characteristics: first of all, it is *communal*; I mean by this that, for it, the proper and specifying end of the city and of civilization is a common good which is different from the simple sum of the individual

---

30. Jacques Maritain, *The Peasant of the Garonne: An Old Layman Questions Himself about the Present Time*, trans. Micheal Cuddihy and Elizabeth Hughes (New York: Holt, Rinehart, and Winston, 1968), 51.

goods and superior to the interests of the individual insofar as the latter is *part* of the social whole. The common good is essentially the right earthly life of the assembled multitude, of a *whole* composed of human persons: this is to say that it is at once material and moral.

But moreover, and for this very reason, this temporal common good is not the ultimate end. It is ordered to something better: the intemporal good of the person, the conquest of his perfection and of his spiritual freedom.

This is why the just conception of the temporal regime has a second characteristic: it is *personalist*. I mean by this that it is essential to the temporal common good to respect and serve the supratemporal ends of the human person.[31]

Maritain affirmed, therefore, that the person is the primary ontological value to which society is subordinate and, at the same time, that the person has ineluctable duties in view of the common good or the good of the city.[32] Thus communitarian personalism is frontally opposed to all types of collectivisms, equally those of the right, fascism and Nazism; and of the left, because both are motivated by the primacy of the collective principle and submit the person to the collectivity. We will not expand on this point because it has already been treated earlier (see chap. 1, sec. 3, above), but it is worth emphasizing that Maritain's theses respond exactly to one of the fundamental needs that gave rise to personalism: to have an anthropology capable of generating a socio-political approach with enough consistency to oppose the two prevailing social models of the 1930s. On this point, Maritain appears not only as a convinced personalist but also as a pioneer in the formulation, probably for the first time, of the philosophical proposal which the personalist awakening needed: Martin Buber's excluded alternative.

---

31. Maritain, "Integral Humanism," 236–37.
32. Maritain maintained an intense debate with some Thomists who, curiously, held to an absolute primacy of the common good: see Charles de Koninck, *De la primauté du bien commun contre les personalistes* (1943; Montreal: Éditions de l'Université Laval, 1952); and Carlos Santamaría, *Jacques Maritain y la polémica del bien común*.

In summary and to conclude, from the personalist point of view, Maritain contributed interesting ideas and perspectives in ethics and anthropology which others would later take up and develop, but his dependence on Thomism kept him from formulating many themes with the necessary force and newness. Nevertheless, in the socio-political domain he appears as one of the great personalists (comparable only to Mounier), since he effectively contributed to the break with an outmoded medievalism and to the adoption of unrenounceable elements of modernity, elaborated a personalist political philosophy of democracy, worked on the intellectual elaboration of the foundations of human rights, and formulated for the first time the theses of communitarian personalism. Therefore it is not strange that his influence in this domain has been so great nor that many politicians of personalist or, more simply, Christian inspiration take his philosophical teaching as a reference point.

2 | Gabriel Marcel (1889–1973): Existentialist Personalism

2.1 | Introduction

Gabriel Marcel is generally framed within the existentialist current and, more concretely, is considered as the principal representative of Christian existentialism (although he rejected this label) in opposition to Jean-Paul Sartre's atheistic existentialism. But he is also frequently framed within a personalism of an existentialist sort.[33] In reality, the difference between the two classifications is subtle, because an existentialism that does not give priority to existence over essence and which conceives the human being as person—as is the case with Marcel—is, without a doubt, a type of personalism. So both classifications are easily interchangeable.

---

33. See Czeslaw Bartnik, *Studies in Personalist System* (Lublin: KUL, 2007); Philip Trower, *Turmoil and Truth: The Historical Roots of the Modern Crisis in the Catholic Church* (Oxford: Family Press, 2003).

Marcel was born in Paris in 1889 and had a difficult childhood because of the death of his mother, a complex relationship with his father and his stepmother, and his peculiar sensibility.[34] Since his youth, he was already inclined toward philosophy; and, initially, his sympathies centered on idealist philosophers, such as Samuel Taylor Coleridge, Friedrich Schelling, Josiah Royce, and Francis Herbert Bradley. Under this influence he resolved to elaborate a philosophical system which he began in the form of notes in a diary. Nevertheless, little by little, his faith in idealism declined under the influence of philosophers such as Bergson and some Americans, and his personal experiences, in particular those of World War I. Marcel was assigned to the department for the missing in action, whose mission was to inform family members about the situation of those soldiers whose whereabouts were not known. He then experienced very intensely the importance of each concrete person and how the happiness of specific persons could depend on a few words: a "yes" or "no." And his faith in global and abstract idealist systems was definitively broken. What was important was the person, each concrete and individual person and not abstractions. If philosophy wanted to respond to reality, it would have to articulate itself around this essential value.

These experiences forged his way of philosophizing and the keys of his thought: horror for abstraction and for all things systematic, which reminded him of the sterility of his initial idealism and, on the contrary, love of the concrete, experience, and expositive thinking. Marcel sought to philosophize about life experience and from that followed his interest in phenomenological analyses. There we also find one of the keys to his interest in theatre and the connection he sought to establish be-

---

34. For Marcel, see José Luis Cañas, *La filosofía personalista de Gabriel Marcel* (2009; unpublished); John B. O'Malley, *The Fellowship of Being: An Essay on the Concept of Person in the Philosophy of Gabriel Marcel* (The Hague: Nijhoff, 1966); Thomas W. Busch, ed., *The Participant Perspective: A Gabriel Marcel Reader* (Lanham, Md.: University Press of America, 1987); Roger Troisfontaines, *De l'existence à l'être. La philosophie de G. Marcel*, 2 vols. (Leuven: Nauwelarts, 1968).

tween thought and drama. Since the person is a being in movement, which unfolds in time, the sole way of existentially knowing a concrete person is to narrate his life. Now, this occurs in novels and in the theatre, and so, both constitute a particularly suitable way to know man and to make him known. Because of this, philosophy should also drink from this source in order to, subsequently, with its peculiar analytical charism, shed light which allows for better understanding of the narrative mystery of the person.

Marcel sought to maintain throughout his life this connection between thought and theatre, and he himself wrote a good number of theatrical works.[35] Nevertheless, what follows is limited to describing his philosophy. We shall begin with his methodological presuppositions and then develop the central aspects of his thought.[36]

2.2 | Methodological Presuppositions

Marcel, with respect to his life and philosophical affiliation, constructed his reflections from the starting point of *existence*, which constituted for him not only the initial datum but also the unavoidable beginning because, "If existence is not at the beginning it is nowhere, for I do not believe that any transition can be made to existence which is not cheating or deception."[37] This declaration of intention certainly corresponds to his life's journey and is also designed to avoid the idealist path, on which he himself began and which is now radically rejected. In fact, for Marcel not even existence was sufficient as a theoretical starting point

---

35. Some of the most relevant are *La Grâce* (1911), *Le palais de sable* (1913), *Le coeur des autres* (1920), *Le Quatour en fa dièse* (1925), *Un homme de Dieu* (1925), *Le Monde cassé* (1933), *L'Emmissaire* (1949), and *Le signe de la Croix* (1949).

36. Marcel's influence extended to Jean Wahl, Paul Ricoeur, Jean-Paul Sartre, and Emmanuel Lévinas, who all came, along with other intellectuals, to his famous Friday meetings.

37. Gabriel Marcel, *Creative Fidelity*, trans. Robert Rosthal (New York: Fordham University Press, 2002), 15. Originally published as *Du réfus à l'invocation* (Paris: Gallimard, 1940), re-issued as *Essai de philosophie concrète* (Paris: Gallimard, 1999), 27.

for philosophy; the beginning must be constituted by a real and concrete existence, by one's own living existence, leading him to state: "I am inclined to deny that any work is philosophical if we cannot discern in it what may be called the sting of reality."[38] Furthermore, he understood that this existence principally responds to *personal* being; thus, it is not a purely objective beginning but also a subjective one, which makes it possible to resolve from the start the dichotomy between objectivity and subjectivity, which has created so many problems in philosophy.[39]

In any case, it is necessary to specify that, although we can speak of a certain methodological reflection in Marcel, this does not mean that he attempted in any way to construct a philosophical system. Nothing was further from his interests and objectives. His passage through Hegelianism cured him of such a pretension, arousing in him a special aversion toward systems and toward any type of "isms," and probably transforming him into one of the most decided and consciously non-systematic personalists. What he attempted to carry out was "his own philosophy" which consisted of *analyzing concrete reality* by way of "successive approximations," "explorations," "perforations" that penetrated little by little, but ever more profoundly, into what is real, discovering and extracting all the streams of riches in concrete existence. This "philosophy of the concrete," which attended to singular existence, obviously did not intend to capture the concrete in its singularity, something which is impossible and anti-philosophical, but rather, in its "concrete generality," that is, as the prototype of a certain type of existence. With this, Marcel attempted to go beyond the limits of purely objective being and to get to personal being with its individual and subjective aspects.[40]

---

38. Marcel, *Creative Fidelity*, 64.
39. This is a concept of experience very similar to that of Karol Wojtyła.
40. Marcel again and again rejects rationalism and "the spirit of abstraction" of idealism, which could lead one to brand his philosophy as irrationalism and to invalidate the scope of these methodological premises. But such an objection is valid only if it is

So it appears that it is possible to speak of a method or hermeneutic proper to Marcel which is personalist in character and about which he does not to go into details, but which would include three elements: wonder, reflection, and exploration. Wonder in face of the being which is given in existence, reflection about what is given—which lifts it to the philosophical plane—and detailed exploration of existence. Exploration seeks objectivity while being fully aware that it can never succeed completely, since each person realizes his own unrepeatable exploration, the result of the fusion of his personal subjectivity with the objectivity of the world. Because of this, each philosophical path is unique and the search for an absolute neutrality, of an absolute objectivity, is simply impossible.

The subject, *par excellence*, of this reflection is the person, a theme that can only be adequately treated when one is aware of its radical originality. The person is essentially distinct from things, and only if our philosophical concepts accept this, can we approach the specifically personal realities without deforming them: corporeality, being and having, problem and mystery, fidelity, hope.... Marcel attempted exactly this type of approach, and his successful reflection unfolded into original contributions to philosophical anthropology which have had a great influence.

2.3 | Marcel's Areas of Interest

Marcel understood *corporeality* as the recognition of the incarnate character of man, which signifies much more than a mere recognition of his evident materiality or the existence of a biological support. It means the recognition of the essentiality of the body in the constitution of the person, surpassing a merely objective view—the body as an instrument for

---

admitted that logical rationality is the only way of employing intelligence. Marcel, on the contrary, had a very broad vision which even led him to recognize "the need for abstraction, understood as the potentiality of grasping profound realities." *Men against Humanity*, trans. G. S. Fraser (London: Harvill Press, 1952).

use—in order to understand it as the complete mediator in the interaction with the world. "To be incarnated is to appear to oneself as body, as this particular body, without being identified with it nor distinguished from it—identification and distinction being correlative operations which are significant only in the realm of objects."[41] The body thus becomes one of the prisms for interpreting reality—I understand the world from my body—to the point that Marcel even stated that "incarnation is the axis of metaphysics."

Another great theme of Marcel's is, without a doubt, *intersubjectivity*, to which he gives the same relevance as other personalists (Nédoncelle, Buber, and so on) and in very similar terms: intersubjectivity is not a point of arrival but of departure. Human existence is, from the start, being-with, being with others, a perspective that affects all aspects of the person including understanding, of which it is the driver and mediator. Nevertheless, intersubjectivity is not a mixing of subjects, still less a fusion of them. If there is no subject, if there is no person, neither is there a relationship or interrelationship. Therefore, Marcel affirms that authentic intersubjectivity is to be understood within these three parameters: immediacy, presence, and *distance*. And, finally, Marcel understands that intersubjectivity points to the divine Thou or to being *par excellence*, which ideally fulfils all the intentions and aspirations that the relationship carries with it but which no relationship in this world satisfies.

Marcel also gave attention to *metaphysics*, something not excessively frequent among personalists. His methodological presuppositions led him initially to reject the concept of being, but, after reading Fr. Reginald Garrigou-Lagrange's *Dieu*, he changed his opinion to the point that, afterwards, he tried to integrate it into his thought. Anyway, he attempted to found or express a personalist metaphysics, that is, an ontological reflection, in a kind of Heideggerian direction, which would begin with the person and would aspire to overcome the abstraction of Aristotelian metaphysics.

41. Marcel, *Creative Fidelity*, 20.

Thus Marcel proposes a peculiar metaphysics or ontology, which could be characterized by two fundamental features. It is a metaphysics of what is human; it investigates the meaning of being in human existence and for human existence. The second feature is its interpretation of being, conceived as a certain *consistence* or permanence that manifests itself, for example, in the permanence of the subject against his possible reduction to Hume's flows of consciousness. The issue, in any case, is very complex and difficult to categorize, so much so that he himself recognized at the end of his life that he did not know with precision to what extent he could use the term "ontology."[42]

One of his more characteristic contributions is the famous and original "Distinguish between the Mysterious and the Problematic. A problem is something met with which bars my passage. It is before me in its entirety. A mystery, on the other hand, is something in which I find myself caught up, and whose essence is therefore not to be before me in its entirety. It is as though in this province the distinction between *in me* and *before me* loses its meaning."[43] A mystery is a reality in which I am personally implicated, and as such, I cannot study it from the outside with total objectivity. I can only analyze with objectivity problems which are external to me, for example, a mathematical problem, but not that which forms a part of my very being, since, by the very nature of the question, I cannot view it from outside, since I am a part of it. Some examples of mysteries are evil, body-soul relations, freedom, knowledge, and love, because I am the one who knows and loves.[44]

Another of the great topics which characterize his philosophy is the distinction between *being* and *having*, which has since been used profusely. The central nucleus of this idea points to the distinction be-

---

42. His metaphysics was not appreciated by the Neo-Thomists. Gilson classified it as "speculative mysticism," and Maritain, who in this respect was basically Thomist, as "not a genuine metaphysics."

43. See Gabriel Marcel, *Being and Having: An Existentialist Diary*, trans. Katherine Farrer (New York: Harper & Row, 1965), 100. Originally published as *Être et avoir I (1928–1933)*.

44. Ibid., 162.

tween possessive having linked to the world of objects and being proper to personal "existing." Applied to corporeality, it allows us to understand the profound meaning of the fact that man does not have a body, but rather *is* a body, in this Marcelian sense, since corporeality is not something inert and passive at the disposal of the subject, but the man himself. Marcel also used corporeality to criticize the disproportionate development of industrial and technical civilization. Without totally rejecting technological progress, but with a rather negative attitude, he criticized the fact that contemporary man is only concerned about having ever more, instead of making an effort to be more, which only aggravates his crisis of meaning, because in matter alone, in objects, we can never find the fullness of existence nor of meaning.

Marcel is also notable for his suggestive analysis of *fidelity*, *hope*, and *love* (inspired by the three theological virtues). For him, fidelity constitutes "the only means we have of effectively vanquishing time,"[45] and it is sustained in our capacity to commit ourselves, which is possible because we are not identical to our present identity: there is something in us which endures. But fidelity has to be understood not as a routine or submission to a purely formal obligation, but as a creative, personal activity, so that for Marcel "Fidelity can only be shown towards a person, never at all to a notion or an ideal,"[46] and "all commitment is a response. A one-sided commitment would not only be rash but could be blamed as pride."[47]

Marcel's analysis of hope was especially brilliant, so much so that on occasion his thought has been called a *philosophy of hope*. In any case, it is perhaps here that his affiliation to existentialism is most clearly perceived, leading him to insist on the *dramatic* character of hope, to think that its value is especially affirmed when the temptation

---

45. Marcel, *Creative Fidelity*, 152.
46. Marcel, *Being and Having*, 96.
47. Ibid., 46. For Marcel the family is the place *par excellence* for commitment. See "The Mystery of the Family," in *Homo Viator*, trans. Emma Craufurd (London: Harper, 1962).

to despair appears, and to dedicate abundant space to limit situations.⁴⁸ This was not an obstacle to Marcel's insistence on the intersubjective dimension of hope: "I hope in you for us." And, in the end, he places its foundation in transcendence, because "it is planted in a zone of inexpugnable metaphysical security."

We conclude this brief presentation by pointing out that Marcel always conceived his philosophy as a means of social action, of engagement with his contemporaries. Not in Mounier's sense of direct social action, but in the sense of an explicit commitment, although as a philosopher, to the problems of his time. In fact, his philosophical motto, inspired by the world of theatre, which he so liked, consists of the rejection of the perspective of the *spectator*. Philosophy could and should be theoretical, but not in the manner of the spectator who is outside and safe from what happens on the stage; it would have to be active, playing its role in the theatre of the world and involving itself fully in the vicissitudes of its own age. In this sense he affirmed on one occasion: "All my activity is oriented toward so many and so varied creative and critical efforts that I would like to channel into action, but without losing sight of what constitutes the center of my longings: to contribute to improving a world which is threatened with losing itself in hate and abstraction."⁴⁹

---

48. "One could even say that, in this sense, the permanent possibility of suicide is an essential starting point for authentic metaphysical thought." Marcel, "Concrete Approaches to Investigating the Ontological Mystery," in Marcel, *Gabriel Marcel's Perspectives on the Broken World*, trans. Katharine Rose Hanley (Chicago: Marquette University Press, 1998), 183, originally published as *Positions et approches concrètes du Mystère ontologique* (Paris: J. Vrin, 1949).

49. Gabriel Marcel, *Dos discursos y un prólogo autobiográfico* (Barcelona: Herder, 1967), 13.

3 | Emmanuel Mounier (1905–50): Communitarian Personalism

3.1 | Life and Works

Mounier was born in Grenoble, into a peasant family, and was always proud of his humble origin.[50] From his family he received a profound and simple Christian education which would mark his entire life. He received his primary education at Grenoble, and later, in that same city, he began to study philosophy under Jacques Chevalier, a professor at the university and a great Catholic thinker.

At age nineteen, at the initiative of his parents, he went to Paris to study medicine, but after two years of vacillation and frustration he abandoned these studies in favor of philosophy, his true vocation. They were difficult years. His contact with the Sorbonne greatly disappointed him as he encountered a philosophy cut off from life and ineffective, a situation that continued, as his wife relates, "until the day he found Péguy's works. That was a revelation." Péguy's committed Christian thinking enthused him and exercised a profound influence upon him. Later he met and became friends with other important thinkers of the time, Maritain, Marcel, Nikolai Berdyaev, and Jean Guitton. Maritain's influence was particularly important, although they differed in philosophical perspective and over the adequate approach to social and political action.[51] He was also influenced by the French "philosophy of spirit," by Maurice Blondel and Bergson, existentialism and Marxism.

In 1930 he thought of writing his doctoral thesis on Spanish mysticism, to which end he attempted to learn Spanish and traveled to Spain.

---

50. See Nunzio Bombaci, *Emmanuel Mounier: una vida, un testimonio*, trans. Carlos Diaz (Salamanca: Fundación Emmanuel Mounier, 2002); Paul Ricoeur, "Une philosophie personnaliste," *Esprit* 174 (1950): 860–87, translated as "Emmanuel Mounier: A Personalist Philosopher," in *History and Truth*, 133–162; Armando Rigobello, *Il contributo filosofico di E. Mounier* (Rome: Bocca, 1955).

51. Joseph Amato, *Mounier and Maritain: A French Catholic Understanding of the Modern World* (Tuscaloosa, Ala.: University of Alabama Press, 1975).

In the end, he desisted and returned to the dilemma that agonized him: the choice between a life of academic investigation and a life in which thought motivated action. He chose the latter because of the grave sense of crisis that he perceived in Europe and especially in France, and to which he thought he could not give a solid response in a comfortable and erudite academic setting. The crash of 1929 had caused grave economic problems, and there was also a profound spiritual crisis: liberalism and communism pressed upon men from contrary points of view, while many Christians were either installed themselves comfortably in a series of traditions that had become outdated due to the latest events, or adapted themselves to the new situations without trying to modify these or give them characteristics in accord with the Gospel ("the established disorder"). The international situation, finally, foreshadowed a war that would erupt within a few years.

Mounier perceived with special acuity the nature of this crisis, so much so that he conceived it as an historic crisis which would require exceptional decisions and solutions.[52] In particular, he thought that the only possible way out was a new way of thinking that would propose a fresh and totally renewed humanism, determined to "think with the hands," that is, to transform thought into action because real crises are never resolved merely by thinking. And, to this end, he conceived the idea of founding a review which would bring together those young persons who had the same perception. He thus abandoned the academic world and founded, with Georges Izard and André Déléage, the review *Esprit* in 1932, when he was only twenty-seven.[53]

---

52. "Mounier's initial project is to found a new humanism, in proportion to a total crisis." Jean-Marie Doménach, "La presenza di Mounier nella cultura euopea del dopoguerra," in *Mounier trent'anni dopo. Atti del Convegno di studio dell'università cattolica* (Milano: Vita e Pensiero, 1981), 27.

53. "It can be said, if one wishes to gather a complex reality in simple formulae, that *Esprit* appears in the center of three more or less simultaneous crises: a society disturbed by the war and soon after by the great economic depression; the labor movement, torn by the Bolshevik revolution; a Catholic environment which has yet not found its place in the city." Michel Winock, *Histoire politique de la revue Esprit (1930–50)* (Paris: Éditions du Seuil, 1975), 9.

From this moment on, Mounier's life was identified with the destiny of *Esprit*, understood as the spearhead of the movement with which he proposed to transform society. The programmatic message of the first issue, inspired by Berdyaev, was titled "Remaking the Renaissance"[54] and proposed to recover the humanism of that era, purging it of the individualism that it had generated, under the "the primacy of the spiritual" (Maritain's expression) and of the communitarian. Little by little, thanks to Mounier's genius and the merits of his collaborators, the review grew in importance; and, despite its minority status, it came to have a great intellectual importance. It became a banner of renewal and progressivism, and a point of reference for both Catholics and other intellectuals.

In this period, gathering together articles published in the review between 1932 and 1935, Mounier published his first significant work, *Révolution personnaliste et communautaire* (1935), in which he condensed the essentials of his thought and of the *Esprit* movement. In this text personalist topics appeared for the first time, but in a still somewhat indefinite form, and the limits imposed by the author's youth (age 30) are clearly perceived. Other publications followed, increasingly more mature, among which *Manifesto* (1936), one of his principal works, stands out.

In 1938 he married Paulette Leclerq who became his faithful intellectual collaborator. At the outbreak of the war in 1939 he was mobilized into the auxiliary services (because of total blindness in one eye). After the Armistice he returned to the land of his birth, and, with the permission of the Vichy government, arranged that *Esprit* could reappear in the south of France. After a few months, however, the review (first banned in June 1940) was banned again, and Mounier was incarcerated on an accusation of rebellion and conspiracy with the Resistance. After

---

54. Mounier, "Refaire la renaissance," in *Révolution personnaliste et communautaire*, in *Oeuvres*, vol. 1, *1931–1939* (Paris: Éditions du Seuil, 1961), 11–40. Other ideas proposed are: going beyond the crisis, disassociating the spiritual from the reactionary, the importance of revolution understood as *metanoia*, rehabilitation of the material world, of the community, spiritual realism, etc.

a long trial, he was absolved in 1942 and set free, but he had to live a clandestine life.

After the war came to an end, Mounier once again edited *Esprit* in Paris and published new works. The coming of maturity and the experience of the war moderated to some extent his activism and made him see the need to give a more philosophical character to his writings, seeking a more solid foundation for the ideas presented in his first publications. Along these lines, he published *Treatise on Character* (1946), an extensive work on the study of character and psychology, *Introduction aux existentialismes* (1947) and *Personalism* (1949), the clearest and most synoptic exposition of his thought.[55] In these years the review reached its greatest prestige as the banner of personalism and a vanguard of Christianity. Death overcame Mounier at middle age in 1950 due to exhaustion and a heart attack, He died within the little community he had founded with his family and collaborators.

3.2 | Communitarian Personalism

Mounier's thought is automatically identified with personalism and, in particular, with communitarian personalism, but curiously, neither the word "personalism" nor the expression "communitarian personalism" are his. Mounier himself mentions the existence of a work by Charles Renouvier, published in 1903, titled *Le Personalisme*. We have already pointed out that the origin of the compound term "communitarian personalism" is also a matter of discussion and that Maritain attributed it to himself.[56] But the question is merely incidental. What matters is that

---

55. Also from this period, but less relevant, are *Qu'est-ce que le personnalisme?* (Paris: Éditions du Seuil, 1947), republished in *Oeuvres*, vol. 3, *1944–1950*, translated by Cynthia Rowland as "What Is Personalism?" in *Be Not Afraid* (London: Rockcliff, 1951; New York: Sheed and Ward, 1962), 109–196; and *Feu la Chrétienté* (Paris: Éditions du Seuil, 1950), republished in *1944–1950*.

56. The first person we know about to give the name of personalism to a philosophy was Ramón de Campoamor who, in 1855, published a book titled, *El personalismo. Apuntes para una filosofía* (*Personalism: Notes for a Philosophy*). As for "communitarian per-

Mounier made the term his own, eliminated the pejorative meaning which the term had according to its then-common definition in French—of someone who subordinated everything to himself and his own interests—and converted it into the central slogan of his thought and of the cultural movement that he inspired. And, since this movement acquired a great importance, it is no exaggeration to say that personalism became a current within the history of philosophy thanks to Emmanuel Mounier.

Now, what did Mounier understand by "communitarian personalism" and, specifically, what vision did he have of his own thought? The answer, contrary to what might be expected, is not simple, because Mounier elaborated his idea of personalism over the course of many years. He did not start from a defined concept. Not only that, but in *Remaking the Renaissance*, *Esprit*'s programmatic manifesto, the term does not even appear, although very soon (two years later) it can already be found in some pioneering texts, such as *The Personalist Revolution* (1934) and *The Communitarian Revolution* (1935). Both were soon united in the title of his first important work, which turned into the motto that would be his weapon for combat during the following decade: *The Communitarian and Personalist Revolution*. In this work, however, there is not even a minimally precise formulation of his doctrine, but only a set of key ideas, very vibrantly expressed, that at times comes close to the genre of the pamphlet.

Not until *Manifeste au service du personnalisme* do we find his first systematic presentation of his thought. The book is, without a doubt, important, it contributes new ideas; but his perception of personalism as such is imprecise. "We call personalist," he wrote, "any doctrine, any civilization, which affirms the primacy of the human person over the material needs and over the collective mechanisms which sustain his development."[57] It is, then, not a concrete doctrine, but rather a principle which

---

sonalism," some attribute it to Maritain, who, under this hypothesis, would have already used it in 1928 in conferences which he gave at the University of Santander and were the basis for *Humanisme intégral*. J. Guitton, on the contrary, said that Chévalier had previously used the term in conversations with students.

57. Mounier, *Manifeste au service du personnalisme*, in *1931–1939*, 483. Translated as *A Personalist Manifesto*, ed. Joseph T. Delos et al. (New York: Longman, Green, 1938).

could fit multiple, very distinct doctrines. This leads him to the conclusion that "we must speak, then, in the plural, of 'the personalisms.'"[58]

Another decisive feature of Mounier's personalism is its intrinsically active character. Mounier did not leave academia to construct a pure theory but rather to transform society. Thus his ideology was not only directed towards action but is *thought in action*, a thought which conforms itself structurally in order to achieve concrete objectives and, without that aspect, it loses its validity and strength. This configuration has its counterpart in its theoretical weakness, something very clear in Mounier's writings, in which the brilliant intuitions are seldom followed by a detailed exposition which would give them definition and force.

Mounier maintained this vision of personalism his entire life. In *What Is Personalism?*, written ten years later (and only three years before his death), we find it perfectly in force. With respect to the structure of personalism, he states: "What makes personalism very difficult for some to understand is that they are trying to find a system, whereas personalism is perspective, method, and exigency."[59] This method and an exigency lead necessarily to action: "It is not sufficient to say: person, community, total man, in order to insert personalism into the historic drama of our age. We must also say: end of Western bourgeois society, introduction of socialist structures, the proletarian role of initiative."[60]

One can only perceive a significant change, although an especially important one since it is his most mature text, in *Personalism*, written in 1949, where for the first time he presents it as a *philosophy*.

> Personalism is a philosophy, it is not merely an attitude. It is a philosophy but not a system.
>
> Not that it fears systematization. For order is necessary in thinking: concepts, logic, schemes of unification are not only of use to fix and com-

---

58. Ibid.
59. Mounier, "What Is Personalism?" 193.
60. Ibid., 186.

municate a thought which would otherwise dissolve into obscure and isolated intuitions; they are instruments of discovery as well as of exposition. Since it defines certain positions, personalism is a philosophy and not only an attitude.[61]

This passage, nevertheless, loses strength because it is part of a longer exposition in which Mounier again takes up the idea of "personalisms," although less intensely than in earlier writings.

We have to conclude, therefore, that, although there is no doubt that Mounier popularized the term "personalism" like no one else, giving it a much greater cultural and social visibility than it had possessed up until then, the perception he himself appeared to have of his doctrine was fairly weak. It was simply in a basic scheme, compatible with many others, and which, to make matters worse, was not especially original since it was framed within the long religious and philosophical tradition which had used the concept of person. This conclusion, nevertheless, does not seem to really do him justice. Despite the weakness or indefiniteness regarding the structure of his own doctrine, Mounier's thought has a very definite strength and personality; and it was recognized as such by his contemporaries, having a strong impact of many of them. Also, even though the supposed theoretical amplitude of personalism should have permitted it to accommodate under its mantle very diverse doctrines, that never happened either in Mounier's own time or afterwards.[62] Perhaps Mounier insisted on this point, although ever more weakly, in order to leave a door open to dialogue with other philosophical currents; but those philosophies, independently of whether or not they were interested in taking cover under that umbrella, quickly noticed that the philosophical substrate on which personalism was based—although not technically formulated by Mounier—was very different from theirs, so the path of dialogue was never attempted. And

---

61. Emmanuel Mounier, *Personalism*, trans. Philip Mairet (London: Routledge and Kegan Paul, 1952), vii–viii.
62. At least I do not know any Marxists or relativists or agnostics or Nietzscheans who have had any interest in applying to themselves the name of personalism.

Mounier, ever more conscious of this fact, evolved toward increasingly philosophical proposals, a process which was interrupted by his early death.

With respect to the content of his thought, although we will deal with it in more detail presently, Mounier's communitarian personalism does not differ, in its basic principles, from Maritain's. It seeks to affirm the primacy of the person over any collectivity while affirming that the community is essential for the person. In fact, he used to say that the need to use the terms "personalism" and "communitarian" was due only to the poverty of language, seeing as the person necessarily implies the community.

Mounier's insistence on this term has, in any case, caused the expression "communitarian personalism" to be associated with his specific way of understanding personalism, that is, a personalism dedicated to direct action, little preoccupied with the theoretical work of articulating foundations, and which demands of its adherents a strong moral and militant commitment to transforming the world in favor of the person (see chap. 4, sec. 2.2, below).[63]

3.3. Anthropology

Mounier's anthropology, like all his thought, is characterized by its force, its newness, its connection with praxis—thinking in order to act—and a kind of diffuse character. It is futile to try to find in it academic elaborations or technical analyses of problems, because they are not to be found. This direction, toward which his last writings appear to point, was cut short by his early death, so that the real Mounier had an

---

63. May the following personal testimony of a militant personalist serve as a confirmation of this point: "In my opinion," affirms Vincent Miquel of the Democratic Union party of the Autonomous Community of Valencia, Spain, "by personalism we would have to understand civic action aimed at applying in society the values and the ideas consequent with the thought of Emmanuel Mounier." Agustí Colomer and August Monzón, eds., *Emmanuel Mounier i la tradició personalista* (Valencia: Universitat de Valencia Press, 2001), 118.

insuperable ambivalence: capacity for inspiration, newness, and indefiniteness.

In the concrete sphere of anthropology, this characteristic of his thought is manifested in at least two facts. The extension of his work expressly dedicated to this topic is, contrary to what might be expected, relatively scarce. In *Manifeste au service du personnalisme*, for example, one of his central works, the treatment of this topic hardly amounts to twenty pages. All the rest are dedicated to sociological or cultural analyses or to designing methods for action. All of this, of course, implies a determined vision of the person, *but it is not a theory of the person*. And something similar occurs in *Personalism*, his most mature work. There, the attention to philosophical anthropology is greater, but the extension is limited.[64]

The second fact is that his scheme for expounding the essential elements of the person varies from work to work. In *Révolution personnaliste et communautaire*, he proposes three dimensions: vocation, incarnation, and communion. In *Manifeste au service du personnalisme*, five: incarnation and commitment, integration and singularity, overpassing, freedom, and communion. And in *Personalism*, seven. Having made these observations, which seem to us to be important in order to evaluate the character of Mounier's anthropology, we turn to setting out some ideas in outline.

First, Mounier's general vision of the person is open and modern and very similar to that of the rest of the personalists. On the one hand, the person is an ontological and subsistent reality, located in the world and with the capacity of modifying it through his freedom. On the other hand, this ontological character simultaneously conceals and reveals the other essential dimension of the person: his subjectivity, his singular, unique, and unrepeatable character. From this perspective, attempting to define the person ceases to be meaningful since, due to his

---

64. We could consider *Traité du caractère* an exception to this rule, although it is above all about psychology.

singular character, the person goes beyond all conceptualization. "But one can only define objects exterior to man, such as can be put under observation. However, the person is not an object."[65] In this case, we are not dealing with a lack of academic precision, but, on the contrary, with the lucid and meditated recognition of a fact: subjectivity and the richness of personal being impede any possibility of a definition in a literal sense. Therefore, Mounier opts, like many other personalists, for a *description-definition* of the person. The best known is the following: "A person is spiritual being constituted as such by a form of subsistence and independence in his being. He maintains this subsistence by his adhesion to a hierarchy of values freely adopted, assimilated, and livedby a responsible commitment and a constant conversion. Thus he unifies all his activity in freedom and develops, motivated by creative acts, the uniqueness of his vocation."[66] This uniqueness, on the other hand, is not incompatible with the communitarian character of human nature; on the contrary, it demands it. On this point, Mounier decidedly distances himself from Sartrean existentialism which so emphasized the singularity of the subject and the radical nature of his freedom that it ends up dissolving the subject. "It is one thing to refuse the tyranny of formal definitions and quite another to deny, as existentialism sometimes does, that man has any one essence of constitution. If every man *is* nothing but what he *makes himself*, there can be no humanity, no history, and no community."[67]

On these bases rest the three essential features which constitute and manifest the person: vocation, incarnation, and communion. These dimensions are simultaneously constitutive and operative, because man must recognize and exercise them in order to be faithful to himself.[68]

---

65. Mounier, *Personalism*, vii.
66. Mounier, *Manifeste au service du personnalisme*, 523.
67. Mounier, *Personalism*, 30.
68. For Mounier, as we have said, thought is operative, so his anthropological categories are not static or even strictly academic, but only principles of personal and social action. "These formulae are not unrelated to the movement by which man proceeds towards a 'world' to be promoted. They are less definitions of the person than signs indicating

Vocation is the principle of "progressive unification of all my acts and, by means of them, of my situations: it is the person's proper act." Man, each man, has to discover what is, for him, this principle or center, and to act coherently. Thus he is able to confer unity on his life and also meaning because he discovers his place and mission in the world. *Incarnation* puts in relief his bodily dimension, a manifestation of personalist realism. Man is not a mere spirit, but an incarnate spirit, which is not a curse in the Platonic sense, but his way of being real, with its limits and positive aspects.

> I cannot think without being, nor be without my body, which is my *exposition*—to myself, to the world, to everyone else: by its means alone can I escape from the solitude of a thinking that would be only thought about thought. By its refusal to leave me wholly transparent to myself, the body takes me constantly out of myself into the problems of the world and the struggles of mankind. By the solicitation of the senses, it pushes me out into space; by growing old, it acquaints me with duration; and by its death, it confronts me with eternity. We bear the weight of its bondage, but it is also the basis of all consciousness and of all spiritual life, the omnipresent mediator of the life of the Spirit.[69]

Finally, *communion* attends to the social and communal character of the person, to which, because of its importance, we shall devote the next section.

To achieve the full development of these dimensions, determined actions and attitudes are necessary among which are *meditation* to discover one's vocation, *commitment* which confronts the heaviness of fleshly existence, and *detachment* from self in order to live in *communion*. When communion adequately unfolds and achieves its most elevated aspects, it opens the way to love. This is, for Mounier, "the surest

---

a civilization to be made. Thus, vocation has meaning only for a world of 'meditation,' incarnation only for a world of 'engagement,' communion only for a world of personal 'renunciation.'" Ricoeur, "Emmanuel Mounier: A Personalist Philosopher," 139.

69. Mounier, *Personalism*, 11.

certainty that man knows; the one irrefutable, existential *cogito*: I love, therefore I am; therefore being is, and life is worth the pain of living."[70]

3.4 | The Person in Community

Mounier's personalism is communitarian, among other things, because of his special insistence on the relevance of the community in the existence of the person. Both appear at the same time and both are mutually necessary. "The *we* follows the *I*, or, more precisely, since one cannot be constituted without the other, the *we* follows from the *I* since it could precede it."[71] But not every relation, not every grouping of persons, forms an authentic community. On the contrary, the community is more like the ideal grouping, which is only possible by overcoming or rejecting other types of union that are frequently the most common and habitual. There are groupings in which depersonalization predominates: the anonymous mass in which the important word is "everybody says it" or "everybody does it," and is the world of impersonality. There are also societies based on camaraderie and companionship; "life" societies, biological in orientation, such as the family when it is not founded on love; "reasonable" societies, composed by the union of intelligences, and legal societies based on contracts. All these have their value and meaning, but none achieves the category of community.[72]

In order to speak of community, it is necessary to take the person completely seriously, accepting his dignity and unrepeatability. It is necessary to see in the other a "thou," a neighbor, and not someone merely similar, to relate in such a way that a "we" is created, the result of living a common project, of valuing the one facing us, of opening ourselves to him in order to receive him and involve him in our ideals. And only love can make this type of relation possible. "The relationship of the *I* with the *thou* is love, by which my person is, in some way, de-

---

70. Ibid., 23.
71. Mounier, *Révolution personnaliste et communautaire*, 190.
72. This categorization is inspired by Scheler. The use of "thou" comes from Marcel.

centralized and lives completely in the other person, being possessed and possessing his love. *Love is the unity of the community, as vocation is the unity of the person.*"[73]

This is the personalist community endorsed by Mounier, a community whose ties are not merely utilitarian or self-interested, but personal because they are formed by a network of *thou-I* relationships, lived in fullness and founded on love. That is why he occasionally speaks of the personalist community as a "person of persons." This community, nevertheless, is difficult to achieve because what is governed by the principle of love is always beautiful but at times inaccessible. Mounier admitted this. This type of community "dreamt by the anarchists and sung by Péguy in his *Cité harmonieuse*, is not of this world. Christians believe that it lives in the community of the saints, which unites humanity in the mystical body of Christ."[74] But, the fact that something is not easily achieved does not exempt us from struggle, tension, and effort towards an objective to which we must tend and for which we must struggle. Such an ideal is also the guide that can direct the social action of the personalist who must try to modify society, approaching, as closely as possible, the ideal model.[75]

3.5 | Socio-Political Thought

In a certain sense, we have already presented Mounier's socio-political thought when, in chapter 1 above, we described individualism, collectivism, and the personalist reaction, since Mounier was one of the principal thinkers who collaborated in the personalist analysis of these currents and the consequent responses. For this reason, instead of repeating it, which would not add anything new, we shall consider the specific characteristics of Mounier's position, what is proper to him in the common personalist perspective.

---

73. Mounier, *Révolution personnaliste et communautaire*, 193.
74. Ibid., 202–3.
75. In *Manifeste au service du personnalisme*, Mounier proposes three fundamental areas in which we must work to transform society: the family, culture, and the economy.

3.5.1 | Individualism

One of the most striking features of Mounier's thought is his absolute hostility to bourgeois or liberal individualism. In contrast to his ability to find positive elements in Marxism and even in fascism, he finds none in individualism. It appears in his writings to be an absolute evil. And, although it is true that the individualism of the time had caused terrible evils and was one of the factors in bringing about the Second World War, it seems that such an absolutely negative evaluation is excessive.

Whatever the case, this was Mounier's position. The individualist, and the society that he generates, is the man concerned only with himself and his goods, and indifferent to the needs and demands of the poor, marginalized, and exploited, an attitude totally antithetical to a communitarian society. And his principal product and manifestation, capitalism, is the principal motor that feeds these evils. It is true that technology arises from within him, but Mounier takes these two realities to be independent. Technology is positive but capitalism is against work, responsible consumption, property, and freedom.[76] Why? Because it starts with a basic error: the use of money as a means of enrichment. "The primacy of profit was born on the day that money, the simple sign of exchange, was made by capitalism into an asset, capable of causing fecundity into the era of exchange, merchandise that could be bought and sold. This monstrous speculation of money, which used to be called *usury* or *windfall*, is the source of what we now call *capitalist profit*."[77]

On this basis Mounier founds his proposal for a personalist economy or one at the service of the person in which there are pioneering ideas such as the primacy of work over capital, the consideration of work as a personal activity, the option for a decentralized economy and criticisms of collectivist economies, united with his radical anticapitalism which

---

76. See Mounier, *Manifeste au service du personnalisme*, chap. 3, sec. 4, "Une économie pour la personne," 579–610.

77. Ibid., 587.

denies that any capital not directly associated with labor has any benefit. Another new idea in Mounier, and especially significant in his time, is his decentralized and instrumental vision of the State, understood as a social system at the service of the person, and not the reverse, as happens in the collectivisms.[78]

3.5.2 | Nazism and Fascism

Mounier's opposition to any sort of totalitarianism was radical, and for that reason, he opposed both Nazism and fascism with all his strength. In these systems the individual did not count and was merely an instrument at the service of something greater: the State, the race, the spirit of the people, or other such abstractions. Also, some specific features of this collectivism were repugnant to Mounier, such as the mystique of the Leader which magnifies one person beyond all reasonable measure, or the claims of anonymous collective doctrines and ideals such as the nation or the race. He thought that men were inevitably degraded if they put their lives at the service of ideals in which the obscure forces of biology and blood prevailed over concrete persons.

This did not stop him from noticing also some positive factors, such as the appeal to the "spirit" in the face of bourgeois economicism, and he entered into dialogue with thinkers of these movements when they appeared in the 1930s.[79]

---

78. Mounier was also in favor of a federalist type of attitude that influenced the construction of the European Union despite, paradoxically, his opposition to large political groupings.

79. But to deduce from this, as some have done, that he was sympathetic to fascism is nonsense. Also, he has been accused of collaborating with the Vichy regime in France, but Mounier limited himself to getting *Esprit* published in the prevailing circumstances, and, precisely for this, he was imprisoned.

3.5.3 | Anarchism

While Mounier recoiled from Nazism and fascism, he professed an innate sympathy for anarchism and Marxism, although this did not inhibit him from being aware of their limits or the problems that they presented. He appreciated anarchism's enthusiasm for freedom, its interest in the poor, its scathing criticism of capitalism, and some of the economic solutions or models which it proposed. Without a doubt, the vein of utopianism in Mounier made him feel comfortable in this rebellious, independent, and free atmosphere. Mutual support among workers, self-management, and federalism at the national level are some of the ideas that he took from anarchism and put forward in a different form in his social writings.

Nevertheless, although he recognized the value of anarchist criticisms of power, he indicated that this criticism could only be accepted on the condition that it be applied exclusively to the deformation of power and not to power as such.[80] Moreover, this power could and even must be opposed to the individual will if the common good so required: "The purpose of power is the common good of persons, which is not the sum of individual interests, and for this reason can mock simply individual interests, enforce limits, and prohibit external activities. But the common good cannot crush any person as such or refuse a place for any act of authentic spiritual liberty."[81]

---

80. See Mounier, *Communisme, anarchie, personnalisme* (Paris: Éditions du Seuil, 1966), comprising *Anarchie et personnalisme*, comprising articles from *Esprit* (1937), republished in *1931–1939*, 653–725; and *Le Communisme devant Nous*, other articles from *Esprit* (1934–50) republished in *Oeuvres*, vol. 4, *Recueils posthumes et correspondances* (Paris: Éditions du Seuil, 1962), 107–89.

81. Mounier, *Anarchie et personnalisme*, chap. 2, "Pour une doctrine personnaliste de l'authorité," in *1931–1939*, 667.

3.5.4 | Marxism: "The Unresolved Anguish"

Mounier's attitude toward Marxism was very complex because it oscillated between two opposed but equally strong tendencies: attraction to the Marxist movement and its social ideas, and, on a theoretical level, the need to reject its materialism and anthropology. In fact he never succeeded in overcoming this dilemma which he himself called an "unresolved anguish"[82] and which was notably intensified after World War II, when Marxism appeared as a triumphant force which had to be taken into consideration and which, in addition, had fought against Nazism and fascism. At that moment, Mounier did not oppose Marxism as directly as he had before the war.

We shall treat this point with some detail because of its importance. Mounier always considered himself as a man of the Left; and from that common spiritual basis, he sympathized with many of the features of communism. Communists' radicalism and militancy were perfectly in concordance with his impetuous spirit, distant from any compromise. And their revolutionary character and opposition to the rich bourgeoisie and individualists worked in the same direction. He, too, wished to eliminate all things bourgeois from French society, the West, and Christianity; in fact he systematically used the term "revolution," although he gave it a moral content. Also, he was attracted to communism by its political effectiveness and its intellectual forcefulness in contrast to the socialists of the period who appeared as bland and lacking ideas.

This profound attraction always exercised upon him a potent influence, countered by his awareness of the differences of a similar or even greater importance that separated him from Marxism: its crass materialism; its limited anthropology;[83] the impossibility of postponing the

---

82. Mounier, "Débat a haute voix," in *Le Communisme devant Nous*, in *Recueils posthumes et correspondances*, 135.

83. "Marxism forms part of the great current of reaction against idealism and subjectivism that personalisms and existentialisms have developed—perhaps less profoundly than it—in the analysis of *homo faber*, but have led in essential directions, abandoned by

moral question until after the revolution because it was only feasible by creating a new morality subjected to the revolution; particular attitudes in little agreement with his ideal of personalist conduct, such as systematically using bad faith in politics (and boasting of it), being intolerant dogmatists with respect to dialectics, and so forth.

Before the war this delicate equilibrium oscillated toward anticommunism. In 1936, for example, he wrote: "I am, without any possible ambiguity, anti-Marxist." Above his innate sympathy with that doctrine, his consciousness prevailed that, in spite of it all, it was a type of collectivism and, as such, against the person. However, after World War II, a complex set of factors made the balance shift in the opposite direction.[84] Marxists had fought against fascism, which put them on the side not only of the *de facto* victors, but also of the companions in the struggle of the Resistance against the evil represented by Nazism.[85] He was also drawn by communism's intellectual weight, which managed to include in its ranks persons of great prestige; the mystique of the labor movement, very conspicuous in those years; and, finally, the weight that the French Communist Party had acquired, both in number and from the moral point of view, appropriating to itself the idea of the

---

it. An acute description of the social and technological status of man, Marxism is a coarse philosophy in other instances." Ibid., 121.

84. John Hellman, *Emmanuel Mounier and the New Catholic Left 1930–1950* (Toronto: University of Toronto Press, 1981). See esp. chap. 4, "*Esprit* Launched," 52–70.

85. "There are some today who ask how some young Christians could have been fascinated by Marxism between 1940 and 1950, and who do not fear to use psychoanalysis to explain this perversion. The reality is much simpler. It is impossible to imagine, if one has not lived through it, the strength and enthusiasm presented to us, when we were twenty, by those survivors of anti-fascism, those old militants of the strikes, those defeated in every battle, proscribed in Italy and Germany, who, in the middle of the collapse of our country, did not doubt victory for a moment. With them we learned to fight. With them we sang the hymn of the Thaelmann Brigade: 'Oh distant homeland / We shall fight and conquer for thee / Liberty.' I know only too well how fanaticism justifies nothing, and one can die *en masse* for the vilest causes. But the men of whom I speak were beings of hope, lucid, realists, consecrated to brotherhood, sacrificed to a better destiny; and anyone who has not known those men could never grasp the hope Communism has produced beyond a regime or a dogma." Jean-Marie Doménach, *Dimensiones del personalismo* (Barcelona: Nova Terra, 1969), 337–38.

workers' revolution. This whole complicated set of factors led Mounier to conclude (1) one had inevitably to take the Communist Party into account; (2) it was not good to attack it because that would put a brake on the workers' revolution which Marxism could carry out; and (3) the existence of strong communist parties was, to a certain extent, positive because it could prevent the return of fascism.

We can conclude from this that Mounier changed his forthright rejection of communism in the 1930s for a certain indirect support, manifested in not directly attacking communism, not supporting or collaborating with those who did so,[86] and promoting dialogue between communists and Christians in the hope that "an open Marxism could not be very far from a personalist realism."[87] But at the same as he moved toward this position, Mounier was perfectly aware that the theoretical problems remained and that the political attitudes of the communists presented many problems: in France, the wholesale following of the directives from Russia; in Russia, similarities with fascist structures (one party, police state, lack of freedom of information); the danger of a new Russian imperialism; and the committing of atrocities such as deportations, torture, and mass executions.

This profound inner split, this unresolved anguish, was perfectly reflected in his reaction to the reports that, little by little, cleared up the lack of information about the atrocities which were committed in Russia: "I want those reports to be false."[88] And, more generally, about the serious problems that communism presented, he said: "Our difference with many others is, without a doubt, that we desire with all our hearts that they may be groundless concerns."[89] It appears, in the end, that these feelings and, above all, his visceral anti-capitalism played a bad trick on Mounier at this historical juncture, leading him to an exces-

---

86. In fact, he understood that the Communists considered it offensive that they were compared with the fascists.
87. Emmanuel Mounier, *Oeuvres*, vol. 3, 183.
88. Mounier, "Débat en haute voix," 132.
89. Ibid., 137.

sively indulgent attitude towards communism,[90] an attitude that would already weaken in 1948–50 due to the exhaustion of the mystique of the labor movement, the exclusion of the French Communist Party from the government, some ill-tempered debates with communist intellectuals, the start of the Cold War which showed ever more clearly the politics of the communist empire, and so on.

One must note, finally, that, in spite of his desire for collaboration, especially intense after World War II, Mounier always maintained a theoretical rejection of communism and avoided any subordination of *Esprit* to party interests. What happened soon after the foundation of *Esprit* is significant in this respect. Georges Izard and André Déléage were sympathizers of the Communist Party and in favor of subordinating the review to a political party oriented in that direction. Mounier, nevertheless, was opposed, defending the primacy of the review over any direct political action; because of this disagreement they ended up separating and forming a new movement under the name of *Troisième Force*. This later merged with the *Front commun* from which was born the *Front social* which, in the end, was absorbed by the Communist Party. *Esprit*, however, maintained its independence.

3.6 | Mounier's Personalism and Christianity

Mounier lived his Christianity in the radical manner which characterized him, internalizing it to its final consequences in every sphere of existence, theoretical and practical. Now we shall focus on its effect on his thought.

Christianity was, in the first place, a very important source of inspiration for his personalism. Mounier noted very clearly that Christianity not only could but must be the source of the new humanism which he sought because its message regarding man bore very profound contents

---

90. This is the opinion of Winock, *Histoire politique de la revue Esprit (1930–50)*; and others.

which were superior to Greek philosophy.[91] And so Mounier approached the gospel more or less directly for inspiration, to forge or give consistency to some of his principal philosophical concepts: love as the bond of the community, interpersonality, incarnation, vindication of corporeality, a necessary corollary to a God made flesh, and so forth.

At the same time, and in a different direction, he was a tough critic of the Christianity of his age, which, in his opinion, had become bourgeois and accommodated, allying itself with the "establish disorder," the system imposed by the individualist bourgeoisie. This was an especially painful point in his life, and against it he fought bravely. That many Christians, in the battle for the transformation of society and for the moral renewal of the West, were *de facto* allied with the comfort provided by the bourgeoisie wounded his conscience profoundly. That is why his work and writings promoted, along the lines of Péguy and Bloy, a profound transformation of the Church, and sharply denounced all the defects which he noticed, including conformism and lack of struggle; identification with bourgeois principles to the neglect of the radicalism of the Gospel; and a cheap and shallow pietism which did not demand of the young any more than a series of pious exercises instead of profound decisions.[92] As elsewhere, Mounier stood out for his intuition and radicalism. His criticisms were often accurate and profound, but the verve with which he presented them and the utopian-prophetic character which accompanied them did not always facilitate their widespread assimilation.

Both aspects, his intellectual openness and his acute and sometimes merciless criticism, caused him difficulties with ecclesiastical authorities. In fact, it appears that in *Esprit*'s beginnings, the possibility of a condemnation of the review was floating around, but it never mate-

---

91. "The Greeks stumbled twice when they tackled the problem of man: first, with the multiplicity of souls, which seemed to them to fragment the pure essence of thought into space; second, with the origin of souls, which seemed to them an attack on the course of eternity. The Christian affirmation attacks the pagan soul at both of these sensitive points." Mounier, *Personnalisme et christianisme*, 735.

92. See, for example, Mounier, *L'affrontement chrétien*, in *1944–1950*.

rialized, in part, due to the good work of Maritain who had contacts within the hierarchy. But, strictly speaking, such a condemnation did not appear to have any justification. Although Mounier could lean, intellectually and in practice, toward a Christianity of somewhat extreme features, it was just one more type of Christianity among the many possibilities that fit within the Church. And with respect to its intellectual aspect, the service that Mounier gave to the cultural renewal of Catholicism was formidable.

The more negative aspect was probably his decision in favor of dialogue between Marxism and Christianity, the results of which were generally bitter since not a few Christians who participated in these projects ended up, through the influence of Marxism, very distant from the Church, while Marxism remained immune to any influence that would try to make it renounce its materialism.

In summary, Mounier appears as one of the central figures of personalism, if not the most important. It was because of him that it gained visibility as a cultural and philosophical movement recognized throughout Europe, and in his writings many of the principal personalist intuitions were powerfully and vividly expressed. Also, he was a splendid example of coherence, of devotion to his own ideals, and of the union between philosophy and action. The principal limitation of his work is the lack of philosophical consistency of his ideas, in which the brilliance of his exposition does not run parallel to the detailed analysis or to the effort at synthesis, both factors being essential for the construction of a doctrine.

4 | Maurice Nédoncelle (1905–76): Metaphysical Personalism

4.1 | Life

Maurice Nédoncelle was born in Roubaix in 1905 and died in 1976. Unlike Maritain, Mounier, and also Gabriel Marcel, Nédoncelle's life had a markedly academic profile. He studied at the seminary of Saint-Suplice in Paris (1922–26), and then at the Sorbonne (1926–28) where he obtained a licentiate in philosophy. Later he obtained a doctorate in philosophy and also in theology, and was ordained a priest. Philosophically he was influenced, in the first place, by the scholastic philosophy which he studied in the seminary, and afterwards by authors such as Bergson, Blondel, Léon Brunschvicg, Husserl, and Max Scheler.

When he came into contact with Mounier, he joined the personalist movement but chose not to collaborate in the review *Esprit*—although he had many friends there—because he considered himself to be an "apolitical animal." He was not interested in politics or in social activism, but rather in philosophical reflection. So, abstaining from the social and political commitments in which other personalists were involved, he dedicated himself to the academic sphere, teaching and developing his intuitions which centered on the study of interpersonal relations. In fact, around 1960, he felt quite distant from the vision of personalism which had become generalized through the influence of Mounier and communitarian personalism, forcefully calling for an emphasis upon reflection:

> Personalism or, if you prefer, interpersonalism, has gained an enviable place in the parliament of contemporary philosophies, but its success has cost it dear. It has become nauseatingly vague and publicizing. It has become caught up in a well-thinking politics whose intentions are respectable, but which has nothing to do with philosophical investigation. In it, the spirit of investigation is dead: it is no more than a slogan. An atrocious desire to renounce such a disappointing label takes hold of me, and thus [to] remain alone.[93]

Nédoncelle thus represents a type of personalist dedicated to deepening and developing the doctrinal presuppositions of personalism and not to social action.

Nédoncelle taught, among other subjects, fundamental theology at

---

93. Maurice Nédoncelle, *Persona y naturaleza humana: Estudio lógico y metafísico*, trans. Carlos Díaz (Salamanca: Fundación Emmanuel Mounier, 2005), 18. We shall analyze this problem in chap. 4, sec. 1.

the University of Strasbourg and was dean of the Faculty of Theology. He was also awarded an honorary doctorate by the Catholic University of Louvain.

4.2 | Love and Interpersonal Relations

The core of Nédoncelle's philosophy can be found in the study of interpersonal relations and consciousness from a perspective that attempts to unite phenomenology with ontology or metaphysics. Because of this Jean Lacroix named him "the metaphysician of personalism," an epithet that became popular, so that it is customary to refer to Nédoncelle in this way, although it would also be perfectly justified, as Battista Mondin has done, to classify his personalism as intersubjective[94] because of the great importance which he gave to interpersonal relations.[95]

In addition, like Marcel and Karol Wojtyła, and unlike other personalists, Nédoncelle is also characterized for his preoccupation with *methodology*, particularly in his attempt to give the phenomenological method an ontological scope not directly dependent on Aristotelian categories. Thus, he moved away both from the procedures of an abstract metaphysics, self-defined as the point of reference for all philosophical categories, and from a strict phenomenology dependent on the *epoché*. With reference to this, he wrote:

> another difficulty has posed itself to the method that I advocate. Some desire for a general metaphysics to precede the philosophy of the person and that, from the results obtained by each of them, one might run the risk of finally determining the nature of love. The order I have followed seems to be almost the reverse of this. It is much more inductive than deductive; it

94. See further, Mondin, *Storia dell'Antropologia Filosofica*, 535–43.
95. Another great theme that occupied him was the concept of person and its history. In fact, he had projected a complete history of the concept of person which he could not complete because of his academic obligations as dean. See Nédoncelle, "Prosopon et persona dans l'antiquité classique: Essai de bilan linguistic," *Revue des Sciences Religieuses* 22, no. 3–4 (1948): 277–300.

presumes a going and coming and even an osmosis between phenomenology and metaphysics. It approaches the method set out in the posthumous work of Louis Lavelle. It is the whole question of the metaphysical experience thus raised and which demands not to be evaded.[96]

The specific starting place of Nédoncelle's reflection was the experience of self-consciousness perceived in communion with other consciousnesses. Nédoncelle sought to construct a philosophy of interpersonal relations which would situate this relation in the very *beginning* of the person. He considered it a mistake to conceive of the person as an isolated entity and *afterwards* to add the interpersonal relation to it, because this relation already existed from the start. Against the solipsist Cartesian *cogito*, he affirmed: "the communion of consciousnesses is the original fact; the *cogito* has before anything else a reciprocal character."[97] In other words, the person is from the start in relation with others and becomes aware of himself by recognizing the existence of other consciousnesses.

In this way, the essential element in Nédoncelle's thought arises: the dyad *I-Thou*. The person finds before his "I" a "thou" and, in order to grow, he must receive that "thou" and form a relationship with him. But this relationship, in order for it to be successful and produce the expected results, requires reciprocity, that is, a similar stance on the part of the other "I" which we observe as a "thou." In other words, between the two persons a bond of love must be established. "To have an 'I,'" Nédoncelle explains,

> it is necessary to be loved by another *I* and, in turn, to love him; it is necessary to be aware, at least obscurely, of the other and of the relations that unite the two terms of this spiritual network which is the original fact of the communion of consciousnesses.... *Another* does not mean *not-I*, but rather the will to promote the *I*, the transparency of the one to the other. It

---

96. Nédoncelle, *Persona y naturaleza humana*, 21.
97. Nédoncelle, *La réciprocité des consciences* (Paris: Aubier, 1942), 310. This is his principal work.

is a coincidence of the subjects, a double immanence.... From then a *collegial consciousness* is constituted or is revealed, a *we*.[98]

As Mounier had already indicated, the other is not a limit whom we must confront in order to be able to develop our personhood; he is, on the contrary, a necessary help for our own progress. He needs, indeed, to enter with us into a relationship of love, that is, of advancement; it is then that the "we" emerges. Nédoncelle's dyad I-thou is not, therefore, exclusivist or localist, but is the cell in which the universality of the "we" is incubated, a "we" which, moreover, is not a concession to collectivism, because it does not consist of a set of anonymous entities, but rather a group of independent persons, self-aware and autonomous, but bound together by love. Love is thus—Nédoncelle defines it as such—a "will of advancement" which unites the consciousnesses in a spiritual community. It is this presupposition which gives meaning to marriage and transforms fidelity into a beautiful task.[99]

Now, even in such elevated cases as these, the love that we find in other persons is finite, limited, and fleeting. There are encounters that reveal themselves as failed and harm us. Also, although the encounters with the persons we love influence us positively and help us to build our identity, this influence is never so decisive that it radically constructs the other person. "Properly speaking, the creation of one person by another does not exist.... It is very clear that a man is not wholly the product of another man, not even in the case of procreation."[100]

These shortcomings and limits are what led Nédoncelle to intuit the presence of and need for an absolute and definitive love which can only be found in God, the "Thou" *par excellence*, the only one who can radically build and advance each person.

---

98. Ibid., 319.
99. See Nédoncelle, *De la fidélité* (Paris: Aubier Editions Montaigne, 1953).
100. Nédoncelle, *Conscience et logos. Horizons et méthodes d'une philosophie personnaliste* (Paris: Editions de l'Epi, 1962), 7–11.

> The possibility of leading us without limit to our total realization, which would also be the total realization of the network of persons with whom we meet in existence, could not be explained by either the efforts of the *I* or the collegiality of all the *I*s. It cannot be explained except by a God, who must be personal. We are not only caused by being, but also loved by a God.... The phenomenology of the concrete *cogito* impels us to recognize this divine priority in us as a conclusion through the reflection on the cause and the end of our loving.[101]

This reference to God through the analysis of the subjective experience of persons, this need for the divine *Thou* in order that a collegial and authentic *we* may exist in all fullness, could be understood as a lapse into ontologism, as an attempt to see the presence of God in the disclosure of the consciousness of reciprocity. For Nédoncelle, however, there is nothing of this. It is more a proof of the existence of God by means of philosophical reflection on persons and on their relational activity. The limitation, insufficiency and fleetingness which these relations manifest in fact, before the fullness of being that they could potentially attain, only finds justification in the existence of that divine *Thou* who creates persons out of love and is determined to radically advance them so that they may achieve their perfection.

101. Ibid., 11–12.

CHAPTER THREE | **Other Personalist Currents**

1 | Italian Personalism

1.1 | From Idealism to Personalism

Italian personalism, as Armando Rigobello (one of its principal investigators) has remarked, arose following its own path: the crisis of neo-idealism.[1] At the start of the twentieth century, the philosophical scene in Italy was dominated by two versions of idealism: the historicist neo-idealism of Benedetto Croce and the "actualist" neo-idealism of Giovanni Gentile.[2] Nevertheless, despite the intellectual quality of both philosophers and of their overwhelming predominance in cultural spheres, its stance became unsatisfactory. Neo-idealism, even in its Italianized versions, was too abstract, too distant; and, therefore, some philosophers independently began to take a path opposite that taken by Georg Hegel. They sought to move from the transcendent and abstract to the concrete and existential, and from impersonal logic to concrete phenomenology close to reality.

The first to venture on this path was Armando Carlini (1878–1959) who, seeking ways to make the transcendent concrete, approached the category of the person, and defined it as "an existentialization of the

---

1. See Armando Rigobello, *Il personalismo*, 2nd ed. (Rome: Città Nuova, 1978).
2. See Battista Mondin, *Storia dell'Antropologia Filosofica*, vol. 2, *Da Kant ai giorni nostri* (Bologna: Edizioni Studio Domenicano, 2002), 378–93, "An Idealist Humanism."

transcendental." That is, Carlini still remained within a structure of an idealistic type—the fundamental category was the transcendental. But he already introduced the idea that this transcendental had to be existentialized and made concrete, and if this operation was to be carried out, the category that had to be used was that of the person. Carlini thus took the first steps from neo-idealism to personalism, but only stutteringly. So, even though there are a good number of personalist elements in his work, he never defined himself as a personalist nor established relations with the European personalists.[3]

Luigi Stefanini (1891–1956) completed the journey from neo-idealism to personalism, and, according to Rigobello, he is "the founder and principal representative of the personalist movement in Italy."[4] He was born in Treviso, and his career was not easy because he had to suffer the limitations placed upon a Catholic in a secularist academic atmosphere also impregnated with neo-idealism and immanentism. He fought in the First World War and worked diligently in the Catholic youth movement. He was a high school teacher in Mantua and in Padua, and in 1937 succeeded to the chair in theoretical philosophy at the University of Messina. Then he went again to Padua where he developed the greater part of his work and where he died prematurely in 1956. His thought, which was reaching its maturity at that time, was irremediably cut short.[5]

Stefanini can be said to have arrived at personalism from historiography. In effect, it was his studies of Vincenzo Gioberti and existentialism which led him, little by little, to center on the category of the person.[6] And, differently from Carlini, this evolution led him to a fully personalist philosophy which he would develop principally after the Second World War.

3. See Rigobello, *Il personalismo*, 46–53.
4. Mondin, *Da Kant ai giorni nostri*, 566–86, "Italian Personalists." Mondin discusses Stefanini, Rigobello, and Melchiorre.
5. Stefanini's principal works are *Personalismo sociale* (1951); *Personalismo educativo* (1954); *Trattato di estetica* (1955); and *Personalismo filosofico* (1962).
6. Vincenzo Gioberti was a nineteenth century philosopher who promoted a liberal Catholic political philosophy and supported Italian unification.

His thought can be structured around two great axes. The first is the elaboration of a *metaphysics of the person*, that is, a rethinking of metaphysical categories from a personal perspective. It was not a matter, as in Carlini, of attempting to existentialize the transcendental, nor even to do an ontological analysis of the person that would include his activity, his capacity to create images and meanings, and his transcendent openness to men and God, among other factors. It was a matter of reworking the traditional metaphysical categories of an Aristotelian stamp, which structurally depended on the notion of *ens*, and taking a step further into other, new categories that derived from the notion of the person, beginning with the first of them, the category of "being." It is in this sense that he stated: "Being is personal; and everything that, in being, is not personal is the result of the productivity of the person, as the means of manifestation of the person and of communication among persons."[7]

The metaphysics of the person is, then, the anchor-point of Stefanini's thought, but when he found *terra firma* he made an effort to draw the consequences. This is the second axis that we referred to: *the elaboration of a personalist "summa"* that was to be cut short by his early death. Some of its elements are very similar to those already mentioned in speaking of French personalism.[8] But Stefanini also began new approaches, a good part of which can be found in one of his most important works, *Personalismo sociale* (1952).

In this work he reflected, for example, on the relation between moral *autonomy* and *theonomy* (God's moral laws); and, instead of opposing the two concepts, as is habitual, Stefanini considers the possibility that they may support each other. Thus, on the one hand, he insists on the autonomy of personal conscience. We are our own masters and should act in accordance with what we judge in conscience, with the vision we

---

7. Luigi Stefanini, *Personalismo sociale*, 2nd ed. (Rome: Studium, 1979), 7. A similar project can be found in Leonardo Polo, Josef Seifert, Xavier Zubiri, etc.

8. For Stefanini, the essential properties of the person are (1) primacy of the spiritual over the empirical and bodily; (2) substantiality; (3) unity and uniqueness; (4) rationality; (5) openness; (6) lack of proportion; (7) transcendence.

have formed of ourselves. However, it is this very capacity of being our own masters, of fully exercising freedom and rationality (that is, autonomy), which leads us to transcendence, because man is aware in each moral action that, despite the dominion which he has over himself, he is not entirely founded on himself and requires, therefore, another being who has founded him in a radical way (theonomy).

Stefanini also analyzed the *relations between intimacy and institution*, advocating a position of equilibrium which would not leave the subject completely helpless in a way that would have him continually reconsider his actions, but would enslave him to neither the automatic laws of institution nor of custom. Another question which he tackled is the need to study the human act in general. Stefanini thought that some philosophies, in trying to deepen the study of man, had committed the error of dividing the human act into so many parts and sections that, although they advanced an analytic knowledge of action, they had lost an overall vision. The human act no longer looked like an action of man but rather like a sort of mechanical device consisting of numerous pieces which were attributed either to the intelligence or to the will, and which would end in complex vicious circles. To solve this problem Stefanini suggested reconsidering the initial facts, that is, avoiding the division of the act of the person into numerous watertight compartments which, in reality, do not exist. It is the person who exists and acts, not the will nor the intelligence nor the appetitive faculty. In this sense, he thought that,

> to re-establish the human act in its indissoluble fullness of vision and production (it is naturally a consideration of the *actus humanus*, and not just of any *actus hominis*) is to escape from a decomposition which ends up in ephemeral and unhealthy aggregations. Thought, will, and love are never separate from each other, but rather indicate the co-presence of the three aspects on the indivisible plane of one unique reality.[9]

---

9. Stefanini, *Personalismo sociale*, 43. It is an approach very similar to that of Karol Wojtyła in *The Acting Person*, although the latter develops a much more powerful and complete theory.

As for society and forms of government, Stefanini defended parliamentary democracy and proposed a vision of society based on solidarity which took up again ideas from the "mystical body" of Christianity.[10] However, his study of *psychoanalysis* is new. He opposed its radical and orthodox versions, even comparing it with Marxism. "To the rigid Marxist determinism, which moves the events of history in function of economic factors, is associated Freud's psychical determinism, which finds the ineluctable causal conditioning for each conscious psychical factor in an unconscious psychical event without allowing any margin to human freedom."[11] We also find aesthetic analyses. For Stefanini, art can be considered an absolute language in which man expresses himself completely but momentarily. It is an instant in which the mystery of the person is revealed emotionally and completely creating a highly full and satisfactory experience. But it is only for an instant and in one sector of life. To want to extend this experience to the whole sphere of human existence would mean to fall into aestheticism.[12]

An author whose itinerary was similar to Stefanini's was Luigi Pareyson (1918–91).[13] He began in the neo-idealistic atmosphere, but his first personal interests led him to existentialism. In this vein he studied authors such as Søren Kierkegaard and Karl Jaspers, and he came to define himself as an existentialist. However, little by little he began to glimpse limits in this current, above all in its negative view of the concrete and finite; and he slowly moved towards personalism. Finally,

---

10. This is one of the points of difference with Mounier, who was much more critical of parliamentary democracy and advocated a type of direct democracy. The other points—according to Rigobello—were Stefanini's metaphysical perspective in contrast to the phenomenological one in Mounier, and Stefanini's character as a mediator and reconciler, in the Italian style, as against Mounier's French radicalism.

11. Stefanini, *Personalismo sociale*, 88.

12. See Rigobello, *Il personalismo*, 53–57, 89–90.

13. For details on Pareyson's life and work, and extracts from his writings, see Paolo D. Bubbio, ed., *Luigi Pareyson: Existence, Interpretation, Freedom: Selected Writings*, trans. Anna Mattei (Aurora, Colo.: The Davies Group, 2009). For more on Pareyson's personalism, see Dan Lazea, "The Ontological Personalism of Luigi Pareyson: from Existentialism to the Ontology of Liberty," *Appraisal* 6, no. 1 (March 2006): 7–16.

when his philosophical position was definitively settled, he stated that his intellectual journey consisted in a transition from existentialism to "ontological personalism," also indicating that, within personalism, his position was original, since he had proceeded "independently of other forms of personalism, such as the Italian personalism of an actualist origin or German phenomenological personalism or French spiritualist or communitarian personalism."[14]

In spite of this, his philosophy has many points in common with French personalism. So as not to be repetitive, we shall mention only a few. For example, Pareyson's attitude to Christianity is similar. He affirmed, "Respect for the person is a demand so typical of Christianity that not only can it be said that only a Christian philosophy can provide a theoretical foundation for it and justify it, but also that any philosophy which gives [such a] theoretically based justification is thereby Christian."[15] In his anthropology he stresses the well-known dimensions of the person: dynamic, operative, and subjective. For example, he thought that the person can be defined by means of four notions: existence, task, work, and "I." And he emphasized the person's capacity for initiative and his dynamic and moral response with respect to himself: "In the man's being there is an implicit commitment of the individual to fulfill his essence. Man's essence is an 'ought-to be,' and the affirmation of one's own humanity depends on the individual."[16]

Pareyson gave particular attention to the question of interpretation, both because of his personal interest in it and because his thought is framed within a period dominated by hermeneutics, initiated above all by Hans-Georg Gadamer. Hermeneutics presented itself as overcoming a "naive" rationalism which had believed itself able to arrive at completely objective, rational, and scientific knowledge by way of a method (with Cartesian roots) which could eliminate all presuppositions. Gad-

---

14. Luigi Pareyson, *Esistenza e persona* (Genoa: Il Melangolo, 1985), 173.
15. Ibid., 174.
16. Ibid., 175.

amer, in *Truth and Method*, criticized this position and showed that all knowledge is conditioned both by personal factors and by the influence of the cultural and philosophical tradition on which it depends.[17]

Pareyson approached this new attitude from his personalist perspective. For him, knowledge is always something personal, because it is the whole person, with his history and personal context, rather than an abstract and non-existent intelligence, who seeks to arrive at the truth. But, contrary to what may at first be thought, he considers that this point of departure not only does not lead to subjectivism, but it even makes it possible to overcome the old artificial schemes of confrontation between objectivism and subjectivism, that is, between true but impersonal (and thus unreal) knowledge and knowledge that is subjective (and thus real) but lacking the dimension of truth. "With the concept of interpretation," he affirms, "subjectivism is definitively overcome; moreover, it can be said that the concept of interpretation was born precisely to eliminate subjectivism and to get rid of forever the antithesis between subjectivism and objectivism."[18]

Pareyson also strongly emphasized the need for commitment in the search for truth. "Knowing and possessing the truth are impossible without commitment, without taking a side, without personal exposure. This occurs not only in philosophy understood as the formulation of truth, but also in every single interpretation worthy of the name, no matter how marginal and insignificant it might be, because truth is engaged in every hermeneutic process, and even the most meager interpretation carries an ontological import."[19]

Pareyson furthermore produced interesting reflections on art, language, and religious experience, which we cannot consider because of

---

17. On the concept of cultural tradition, see Alasdair MacIntyre, *Three Rival Versions of Moral Enquiry* (London: Duckworth, 1990).

18. Luigi Pareyson, "Filosofia e Verità (interview with Marisa Serra)," *Studi Cattolici* 193 (1977): 175.

19. Luigi Pareyson, *Truth and Interpretation*, trans. Robert T. Valgenti (Albany, N.Y.: SUNY Press, 2013), 73. Originally published as *Verità e Interpretazione* (Milan: Mursia, 1982), 86.

space limitations.[20] However, we will now look at a unique aspect of Italian personalism: the great influence that it had and still has on Italian society, something that, in our opinion, has only happened in such a marked way in this European country.

1.2 | Personalism as a Cultural Matrix

The Italian version of personalism that arose out of neo-idealism brought with it interesting and creative thinkers, such as those we have just mentioned, but, in our opinion, this is not the most important or the most significant characteristic of personalism in Italy. Personalism in that country is characterized above all by its wide dissemination, much greater than in France, and by its creative assimilation by numerous social and intellectual groups. We shall attempt to describe this phenomenon in more detail and explain the reasons that brought it about.

During the first half of the twentieth century in Italy, as we have seen, there was an *individual* evolution of some philosophers towards personalist positions, but this had no significant social relevance. It may seem surprising that this occurred in a Catholic country which, thus, could have an interest in this sort of philosophy, but one must account for the fact that, in the first half of the century, Italy was governed by a secularist government that emerged from the *Risorgimento*, and then by a fascist regime. Neither of them was inclined toward this sort of philosophy, so we must wait for the end of the Second World War to see a change in the panorama, and this, in a radical way.[21]

With the end of the war, Italy, in the first place, opened itself completely to Europe; and so the free interchange of ideas was assured. But the fundamental event was the coming to power of the Christian Democrats and with them the massive inrush into public life of numer-

---

20. See Bubbio, *Existence, Interpretation, Freedom*, esp. 114–40.

21. This does not mean that during those years the French personalists were not known (the future Pope Paul VI, for example, promoted the translation and wrote the introduction of the first Italian version of *Three Reformers* by Jacques Maritain), rather that knowledge of them was much more restricted.

ous Catholics who had remained on the margin of social life during the preceding decades, thanks to the famous "Roman Question." Pope Pius IX had prohibited participation in Italian national politics as a consequence of the loss of the Papal States. The prohibition was formally lifted only in 1919. Within this context, two factors coincided. On the one hand, the discrediting of the neo-idealism which had dominated the previous historical phases and which, precisely because of its links to the governing regimes of those periods, was now completely emptied of prestige. On the other hand, there was a certain lack of proposals on the part of Catholics, whose distance from public life had left them without the cultural arms for forming projects for the future. Finding new proposals was especially urgent since the task which Italians faced consisted not only in constructing a new state and a new society over the ruins left by the war, but also a state and a society in which a war like that would never again be possible.

In these circumstances French personalism began to enter Italy with renewed strength, and it is easy to understand that many saw it as a splendid and providential instrument for gathering ideas for the task that they had to tackle. Jacques Maritain and Emmanuel Mounier, in particular, were especially well received. Their works were published in successive editions, and were studied and assimilated by a large part of the Catholic laity desiring to find cultural resources for the construction of the new society. Their writings were widely used in the FUCI (Italian Catholic Federation of University Students) and in the educational organisms of the Christian Democrats. They influenced the constitutional texts of the new State, so much so that, according to Paolo Balboni, "It can be said that, thanks to the decisive contribution of Catholics elected to the Constituent Assembly, a group in which [Giorgio] La Pira, [Giuseppe] Dosseti, [Aldo] Moro, and [Giuseppe] Lazzatti were prominent, the distinctive feature of the Republic is that it is founded, at least on the level of the wording of the Constitution, as a personalist State."[22]

---

22. Paolo E. Balboni, "Annotazioni storico-guiridiche," in *Mounier trent'anni dopo. Atti del Convegno di studio dell'università cattolica* (Milan: Vita e Pensiero, 1981), 177. La

And, finally, via Alcide De Gasperi they intervened significantly in the launching of the movement for the construction of a new united Europe. In this way, French personalism (and, perhaps above all, Maritain), paradoxically, made its most relevant achievement in Italy where it was able to form and influence a good part of the leaders of society.[23]

The degree of personalism's penetration and assimilation was so strong that it achieved the necessary "critical mass" for Italian personalism to begin its own life and form what we may call a "personalist cultural matrix," that is, a living framework of ideas, shared by many and capable of orienting new generations of intellectuals who, in addition, have creatively and ingeniously applied them to new spheres. Among the many Italian personalists and personalist initiatives are: the FIBIP, the International Federation of Bioethics Centers and Institutes of Personalist Inspiration created by Elio Sgreccia; the international network of personalism coordinated by Giulia P. di Nicola and Attilio Danese, whose journal is *Prospettiva Persona*, published since 1991; the International Jacques Maritain Institute, which publishes the review, *Notes et documents: Pour une recherche personaliste*, directed by the historian Phillipe Chenaux; the personalist philosophers Armando Rigobello, Vittorio Melchiorre and Vittorio Possenti, a follower of Maritain, and so on.[24]

2 | Polish Personalism

2.1 | The Origins

Polish personalism was born in the context of the intellectual movement subsequent to the end of World War II because, at the time when Poland

---

Pira, in particular, was inspired by the "Project on a Declaration of Rights" elaborated by Mounier and his group, and published in *Esprit* in 1944.

23. An example of this influence is the International Jacques Maritain Institute, founded in 1974, which has always operated from Rome.

24. Others who take inspiration, in one way or another, from personalist sources include Francesco d'Agostino and Giuseppe dalla Torre in bioethics and philosophy of law; Giorgio Campanini in political philosophy and philosophy of the family; Pier Paolo Donati in sociology; and Stefano Zamagni in economics.

fell under Russian domination, the Polish Church decided in favor of a renewal-minded Catholicism and encouraged currents of thought close to personalism, with the understanding that it contained a powerful source for setting forth an idea of man that could compete with Marxist anthropology.[25] To this end, Cardinal Adam Stefan Sapieha of Krakow promoted two cultural publications that were very important for Polish Catholicism. One of them was the weekly journal *Tygodnok Powszechny* (*The Catholic Weekly*), which began in March 1945 and was edited by an emblematic figure of Polish culture, Jerzy Turowicz. The other, *Znak* (sign or symbol), appeared a year later and was probably inspired by *Esprit*. Around them, as also around *Esprit*, an important group of Catholic intellectuals was formed, Karol Wojtyła among them. This group was able to maintain an independent and creative intellectual movement in the post-war era, supported by the strength of Polish culture, which is the basis of Poland's national identity.

It is interesting to note that this group of intellectuals, despite their progressivist outlook, did not slip over time into quasi-Marxist positions or into confrontation with Catholicism, as happened in France and, more generally, in Europe. Their motives are easy to identify. In contrast to the fascination that Marxism produced in Europe, surrounded by the aura of the fight against Nazism and capitalism, and a prestige strengthened by the presence of notable intellectuals, in Poland personalism appeared as the ideology of the country which militarily subjugated its citizens and, among many other atrocities, had allowed Warsaw to be destroyed during the Polish insurrection. Because of this, although the Poles had to battle, in any case, with the ideological brilliance of Marxism, the latter started from a substantially weak and negative cultural position. Furthermore, since religion is an inherent part of Polish culture, the Marxist attack on whatever smacked of transcend-

25. See Rocco Buttiglione, *Karol Wojtyła: The Thought of the Man Who Became Pope John Paul II*, trans. Paolo Guietti and Francesca Murphy (Grand Rapids, Mich.: Wm. B. Eerdmans Publishing Co., 1997). Also, Nancy Mardas, Agnes B. Curry, George F. Mclean, eds., *Karol Wojtyła's Philosophical Legacy* (Washington, D.C.: Council for Research in Values and Philosophy, 2008).

ence had the effect of reinforcing the identification between religion, culture, and the Polish nation. Consequently, while in Europe a good part of the renewal movements lost their direction after Vatican Council II, in Poland the contrary happened. Polish Catholicism knew how to maintain an advanced ideology, but without any concessions to Marxism; and existentialism maintained a Christian and religious character, nourished by authors such as Maritain, Gabriel Marcel, Georges Bernanos, Charles Péguy, and Mounier. A significant part of the success of this process was, doubtless, due to the presence of the gigantic figures of Cardinal Stefan Wyszyński[26] and Karol Wojtyła, who, with their moral and intellectual authority, helped Catholic intellectuals keep course in very adverse conditions.

It is easy to note that this context represented a fertile ground for personalism, but it did not arise because of socio-religious motives alone; rather, as in other countries, it arose as a philosophical response to questions that traditional philosophy could not resolve. In this sense, Gilson and Maritain were read as authors who introduced the new issues, but the more properly personalist philosophers, such as Wojtyła, took a step further, attempting to elaborate a new scheme of thought with the aid of phenomenology and, more particularly, of two realist phenomenologists, Max Scheler and Roman Ingarden, himself Polish.

The different intellectual groups formed under these influences came together at the Catholic University of Lublin, since it was the only Catholic university that could operate freely in all of Eastern Europe, giving rise to what would later be called the Lublin School.[27] Taken

---

26. In Poland Wyszyński is usually given the credit for having applied the innovations of Vatican II gradually, which, although it initially made him the target of some criticisms for being conservative, in the long term it proved to be a good strategy, since it gave the Polish Church a serene and not convulsive and traumatic assimilation of the council's measures. Wojtyła also actively worked in the same way in his diocese of Krakow.

27. See Czesław Bartnik, *Oeuvres rassemblées*, vol. 16, *Le Phénomène de la Nation* (Lublin: Standruk, 2005), for a brief summary in English of philosophical trends in and around personalism in Poland.

in a wide sense, this school united several tendencies with important differences among them: a traditional Thomism led by the professor of metaphysics Stanisław Adamczyk; existential Thomism, that is, Thomism renewed by the contributions of Maritain and Étienne Gilson and with openness to phenomenology, whose principal representative was Stefan Swieżawski; a Polish version of the transcendental Thomism of Louvain led by Mieczysław Krąpiec, OP, which still continues to be active today; and the more strictly personalist tendency of Karol Wojtyła, Wincenty Granat, and Czesław Bartnik.

The cohabitation at Lublin of these currents was not always easy, but

> among all of these divergent methodologies, each of which contributed to a vibrant intellectual interchange, the Lublin philosophy school was united in these years in a fundamental commitment to the defense of human rights against all theories which would dissolve the unique dignity of human beings in the infinite currents of history, and also in the decision to exhibit the profound alliance between human reason and Christian faith. There was thus a fundamentally personalistic philosophy, Thomistic in inspiration (in a more rigid sense in Krąpiec's case and a more open one in Wojtyła's), but welcoming dialogue with any thought which took seriously the problem of being human.[28]

2.2 | Karol Wojtyła (1920–2005)

Karol Wojtyła is the principal representative of Polish personalism.[29] This is principally due to his genius and creativity, since he was the soul of the Lublin School of Ethics and elaborated a richer, more profound, and more original philosophy than his colleagues, but clearly one cannot ignore the repercussion which his election as pope had,

---

28. Buttiglione, *Karol Wojtyła*, 38.
29. The principal biography of John Paul II is George Weigel, *Witness to Hope: The Biography of Pope John Paul II* (New York: Harper Collins, 2001). See also, Tad Szulc, *Pope John Paul II: The Biography* (London: Simon and Schuster, 2007). For his philosophy, see note 25 above; and Adrian Reimers, *Truth about the Good: Moral Norms in the Philosophy of John Paul II* (Ave Maria, Fla.: Sapientia Press, 2011).

helping him to overcome the linguistic barrier of the Polish language and facilitating the dissemination of his ideas.

Wojtyła united all the characteristics necessary to be considered a "typical" representative of personalism, not only because his thought is fully framed within the course of this current, but also because his life united that blend of action and reflection characteristic of many of its representatives.[30] Initially he thought about dedicating himself to the theatre, and he studied the Polish language and Polish literature at the Jagellonian University, and presented theatrical works. But the Nazi invasion of Poland and the Second World War changed his plans. He had to do manual work in order to escape deportation and decided to become a priest, which led him to begin to study philosophy. After his ordination, he succeeded in combining his studies of philosophy and theology, and his publications, with his pastoral duties, which were soon very important. At only thirty-eight years of age he was elected as a bishop and had to firmly take on Marxism on a pastoral and intellectual level. Later, and also very young, he was named a cardinal and, after that, pope in 1978. He died in 2005.

The best way to present his thought is, doubtless, biographically, since it underwent a significant evolution before arriving at its mature and definitive position.[31]

2.2.1 | Formation and Evolution in the Thought of Karol Wojtyła

Wojtyła's philosophical journey began with Thomism because it was, at that time, the philosophy taught in the seminaries (see chap. 1, sec. 4.4,

---

30. "Circumstances never left me much time for study. By temperament I prefer thought to erudition. I came to realize this during my short career as a teacher at Crakow and Lublin. My conception of the person, 'unique' in his identity, and of man, as such at the center of the universe, was born much more of experience and of sharing with others than of reading. Books, study, reflection and discussion ... help me to formulate what experience teaches me." John Paul II with André Frossard, *Be Not Afraid*, trans. J. R. Foster (New York: St. Martin's Press, 1984), 17–18.

31. For the author's distinctive view of Wojtyła, see Juan Manuel Burgos, *Para comprender a Karol Wojtyła: Una introducción a su filosofía* (Madrid, BAC, 2014).

above). The move from philology to metaphysics was not easy, although certainly very enriching, as he himself recounts, remembering his first steps as a philosopher: "When I passed the examination, I said to the examiner that, in my judgment, the new view of the world that I had conquered in that full-contact wrestle with my metaphysics textbook, was more precious than the grade obtained. And I was not exaggerating. What my intuition and sensibility had taught me about the world up to that point had been solidly corroborated."[32] The Thomistic path continued, reaching its peak when, at the age of twenty-eight, he defended his doctoral thesis in theology on *Faith According to St. John of the Cross*, at the Angelicum in Rome, under the direction of the eminent Thomist, Fr. Reginald Garrigou-Lagrange.[33] On his return to Poland, however, one event decisively modified his outlook, the writing of his philosophical thesis on Scheler in 1954. On several occasions he related the impact of this work: "This research [the thesis on Scheler] benefited me greatly. My previous Aristotelian-Thomistic formation was enriched by the phenomenological method, and this made it possible for me to undertake a number of creative studies. I am thinking above all of my book *The Acting Person*. In this way I took part in the contemporary movement of philosophical personalism, and my studies were able to bear fruit in my pastoral work."[34]

In studying Scheler, Karol Wojtyła discovered a new panorama to which he had not had access in his studies in Rome: contemporary philosophy in an especially interesting version, the realist phenomenology of Scheler. His interest in this path had its roots in the fact that some type of integration seemed to be possible between Scheler's phenomenology and traditional Christian thought and even with Thomism, which at that time was what the young Wojtyła professed. In fact, the objective of his thesis was to determine the validity of Scheler's theory,

---

32. Wojtyła, *No tengáis miedo*, 16.
33. See Wojtyła, *Doctrina de fide apud S. Joannem a Cruce* (STD diss.; Rome: Pontifical University of St. Thomas Aquinas, 1948), translated by Jordan Aumann as *Faith according to St. John of the Cross* (San Francisco: Ignatius Press, 1981).
34. John Paul II, *Gift and Mystery* (New York: Doubleday, 1996), 93–94.

much in vogue then, for Christian ethics.[35] His conclusion was as follows. Scheler's scheme, as a structure, was incompatible with Christian ethics, among other things, because of its actualist conception of the person and its emotionalism, but Scheler used a method, the phenomenological method, which seemed particularly useful and productive. In addition, he proposed new topics, which could be used to renew ethics: the importance of models, the recourse to moral experience, and so forth.[36] In view of these results, Wojtyła clearly saw that any philosophy which he might develop in the future would necessarily have to take elements from phenomenology into account, that is, it would have to consist of the renewal of the classical perspective making use of phenomenology. And so he went to work.

2.2.2 | The Lublin School of Ethics

Wojtyła began with ethics, above all because it was the principal subject that he had to teach at Lublin, but also because it had always been a particular interest of his. With some collaborators, among whom Tadeusz Styczeń stands out, he formed a research group which later became known as the Lublin School of Ethics.[37] Its aim was to work on the re-founding of the bases of classical ethics using the phenomenological perspective.

Wojtyła did not produce a text synthesizing the results of the research group but we may indicate three principal areas of his work. The first is the analysis of and confrontation with the ethical positions of his four authors of reference: *Thomas Aquinas*, *Kant*, *Hume*, and *Scheler*. In these very analytic and detailed studies, Wojtyła marked out his terri-

---

35. See Wojtyła, *Ocena możliwości zbudowania etyki chrześcijańskiej przy założeniach systemu Maksa Schelera* [Evaluation of the Possibilities of Building Christian Ethics on the Principles of Max Scheler's System] (Lublin: Catholic University of Lublin, 1959).
36. See ibid.
37. See Juan Miguel Palacios, "La Escuela Ética de Lublin y Cracovia," *Sillar* 2 (1982): 55–56.

tory, establishing parallels and differences, discovering problems, and glimpsing solutions and new perspectives. We cannot go into the details of these texts, but especially important is his central observation on Thomistic ethics in which he says,

> The concept of the person to be found in St. Thomas is objectivist. It almost gives the impression that it has no place for the analysis of consciousness and of self-consciousness as truly specific symptoms of the person-subject. For St. Thomas the person is obviously a subject, a very particular subject of existence and action, since he has subsistence in rational nature and the capacity for consciousness and self-consciousness. However, it appears that his objectivist view of reality has no place for the analysis of consciousness and of self-consciousness, about which modern philosophy and psychology are especially concerned.[38]

The second area of investigation was the analysis of *metaethics or ethics as science*. In particular, he dedicated attention to the justification of ethics against the objections coming from hedonism, positivism, and, in another sense, from Kant's apriorism. And, to that end, he turned with profundity and originality to the notion of moral experience. Ethics, he explained, does not arise from any structure external to the subject; it is not a mental construction generated by sociological pressures, but stems from a real and original principle: moral experience, the experience of duty; but not as understood in a Kantian fashion as the formal structure of practical reason, but in a profoundly realist sense as the experience that every subject possesses—in each concrete ethical action—that he should do the good and avoid the evil. This recourse to moral experience enabled him also to propose his thesis that the science of ethics has a relative autonomy in relation to anthropology.

Wojtyła's interest in metaethics even led him to attempt to elaborate a systematic text on these questions in collaboration with Styczeń. But it never took a definitive form and was published only later (1991) as a

---

38. Karol Wojtyła, *El personalismo tomista*, in *Mi visión del hombre*, 6th ed., trans. Pilar Ferrer (Madrid: Palabra, 2006), 311–12.

rough draft titled *Man and Responsibility: A Study of the Concept and Methodology of Ethics*.[39] In it, Wojtyła tackles, from an already mature perspective, the central themes in the structuring of ethics as a science: morality, its practical and normative character of ethics, the personalist norm, and so on. It is a study rich in perspectives and innovations, but unfinished.

The third central theme for research was his attempt *to connect ethics with personal life*. He understood that ethics could not be reduced to a group of norms which are obligatory from a heteronomous perspective, rather, it must implicate the subject, and therefore, in this direction he studied, for example, "perfectionism," which analyzes how ethical actions have repercussions on the person who performs them, perfecting him. Other topics he explored were the need for models in order to effectively motivate ethical actions (following Scheler) and the relations between value and end in acts of will.

2.2.3 | Love and Responsibility (1960)

The studies of ethics led Wojtyła progressively and naturally to his first great original work, *Love and Responsibility*.[40] Its origin, in any case, was not exclusively academic, but rather, as he explained in *Crossing the Threshold of Hope*, the fruit of a necessity and of an experience.

> In those years, my greatest involvement was young people who asked me questions, not so much about the existence of God but rather *how to live*, how to face and resolve problems of love and marriage, not to mention problems related to work.... From our meetings, from my sharing in the problems of their lives, a book was born, the contents of which is summarized in the title *Love and Responsibility*.[41]

---

39. Published in English as Karol Wojtyła, *Man in the Field of Responsibility* (South Bend, Ind.: St. Augustine's Press, 2011).

40. See Wojtyła, *Love and Responsibility* (San Francisco: Ignatius Press, 1981). Originally published as *Miłość i odpowiedzialność* (Krakow: Wydawnicto, Znak, 1960).

41. John Paul II, *Crossing the Threshold of Hope*, trans. Jenny McPhee and Martha McPhee (New York: Knopf, 1995), 200.

Thematically, the book consists of a reflection on the structure of human love in which he attempts to join Thomism and phenomenology from a personalist perspective. Thomism is his basic perspective, phenomenology supplies the tone and the themes, and personalism is the point from which the problems are analyzed and toward which they converge. Here we already find *in nuce* that project which he would develop systematically in *The Acting Person*. We shall now mention some specific characteristics of *Love and Responsibility*, beginning with the point of departure: the person.

In that era, studies about chastity from the perspective of Christian ethics had generally been conditioned by their negative and casuistic perspective.[42] They showed or demonstrated what people must *not* do, and casuistry gave the details. But this approach, for Wojtyła, was insufficient. It was focused on the object: sexuality, the sexual act, and forgot about the subject. The norms, in consequence, lost the capacity to motivate because they became autonomous entities which justified themselves and were seen by the subject as something alien and external. Consequently, they were rejected: Why perform actions governed by laws alien to one's own experience? Because of submission to an external law? Because of irrational obedience to the Church?

Wojtyła was fully aware that this problem could only be overcome with a new overall approach to sexual morality, since the latter would only be accepted if people discovered it within themselves as a positive, stimulating, and integrating principle, and not as merely an external brake on their tendencies. His solution, very original in its time, consisted of integrating sexuality into the wider perspective of the interpersonal relations between a man and a woman.[43] Approached in this way, sexuality ceased to be a mere biological impulse and was trans-

---

42. See Karol Wojtyła, "La experiencia religiosa de la pureza" (1953), in *El don del amor: Escritos sobre la familia*, 5th ed. (Madrid: Palabra, 2006): 69–81.

43. The approach is very similar to the one Julián Marías employed ten years later in *Antropología metafísica* (Madrid: Alianza, 1970). Translated by Frances M. López-Morillas as *Metaphysical Anthropology: The Empirical Structure of Human Life* (University Park, Pa.: Pennsylvania State University Press, 1971).

formed into a tendency that creates a relationship between two persons: the man and the woman. This was the adequate framework in which to understand sexual relations: the personal complementarity between man and woman, not the instinct of procreation or the mere desire to satisfy sexual impulses. The task that remained was to determine the characteristics of that relation, which Wojtyła resolved by means of the implementation of his concept of the "personalist norm" understood as a basic criterion of the orientation of action. This norm begins with Kant's principle of non-instrumentalization of the subject, but elevates and transforms it into a positive rule which maintains that "A person is an entity of a sort to which the only proper and adequate way to relate is love."[44]

2.2.4 | *The Acting Person* (1969)

The Acting Person is undoubtedly Wojtyła's masterpiece. It is a truly copious work that can be interpreted from two points of view. The first perceives it as a natural offshoot of his ethical investigations which gradually led him to a profound conviction: ethics needed a strong anthropological groundwork. It was not possible to work out a potent conception of morality without having, simultaneously, an equally potent anthropological conception of the person. And this meant, in the end, that the rethinking of ethics which Wojtyła had begun could be radically carried out only through an analogous rethinking of anthropology. Otherwise the project would remain unfinished.

But there is also a second possible reading of *The Acting Person*, or rather, if one prefers, a radicalization of the first. Together with the need to construct an effective and innovative anthropology, in Wojtyła's mind the need to unify Thomism and phenomenology affirmed itself ever more forcefully. Only the fusion of both could give rise to the philosophy of the future. And what better opportunity to undertake this

---

44. Wojtyła, *Love and Responsibility*, 41.

plan than the quest for a new anthropological foundation? In this way, the two projects were, in the end, united. *The Acting Person* thus corresponds to a double objective: to fulfill the demands of his ethical investigations and to meld Thomism and phenomenology into a new personalist anthropological formulation. Wojtyła tackled the topic with his characteristic radicality and depth which, in fact, were indispensable, since he was not attempting to merely innovate, but rather to *refound* the architecture of anthropology. Therefore, *The Acting Person* is an enterprise as original as it is titanic, as can be appreciated in the succinct description of some of the fundamental ideas that characterize it.

(1) Contrary to the classical scheme, Wojtyła approached the person by way of the person's action; action will reveal the person, not the other way around. He states in the preface to the English/American edition, "This presentation of the problem, completely new in relation to traditional philosophy (and by traditional philosophy we understand here the pre-Cartesian philosophy and above all the heritage of Aristotle and, among the Catholic schools of thought, of St. Thomas Aquinas) has provoked me to undertake an attempt at reinterpreting certain formulations proper to this whole philosophy."[45]

(2) The concept of experience is very rich, and a particularly suggestive aspect is its use as a methodological instrument to access, integrate, and go beyond the opposing positions of objectivism (truth without a subject) and of philosophy of consciousness (subject without truth). In this sense, he said, "We reach the conclusion that much more important than any attempt to attribute absolute significance to either aspect of human experience is the need to acknowledge their mutual relativeness."[46]

---

45. Karol Wojtyła, *The Acting Person*, trans. Anna-Teresa Tymieniecka (Dordrecht: D. Reidel Pub. Co, 1979), xiii.
46. Ibid., 19.

(3) The perspective of integrality which inspires *The Acting Person* will cause a transition from the *actus humanus* of Thomism to the act of the person (*actus personae*), as the only way to integrate all the anthropological dimensions of the subject, including subjectivity, into action.

(4) Consciousness extends from the mere knowledge of one's own actions (the classical position) to the experience of such actions (modernity). "The essential function of consciousness is to form man's experience and thus to allow him to experience in a special way his own subjectiveness."[47] This is another example of his project of integration between classicism and modernity in the structure of the person.

(5) Another great contribution in this work is the systematic integration of subjectivity into the classical tradition. The conception of consciousness as self-experience opens the way for the thematic elaboration of subjectivity, and this, in turn, clears the way for the consideration of the "I" as the subject's unifying center. All of this, of course, without renouncing the realist ontological platform that Thomism provides.

(6) Freedom is understood not only as choice but as the *self-determination* of the person through his choices, which is anthropologically possible through the structure of self-dominion and self-possession characteristic of the person.[48]

(7) Body, psyche, and feelings are more of the many topics, belonging to the personalist tradition, which Wojtyła incorporates into classical reflections. Man is understood as a bodily being, which means that the structure of the person is mediated by the body or that the body is a personal dimension; the investigation of psyche, for its part, favors the active consideration of corporeality and eliminates the risk of a *de facto* dualism (soul-body) by

---

47. Ibid., 42.
48. The subject is fully developed in chap. 3, "Personal Structure of Self-determination"; and chap. 4, "Self-determination and Realization," in Wojtyła, *The Acting Person*.

incorporating an intermediate dimension which modulates both. Finally, affectivity (along the lines of Dietrich von Hildebrand and Scheler) is incorporated from a highly positive perspective. It is not simply a matter of an unredeemed anthropological mechanism which the higher faculties (intelligence, will) must control, but rather, it is a matter of the way in which the subject lives himself.

2.2.5 | Interpersonal and Social Philosophy and "The Theology of the Body"

After *The Acting Person*, Wojtyła published several studies which developed or clarified some of the concepts in that work. For example, he investigated what is irreducible in man, vindicating the radical specificity of the sphere of what is personal: self-teleology, alienation, and so forth. But in these years his philosophical path was decidedly directed toward the treatment of an eminently personalist topic to which he had not yet given sufficient attention: interpersonality. Certainly, the question had already been approached in *The Acting Person*, but only provisionally and preliminarily, as indicated by the title of the section in which it was studied: "Notes for a Theory of Participation."

It is important to note, in any case, that the fact that Wojtyła reflected first on the person and afterwards on the relationship is not at all by chance, but rather the result of a perfectly defined intellectual position: the *primacy of the person with respect to the relationship*, as he expressly affirmed in response to a criticism on this point:

> In the discussion published in *Analecta Cracoviensia*, vols. 5–6, ... a counterproposition was suggested with regard to both the substantial and the methodological approach in *The Acting Person*. From the position of this counterproposition, the essential knowledge of man as the person is the knowledge that emerges in his relations to other persons. While acknowledging the validity of this epistemological position, this author—after due consideration to the arguments for and against—still holds that a

sound knowledge of the subject in himself (of the person through action) opens the way to a deeper understand of human intersubjectivity; indeed, it would be entirely impossible to establish the right proportion in the understanding of the person and his interrelation with other persons without such categories as self-possession and self-governance.[49]

Now, the fact that Wojtyła affirmed the primacy of the person does not mean that he did not give importance to interpersonality. In fact, we recall that *Love and Responsibility* has this perspective. Thus, once he was satisfied with the instruments for the comprehension of the person which he had developed in *The Acting Person*, he prepared to tackle the problems of interpersonal philosophy, which resulted in the important article *The Person: Subject and Community*, the basic thesis of which is that the "I" is constituted as subject (not as an ontological *suppositum*) through the thou and, thus, the thou is not only the expression of a separation but also the constitution of a unity.[50] The second moment in this process takes place with the formation of the "we" or social dimension of the community, which Wojtyła understood as a collective subject different from the individual subjects, and which has a certain interiority, personality, or social subjectivity, an idea that would appear later in papal documents that demand, for example, the recognition of the "social subjectivity" of the family.

This was, however, his last philosophical contribution, since two years later he was elected Pope, which would interrupt his work as a philosopher. It was not so with his intellectual work, since, in addition to continuing to write poetry, he would present, almost immediately, his brilliant reflection on theological anthropology, which is often called the *theology of the body*. In a series of addresses, he returned to an already familiar topic, human love, but now interpreted in a theolog-

---

49. Ibid., 316n77.
50. See Wojtyła, "The Person: Subject and Community," in Wojtyła, *Person and Community: Selected Essays*, trans. Theresa Sandok, OSM (New York: Peter Lang, 1993), 219–261. Originally published as "Osoba: Podmiot i wspólnota," *Roczniki Filozoficzne* 24, no. 2 (1976): 5–39. A detailed study of this point has been developed by Sergio Lozano, *La interpersonalidad en Karol Wojtyla* (Valencia: Edicep, 2016).

ical key beginning from the texts of Genesis which relate the creation of man and woman.⁵¹

It is not possible to undertake here an in-depth analysis of this important work. We limit ourselves to considering one of the central ideas that emphasizes the importance of interpersonality in relation to a classical question of Christian anthropology: man's likeness to God. Pope John Paul II made the bold suggestion of a new understanding of this ancient doctrine, born from his reflections on the person:

> *Man became the image of God not only through his own humanity, but also through the communion of persons*, which man and woman form from the very beginning. The function of the image is that of mirroring the one who is the model, of reproducing its own prototype. Man becomes an image of God not so much in the moment of solitude as in the moment of communion. He is, in fact, "from the beginning" not only an image in which the solitude of one Person, who rules the world, mirrors itself, but also and essentially the image of an inscrutable divine communion of Persons.⁵²

2.3 | Other Polish Personalists: Wincenty Granat and Czesław Bartnik

In addition to Karol Wojtyła, Poland has had other prominent personalists among whom one may highlight Wincenty Granat and Czesław Bartnik, both professors at the Catholic University of Lublin, whose thought is acquiring increasing notice thanks to the work of Krzysztof Guzowski, the chair of Christian Personalism at that university.⁵³

Wincenty Granat (1900–79) was a philosopher and theologian, and rector of the Catholic University of Lublin from 1965 to 1970.⁵⁴ One may

---

51. See John Paul II, *Man and Woman He Created Them: A Theology of the Body*, trans. Michael Waldstein (Boston: Pauline Books & Media, 2006).
52. John Paul II, *Man and Woman He Created Them*, 163.
53. See Krzysztof Guzowski, "Bartnik, Czeslaw" in *Enciclopedia della persona nel XX secolo*, ed. Antonio Pavan (Naples: ESI, 2008), 85–90; and Krzysztof Guzowski, "Granat, Wincenty," in Pavan, *Enciclopedia della persona nel XX secolo*, 407–409.
54. His principal publications are: *Osoba ludzka* [The Human Person] (1961; Lublin: Wydawnictwo KUL, 2006); *U podstaw Humanizmu chrześcijańskiego* [Towards the Fun-

observe an evolution in his conception of personalism. In *The Human Person* (written in 1951 but published 10 years later), Granat attempted a dialogue with Marxist anthropology, especially with the practical disciplines, such as psychology, pedagogy, ethics, and the social sciences. And, to this end, the starting point was Thomistic anthropology and the Augustinian method, although he emphasizes the value of experience understood as a property of the personal world and not as a phenomenological concept. But, years later, in his final book, titled *Christian Personalism* and written in the same period as the publication of John Paul II's encyclical *Redemptor Hominis*, he openly approached a theological personalism which begins with the observation that Christian anthropology does not have as its starting-point just any biblical conception, but specifically the Person of the Incarnate Word. In the person of the Word, in his humanity united to the divinity, the structure of the person is revealed. In the relationship with the personal God, Creator of created persons, the meaning of the transcendence of the person is displayed. And if, in Christ, it is the Person of the Word who plays the role of the bridge between the divine and the human, in the case of man, his person is a sign and guarantee of openness, of relationship and of transcendence toward the transcendent Persons and human persons. In this way, Granat sought to overcome the separation generated by modern thought between autonomous anthropology and theonomous anthropology, resulting from the annulment of transcendence.

Finally, it is worth stating that Granat affirmed that the Christian *Weltanschauung* is personalist and is structured into seven points: (1) the supreme reality of the Three Divine Persons; (2) human beings are treated as persons, a notion that appropriately reflects their greatness and dignity; (3) the ultimate end of men is participation, not in a generic happiness, but in the life and love of the Divine Persons; (4) Christianity

---

damentals of Christian Humanism] (Poznan: 1976; Lublin: 2007); *Personalizm chrześcijański* [Christian Personalism] (Poznan: 1985). See also Kryzsztof Guzowski, "Different Personalities, One Person? Wincenty Granat's Proposal Concerning Personalism," *Appraisal* 6, no. 1 (March 2006): 28–32.

has a dialogical character; (5) the Christian is a collaborator with God in the work of creation and redemption; (6) Christianity is a social community of persons in the Church, in which the person of Christ acts; (7) the notion of person and personalism as a method and content enables us to comprehend man from the point of view of reason and revelation.

Czesław Bartnik (1929–) has been a professor of fundamental and dogmatic theology and philosophy at the Catholic University of Lublin. His personalist thought is much more developed than Granat's and touches upon more topics than Wojtyła's. His perspective is that of *universalist personalism*, and his most important publications are *Personalism* (Lublin, 1994), *Personalist Hermeneutics* (Lublin, 1994), *Studies in the Personalist System* (Lublin, 2006), and *Christ as the Meaning of History* (Wrocław, 1987).[55]

Bartnik embraces personalism as a method of approaching all reality. In his works he proposes to reformulate epistemology, the method and theory of history, aesthetics, theology, and ontology in a personalist key. His position may be presented in six points:

(1) The starting point. Every system requires a starting point, and, for Bartnik, personalism's starting point is the phenomenon of the person which, since it is accessible from the start in a realist way, becomes the key, the model, and the criterion for understanding being in general. Personalism as a (open) system is not limited to anthropology ("personology"), although this is the foundation of personalism.[56]

(2) Definition. Personalism uses two sorts of definition: the first, or "alphal," definition is the result of the basic experience of the totality of the phenomenon of the person; the person is a "who."

---

55. See Bartnik, *Studies in Personalist System*; and Bartnik, *Le Phénomène de la nation*, collected articles in French and English, including short items on personalism and personalism in Poland.
56. Bartnik distinguishes between "personology" which studies the person in general and "personalism" in the strict sense, which would be the consideration of the person as the criterion for understanding all reality. See Bartnik, *Studies in Personalist System*.

Later, when the end of the process of investigation is reached, one attempts to unite the objective perspective with the subjective conceptions in order to assess the exteriority, the interiority, and the social dimension of being a person. Then the final, or "omegal," definition appears: "subsistence in the form of a 'who.'"

(3) Personalist ontology. According to Bartnik, personalism as a system needs a general vision of being. The person is not only one of many elements which constitute reality, but the source of ontological theory. The knowledge of reality is of a "personal" type because the person not only knows nature, but also transforms and personalizes it. The person is the *third type of being*, in which the "*contractio entis*" takes place, because he not only possesses a material and spiritual dimension but *is* body and spirit.

(4) Theory of knowledge (epistemology). The integral person (spirit and body) is the basis of two forms of experience, exterior and interior. In the interior of the person a certain *perichoresis* and synthesis of these two types of experience takes place. The ontological unity and the unity of the "I" make the contact with reality possible on all levels, and this constitutes the basis of the unity and differentiation of knowledge. Since the person is a relational and social being, personal knowledge is objective and not only subjective ("egoist"). For this reason scientific knowledge always implies a certain ethical commitment.

(5) Method. The personalist method begins with the analysis of the phenomenon of the person in relation to the whole of reality, and of the *perichoresis* of innumerable strata of reality. Since in the personalist method two movements are present (one from persons to reality and another from reality to persons), the passage from the theoretical stage to the practical stage is also produced. Thus the personalist method resembles the hermeneutical method.[57]

---

57. Similar elements can be found in Wojtyła, in particular, with regard to epistemology and method.

(6) Language. According to Bartnik, everything that exists is manifest in persons, created or Uncreated. Thus the entire cosmos consists, in a broad sense, of communication and language, which are made manifest through innumerable groups of empirical and supra-empirical signs which, thanks to the person, continually leave the sphere of nothingness and silence. Language also reveals the interiority of the person: freedom, rationality, transcendence, and creativity.

3 | Personalism in German

Personalism in the German language refers principally to two great currents of thought: realist phenomenology and the philosophy of dialogue. Each can be treated separately or as elements of the personalist movement, since both perspectives are justified. Realist phenomenology is a sector of the wider phenomenological movement and the philosophy of dialogue that arose independently of French personalism, but the intellectual keys of these thinkers not only are personalist keys, but even some of the basic theses of personalism, such as interpersonality (Martin Buber) or affectivity (von Hildebrand), have been developed in an especially profound way by thinkers from these groups.[58] In other words, realist phenomenology and the philosophy of dialogue are two central elements of German personalism.[59]

In addition, we find independent authors, such as Romano Guardini, of great interest and close to the positions of the philosophers of dialogue. Or, in more theological circles, Joseph Ratzinger (Pope Benedict XVI), who proposes a theological personalism of Augustinian roots, as he comments in this autobiographical account:

---

58. In fact, the philosophy of dialogue is occasionally called "dialogical personalism," and Buber is unanimously recognized as one of the key personalists. Buber's influence is present in the thought of almost all the others (Mounier, Marías, Laín Entralgo, Nédoncelle, and so on).

59. We shall return in chapter 4 to the question of the philosophical unity of personalism.

We then found the philosophy of personalism reiterated with renewed conviction in the great Jewish thinker Martin Buber. This encounter with personalism was for me a spiritual experience that left an essential mark, especially since I spontaneously associated such personalism with the thought of Saint Augustine, who in his *Confessions* had struck me with the power of all his human passion and depth. By contrast, I had difficulties in penetrating the thought of Thomas Aquinas, whose crystal-clear logic seemed to me to be too closed in on itself, too impersonal and ready-made.[60]

Now we shall present these two currents very synthetically, asking beforehand the indulgence of the reader for the brevity and concision. To refer to Scheler, Buber, Guardini, Emmanuel Lévinas, and many others in such a short space can be justified only by the introductory character of this book. To Guardini, due to the interest in his work and for biographical reasons, we shall pay greater attention.

3.1 | Realist Phenomenology: Max Scheler, Dietrich von Hildebrand, Edith Stein

Phenomenology is a very complex and differentiated movement to which we can ascribe, in greater or lesser measure, thinkers as diverse as Martin Heidegger, Sartre, Maurice Merleau-Ponty, José Ortega y Gasset, Jean-Luc Marion, Jan Patočka, Emmanuel Lévinas, Paul Ricoeur, Jacques Derrida, and others. We already mentioned (see chap. 1, sec. 4.2, above) the influence that it had on the rise of personalism, which we have been able to confirm in our presentation of some authors (for example, Nédoncelle, Mounier, and Wojtyła). But, in addition to this general influence, a particular set of philosophers, known as the Göttingen group or realist phenomenology, can be strictly ascribed to personalism inasmuch as their philosophy lies fully within personalist parameters. The most rel-

---

60. Joseph Ratzinger, *Milestones: Memoirs 1927–1997*, trans. Erasmo Leiva-Merikakis (San Francisco: Ignatius Press, 2005), 44. Ratzinger was also influenced profoundly by Guardini.

evant authors in this group are Max Scheler, Dietrich von Hildebrand, and Edith Stein.

Max Scheler (1874–1928) was Edmund Husserl's most brilliant and important disciple and one of the most relevant philosophers of his time period. His work is very extensive, but here we shall limit ourselves to indicating some aspects relevant to personalism. The starting point is his best known and most important work: *Formalism in Ethics and the Non-Formal Ethics of Values: A New Attempt Toward the Foundation of an Ethical Personalism*.[61] In this book, and generally in all his works, Scheler presents a decided and powerful criticism of Kant's moral formalism which rejects happiness and concrete realities as valid motives for moral action—the only acceptable motive was duty—opposing it with a "material" (non-formal) ethics of values, that is, an ethics with specific contents and structured around the idea of value. This new notion of value arose from the phenomenological analysis of moral experience which showed that man encounters values before him and that these values are what motivate action. Although we are not able to go into the details of this proposition, it is important to emphasize that Scheler strongly facilitated an anthropology shift in the Kantian proposal which was much more in accord with the personalism which would directly inspire authors such as von Hildebrand and Karol Wojtyła.

In effect, faced with a formalism in which the subject is dissolved into a transcendental ego, Scheler uses the phenomenological method to regain the subject and then the person as concretely and "materially" responsible for a series of actions which interest him and motivate

---

61. See Max Scheler, *Der Formalismus in der Ethik und die materiale Wertethik. Neuer Versuch der Grundlegung eines ethischen Personalismus, 1913–16*, 6th ed. (Berlin: Franke Verlag, 1980); 1st–5th eds. as vol. 2 of *Gesammelte Werke* (Bern: Franke Verlag 1971). Translated by Manfred S. Frings and Roger Funk as *Formalism in Ethics and Non-Formal Ethics of Values: A New Attempt Toward the Foundation of an Ethical Personalism* (Evanston, Ill.: Northwestern University Press, 1973). For a general introduction to Scheler, see Manfred S. Frings, *The Mind of Max Scheler* (Milwaukee, Wis.: Marquette University Press, 1997). NB: "Material" is from "*materie*," meaning "matter" as the counterpart of "form" in Aristotelian ontology, and is best translated as "non-formal."

him and to which he must respond in accord with a specific hierarchy. In this way, Scheler directly introduced the topic of the person as the central axis of his anthropology, starting from phenomenological presuppositions; a path that, with different accents and perspectives, all the realist phenomenologists would follow.

His acute analyses of anthropological and ethical questions are another of Scheler's great contributions to personalism. The continuing publication of Husserl's unpublished writings is showing that he also was interested in questions besides methodology, but in Scheler this interest to go beyond methodology was central, took priority, and led to master works which unveil seldom studied dimensions of interpersonal relations or the individual person in a brilliant and original way. Without doubt, Scheler's best known work in this area is *The Nature of Sympathy*,[62] in which he maintains that the basic structure of the interpersonal relation consists, as its etymology indicates, of sharing feelings with a fellow person but respecting his otherness.

> Sympathy guarantees the autonomy of the person at the same time as it makes it possible to understand the other and to communicate with him. Nevertheless, for Scheler, beyond sympathy, as its ultimate basis, we find love. The lover realizes in himself the maximum union with the beloved, at the same time as he affirms the beloved's radical otherness and intellectual unrepeatability. Through love, the person wills the other and unites himself to the other precisely inasmuch as the beloved is other.[63]

A similar book that had great repercussions is *The Eternal in Man*,[64] which has been considered, along with Rudolf Otto's *The Idea of the Holy*, as one of the classics of the phenomenology of religion. Similar

---

[62]. See Max Scheler, *Wesen und Formen der Sympathie*, 5th ed. (1913; Frankfurt am Main: Verlag G. Schulte-Bulmke, 1948). Translated by Peter Heath as *The Nature of Sympathy* (London: Routledge, 1954).

[63]. Mariano Fazio and Francisco Fernández Labastida, *Historia de la filosofía*, vol. 4, *Filosofía contemporánea*, 2nd ed. (Madrid: Palabra, 2009): 349.

[64]. See Scheler, "Tod und Fortleben" (1911–14). See also *Von Ewigen in Menschen* [*The Eternal Man*] (1921), trans. Bernard Noble (London: SCM Press, 1960).

publications, more specific but equally profound and enlightening, are: "Knowledge and Culture," *Problems of a Sociology of Knowledge,* "Death and the Life Hereafter," reflections on work, and *Shame and the Feeling of Shame*[65]—these last two were used by Wojtyła in the elaboration of *Love and Responsibility.* Together, these and other writings represent a legacy of anthropological and ethical reflections of a richness and profundity so notable that it is impossible to disregard them.[66]

Dietrich von Hildebrand (1889–1977) was born in Florence to German parents and spent his youth in Italy and France.[67] He studied with Husserl and was a friend of Scheler, who was influential in his conversion to Catholicism in 1914. He had to escape from Germany because of his firm opposition to National Socialism, and initially he moved to Vienna but again he had to flee. Finally, after wandering through numerous countries, he ended up in the United States in 1940 where he took up residence and taught for many years at Fordham University in New York.

His extensive work can be roughly divided into religious and philosophical writings. Among the first are *Transformation in Christ, Liturgy and Personality,* and *Marriage: The Mystery of Faithful Love* (1929).[68] The most essential of his philosophical works are: *What Is Philosophy?, The Nature of Love, Ethics,* and *Aesthetics.*[69] Like Scheler, he focused on

---

65. See Scheler, *Problems of a Sociology of Knowledge,* trans. Kenneth W. Stikkers (London: Routledge, 1980); Scheler, "Erkenntnis und Arbeit" (1926); Scheler, "Arbeit und Weltanschuung" (1920–21); Scheler, *Person and Self-Value: Three Essays,* trans. Manfred S. Frings (Dordrecht: Martinus Nijhoff, 1987) includes translation of *Über Scham und Schamgefühl* (1913).

66. It is common knowledge that the intellectual journey of Scheler was complex and had several stages. Here we have limited ourselves to the period (the principal one, to be sure) in which his thought was essentially personalist.

67. A splendid biography, with autobiographical features, since his second wife wrote it on the basis of his notes, is Alice Von Hildebrand, *The Soul of a Lion: Dietrich von Hildebrand, A Biography* (San Francisco: Ignatius Press, 2000).

68. See Dietrich von Hildebrand, *Transformation in Christ* (New York: Longmans, Green and Co., 1948); Dietrich von Hildebrand, *Liturgy and Personality* (New York: Longmans, Green and Co., 1943).

69. See Dietrich von Hildebrand, *What Is Philosophy?* (Chicago: Franciscan Herald

ethical and anthropological issues from an axiological perspective. Perhaps special note should be given to his profound studies on love and affectivity and, in particular, his vindication of the spiritual dimension of affectivity, a question he treated in detail in the marvelous book, *The Heart*, which has received much notice recently.[70]

Von Hildebrand held that the philosophical tradition had systematically devalued the role and importance of affectivity by placing it, under the influence of Aristotle, among the irrational, and not the spiritual, dimensions of the person. In von Hildebrand's view, this led to deleterious effects in anthropology, depriving man of one of the essential characteristics that make him a human "who." Therefore, he strongly vindicated the spiritual character of affectivity, arguing that it is easy to prove by recourse to experience, which shows us that many of the principal events and situations in human life are linked to affectivity, such as aesthetic experiences, happiness, and falling in love. This thesis was further developed with his proposal of the existence of three spiritual centers in the person: intelligence, freedom, and—this is the great innovation—the heart. This concept, in its philosophical version, can have various interpretations. One of them, with Hebrew roots, is to consider the heart as the ultimate center of the person; but von Hildebrand argues that it refers exclusively to the affective dimension of the person. This thesis, which, in several ways, can be found in other personalists, such as Wojtyła or Julián Marías, is very important for working out a complete anthropology, since without a consideration of affectivity as an original and autonomous dimension that reaches all three levels of the structure of the person—body, psyche, and spirit—it is practically impossible to show human subjectivity.

Edith Stein (1891–1942), a Jew who converted to Catholicism and was murdered at Auschwitz-Birkenau, is one of the personalist philosophers

---

Press, 1973); Dietrich von Hildebrand, *The Nature of Love* (South Bend, Ind.: St. Augustine's Press, 2010); Dietrich von Hildebrand, *Ethics* (Chicago: Franciscan Herald Press, 1953); Dietrich von Hildebrand, *Aesthetics* (Steubenville, Ohio: Hildebrand Project, 2015).

70. See Dietrich von Hildebrand, *The Heart* (Chicago: Franciscan Herald Press, 1977).

whose thought is gaining greater recognition each day.[71] Her intellectual journey takes a course which is inverse to Wojtyła's, but coincides with it. Wojtyła began with Thomism, came into contact with phenomenology, and worked to create a synthesis of both from a personalist perspective. Stein took the inverse route. She was educated under Husserl at the University of Göttingen, becoming his favorite student and, from 1916 to 1918, his professorial assistant. But when he turned toward idealism, Stein, along with her companions at Göttingen, decided to leave her teacher. Later, because of her conversion, she was introduced to Thomism and, like Wojtyła, worked on a fusion of these two philosophies. Her principal work in this respect, and probably her masterpiece, is *Finite and Eternal Being* (1936), in which metaphysics and phenomenology merge. Other relevant philosophical texts include *Sentient Causality* (1918), *Individual and Community* (1919), *An Investigation Concerning the State* (English trans. 2006), and *Potency and Act* (English trans. 1998, 2009).

Her anthropological reflections tackle typically personalist topics, such as living corporeality (following Husserl), the person, and interpersonal relations.[72] In this context, one may emphasize her original reflections on empathy which constituted her doctoral thesis, defended in 1917, in which she explored this way of accessing the interior *ego* of others: "I feel my joy while I empathically comprehend the others' and see it the same.... If the same thing happens to others, we empathically enrich our feeling so that 'we' now feel a different joy from 'I,' 'you,' and 'he' in isolation. But 'I,' 'you,' and 'he' are retained in 'we.' A

---

71. Edith Stein's *Collected Works* are being translated and published by ICS Publications, http://www.icspublications.org. See Stein, *Collected Works*, vol. 1, *Life in a Jewish Family: An Autobiography, 1891–1916*, trans. Josephine Koeppel (Washington, D.C.: ICS Publications, 1986); and Alasdair MacIntyre, *Edith Stein: A Philosophical Prologue* (Lanham, Md.: Rowman and Littlefield Publishers, 2006).

72. The following philosophical books in the English translation of the *Collected Works*, are currently available: *On the Problem of Empathy* (vol. 3); *Philosophy of Psychology and the Humanities* (vol. 7); *Knowledge and Faith* (vol. 8); *Finite and Eternal Being* (vol. 9); *An Investigation Concerning the State* (vol. 10); *Potency and Act* (vol. 11); *Letters to Roman Ingarden* (vol. 12).

'we,' not an 'I,' is the subject of the empathizing."[73] Also important are her reflections on woman, pioneering in her time and in part based on her sorrowful personal experiences, for example, the impossibility of achieving university tenure because she was a woman.[74] She also tackled the subject of pedagogy, although not with the same profundity and dedication as in her properly philosophical writings.

When, in 1936, she finished *Finite and Eternal Being*,[75] her great mature work of philosophy, a conciliation of Thomism and phenomenology, she began to write on spirituality and predominantly on mysticism, in the context of her life as a Discalced Carmelite nun from her entering the Carmel in 1933 until her death.

3.2 | The Philosophers of Dialogue

The philosophy of dialogue had its moment of splendor between 1920 and 1930, and is very important within personalist thought because it is the principal cause of the relevance which personalism has given to interpersonality. In fact, although an "independent" discovery of the topic of interpersonality cannot be disregarded in a particular author, as is the case with Guardini, the majority of personalists are directly or indirectly influenced by the profound development of the "I-Thou" relationship by the philosophers of dialogue in this period immediately prior to the emergence of the greater part of the principal personalist writings. This development was not limited to accentuating the philosophical importance of the "I-Thou" relationship, that is, to overcoming "it-ism" or the unilateral and exclusivist consideration of objects, which

---

73. Edith Stein, *On the Problem of Empathy*, trans. Waltraut Stein (Washington D.C.: ICS Publications, 1989), 17–18. Originally published as *Zum Problem der Einfühlung* (Freiburg i. Br.: Univ., 1916). .

74. See Stein, *Collected Works*, vol. 2, *Essays on Woman*, trans. Freda Mary Oben (Washington, D.C.: ICS Publications, 1987).

75. Edith Stein, *Collected Works*, vol. 9, *Finite and Eternal Being: An Attempt at an Ascent to the Meaning of Being*, trans. Kurt F. Reinhardt (Washington, D.C.: ICS Publications, 2002).

had been in vogue for centuries in European philosophy. The philosophers of dialogue went further by postulating the foundational relevance of the "thou" in the constitution of the "I." In effect, the I-subject, the I-person, is constituted as such, for the dialogical philosophers, through relationship and in relationship. That is the reason for the importance of the intermediate configurations or of the relational structures which exist between subjects, such as Buber's "between." These configurations, in the dialogical perspective, acquire a primary importance since they are the vehicles of the constitution of the subject's identity with a necessity and consistency which varies according to the individual positions in a scale which, more or less, goes from Ferdinand Ebner (1882–1931), the initiator of dialogical philosophy, to Emmanuel Lévinas (1906–95), a generation after its other classic representatives, Martin Buber (1878–1965) and Franz Rosenzweig (1886–1929).

3.2.1 | Ferdinand Ebner and Franz Rosenzweig

Ferdinand Ebner is normally considered the initiator of the movement. He was an Austrian teacher and a Catholic, who recovered his faith in his maturity. He was inspired by the works of Kierkegaard and John Henry Newman.[76] From the former he adopted an existentialist and somewhat extreme tone; and from the latter the processes of the search for God. His thought is difficult to explain, since it is not structured systematically; rather, he expressed himself through reflections and aphorisms, but in these writings, frequently enigmatic, he advances, for the first time, toward overcoming the unilateral objectivism, present up to then in European philosophy, by means of the discovery of the

---

76. His most important work is *Das Wort und die geistigen Realitäten: Pneumatologische Fragmente. Die Geschichte der Fragmente*, ed. Richard Hörmann (Berlin: LIT-Verlag, 2009). Translated by Harold Johnson Green as *The Word and the Spiritual Realities: A Translation of and Critical Introduction to Ferdinand Ebner's "Das Wort und die geistigen Realitäten" and a Comparison with Martin Buber's "Ich und Du"* (Evanston, Ill.: Northwestern University, 1980).

conceptual and anthropological relevance of the "I-Thou" relationship or, in other words, of the essential relationality of the human person. Ebner studied this relationship principally by way of two phenomena: word and love. "There are only two phenomena in the spiritual life," he affirms, "two phenomena which occur between the 'I' and the 'Thou': word and love. In them lies the salvation of man, the liberation from his 'I,' and from his self-confinement in himself."[77] Love is the soul of intersubjectivity, its justification, which makes it possible to respect the other as a "thou" identical to my "I." And the word—understood in the broad sense—is the way in which this relationship is configured and formalized, a fact to which Ebner, inspired by the *Logos* of St. John's Gospel, gave a theological relevance: "Created by the miracle of the Word, amazed by the miracle of the Word, this is how man lives. My thinking consists in this thought; in this thought I have my life and my life's support."[78]

Franz Rosenzweig (1886–1929), who had read Ebner and was influenced by Hermann Cohen,[79] contributed to the development of this current of thought and gave it consistency with what he called "New Thinking" (*Neue denken*), into which, in addition to the principle of dialogue, other elements flowed: a different approach to the principle of God since, "When, for instance, the old [thinking] poses the problem of whether God is transcendent or immanent, the new [thinking] tries to say how and when He turns from the distant to the near God and again from the near to the distant one"; a sharp perception of temporality which leads to the conviction that "it cannot know [anything] independently of time";[80] one of the first expositions of the failure of the Enlightenment project; the need to look to Israel and not to Athens

---

77. Ferdinand Ebner, *Wort und Liebe*, 26, quoted in Alfonso López Quintás, *Pensadores cristianos contemporáneos* (Madrid: BAC, 1968), 118.

78. Ferdinand Ebner, *Das Wort ist der Weg*, 211; quoted in López Quintás, *Pensadores cristianos contemporáneos*, 113.

79. Cohen (1842–1918) was founder of the Marburg school of neo-Kantianism.

80. Franz Rosenzweig, *Franz Rosenzweig's "The New Thinking,"* trans. Alan Udoff and Barbara E. Galli (Syracuse, N.Y.: Syracuse University Press, 1999), 82, 83.

in order to overcome Greek substantialism, present in philosophy since Aristotle, and so on.

His particular position in relation to principle of dialogue was theo-anthropocentric since, for him, an adequate perspective of relationality would be possible only in God. For Rosenzweig, the "I" is not a foundation; when the "I" ignores the "thou," it reduces the "thou" to the condition of a thing. The authentic "I" appears with the discovery of the "thou," and this happens in God. There man learns to say "thou" to the "he"; thus, the relational "yes" only occurs without conditions when it is a "yes" whose guarantee is God.

3.2.2 | Martin Buber

The representative *par excellence* of dialogical personalism is the great philosopher and thinker Martin Buber.[81] Born in Vienna in 1878, he spent his adolescence in Lemberg (Lviv), in the house of his grandfather, Salomon Buber, one of the most distinguished leaders of the rationalist and enlightenment movement within the Jewish communities of that region. Martin soon made contact with groups of Hasidic Jews, inspired by mysticism, whose influence can be noted in his works in the form of spontaneity, a positive vision, and a certain anti-institutional attitude that would permeate his experiences and, in general, his profound and personal attitude to religion which was at the same time distant with regard to regulated practices and norms and official rites. The first stage of his academic life transpired at Frankfurt, where he was a professor from 1923 to 1933.

Like other personalists he was actively engaged in cultural and political issues. In particular, he worked for the construction of the State of Israel which congealed in the years of his maturity. In 1938 he fled

---

81. For an overview of Buber's life and work see Michael Zank and Zachary Braiterman, "Martin Buber," *The Stanford Encyclopedia of Philosophy*, Winter 2014, ed. Edward N. Zalta, http://plato.stanford.edu/archives/win2014/entries/buber/.

Nazi Germany and moved to Palestine. In Jerusalem, he was a professor of "general sociology" in the Hebrew University, although it was not easy for him due to suspicion of his credentials from the academic world. At first he supported the constitution of a bi-national (Jewish and Palestinian) State, but after the war of 1948, when the State of Israel was founded, he accepted the *status quo* which resulted from the Israeli victory.

The dissemination of his proposal regarding interpersonality and his status as a teacher of social philosophy turned him into an important social theorist, becoming one of the principal ideologists of the kibbutzim and an influence on relevant sociologists of a communitarian outlook, such as Amitai Etzioni.[82] In the last decades of his life he achieved international renown which led him to give conferences throughout the world, increasing his intellectual influence, which grew uninterruptedly until his death in 1965.

Buber's writings are many and varied and can be divided into three groups, as he himself did in the edition of his *Collected Works*, on which he labored at the end of his life:

(1) Writings on the Bible (*Schriften zur Bibel*), the most notable of which is the German version of the Hebrew Bible, translated in collaboration with Franz Rosenzweig and famous for its beauty and fidelity to the original;

(2) *Schriften zum Chassidismus*, consisting of translations and writings about Hasidic thought, such as *Tales of Rabbi Nahman* (1906), *The Legend of the Baal-Shem* (1907), *The Great Maggid and His Succession* (1921), and *The Occult Light* (1924); and

(3) Philosophical writings (*Schriften zur Philosophie*), the most relevant among which we may mention: *I and Thou* (1923), "What Is Man?" (1942), in *Between Man and Man*; *Paths in Utopia* (1950), "Images of Good and Evil" (1952), in *Good and Evil: Two Inter-*

---

82. See Amitai Etzioni, *My Brother's Keeper: A Memoir and a Message* (Lanham, Md.: Rowman and Littlefield, 2003).

pretations; and *Eclipse of God* (1997), in addition to others on education and psychology.

Within the context of his broad intellectual production, Buber's work stands out thanks to his extensive and profound formulation of dialogical thought, emblematically expressed in his most famous book, *Ich und Du* (*I and Thou*) (1923).[83] The work is not always easy to interpret, because of the use of a poetic and occasionally enigmatic language, reflecting his taste for this literary style. In it he gathers together, in any case, the essentials of his dialogical proposal. Therefore, we shall use this work to explain his philosophy.[84]

One may say that there are two basic, interrelated theses of these works: (1) the recognition of the importance of interpersonal relations, which implies, in a parallel way, the overcoming of the "I-It" relationship (person-object), typical up to then in philosophy, by the "I-Thou" relationship (person-person); and (2) the importance that is given to this relationship which, in a way not always easy to specify, gives the "I" its constitution.

Both topics are strongly stated from the very beginning of the book: "The basic words are not single words but word pairs. One basic word is the word pair I-You. The other basic word is the word pair I-It; but this basic word is not changed when He or She takes the place of It. Thus the I of the basic word I-You is different from that in the basic word I-It."[85] In these terse phrases, and with the same style, peculiar to the entire work—and different from his other works—Buber suggests one basic idea of great force: the relevance of interpersonality, which must

---

83. See Buber, *I and Thou*, trans. Walter Kaufmann (New York: Scribner's Sons, 1970).

84. *I and Thou* needs to be supplemented by other texts, occasionally clearer and more explicit: Buber, "Distance and Relation," in *The Knowledge of Man: Selected Essays*, trans. Maurice Friedman and Ronald Gregor-Smith (Amherst, N.Y.: Prometheus Books, 1998); Buber, *Between Man and Man*, trans. Ronald Gregor-Smith (New York: Routledge, 2002), includes "Dialogue," and "What Is Man?"; Buber, *Paths in Utopia*, trans. R. F. Hull (New York: Syracuse University Press, 1996); and Buber, *Gog and Magog: A Novel*, trans. Ludwig Lewisohn (Syracuse, N.Y.: Syracuse University Press, 1999).

85. Buber, *I and Thou*, 53–54.

not be confused with the social character of man, a topic present since antiquity (beginning with Plato and Aristotle). It is not a question of the I-society relationship, which could be included in the I-It. It is a question of the recognition that, in the lives of persons, the relation of one subject to another subject, of one person to another person, and, therefore, of an "I" to a "thou" understood as a personal interlocutor of the "I," is as relevant as, conversely, it has been neglected in philosophy.

In effect, because of its objectifying gaze, philosophy has transformed all external realities into non-personal entities, into things, objects, of greater or lesser transcendence, from merely physical things to persons, with which one cannot enter into a personal dialogue since they are also considered as "other" objects: he or she. But the authentic inter-personal relationship, of subject to subject, is completely different because it puts into play two unrepeatable subjectivities who interact from their most intimate nuclei, if an authentic encounter, that is, a connection of two interior worlds, is produced.

But Buber goes a step further, typical of dialogical thought, and emphasizes not only the importance, but also the priority of the relationship. For Buber, the interpersonal relationship is not just important, rather, he argues that the "I" does not exist without the "thou." In other words, the "I-Thou" relationship gives constitution to the identity of the subjects. "There is no I as such but only the I of the basic word I-You and the I of the basic word I-It."[86] "Only when the primal encounters, the vital primal words I-acting-You and You-acting-I, have been split and the participle has been reified and hypostatized, does the I emerge with the force of an element."[87] "Man becomes an I through a You."[88] "In the beginning is the relation—as the category of being, as readiness, as a form that reaches out to be filled, as a model of the soul; the a priori of relation; *the innate You.*"[89]

86. Ibid., 54.
87. Ibid., 72–73.
88. Ibid., 80.
89. Ibid., 78.

What meaning should one give to these expressions? Is it right to understand that for Buber the "I" does not exist in the proper sense, but rather the "I-Thou" relationship? It is a central question in dialogical thought and in personalism, which insists on the dialogical dimension of the person. And there has been much discussion about it. Due to its importance, we shall offer some brief considerations. The first is that *I and Thou* is a philosophical text but expressed in a poetic form, and consequently the ideas are forced into analogies and symbols that, if they were to be expressed in a more analytic way, would require more nuances. It is not the same to hold that "the human being becomes an 'I' in the 'thou'"—which could be understood as the recognition of the central importance of the relationship for a meaningful personal existence and for self-knowledge—as it is to affirm that "no 'I' exists in itself, but only the 'I' of the basic word 'I-thou.'" Nor, on the other hand, is this last expression univocal: Does it mean that no individualities exist or that, in fact, these individualities occur in relationship? Finally, Buber himself makes important clarifications which point to the ontological meaningfulness of the "I" as when, for example, he affirms that "What has been given up is not the I, as most mystics suppose: the I is indispensable for any relationship, including the highest, which always presupposes an I and You."[90] And, equally, he has not failed to say that the It, as limited and insufficient as it may be, is also necessary for human existence.

Finally, in several contexts, as in his dialogues on life in the kibbutzim, he has decidedly opted to defend distance and otherness as irreplaceable for an adequate life in community.[91] In 1961, Nachman, a young Jewish educator from a kibbutz asked him this question: "When we want to take on fundamental principles of your thought, such as 'pure conversation,' 'reciprocal relationship,' or 'dialogue,' we run into the burning issue of how it is possible to construct a pure relationship

---

90. Ibid., 126.
91. The concept of "distance" also appears, as we saw, in Nédoncelle.

between human beings who live and create in community, in a way that, notwithstanding, the uniqueness of each person remains respected and does not disappear into the group." Buber replied:

> I do not speak of proximity, but of relationship. There is a clear, simple, but very important difference between the two. In no way does mere membership in a group already mean an essential relation of the members among each other. Indeed, every human relationship has to maintain a certain distance: a person must be himself in order to be able to enter into relationships with others. However, precisely that person who has become genuine [*Einzeln*], who has developed a proper personality, can achieve an essential and full community with others.[92]

Following from all this, it seems feasible to conclude that, in Buber, the discovery of interpersonality co-existed *de facto* with the affirmation of individual persons.

Buber, finally, showed the potentiality of this idea in the religious experience understood as a relationship with a transcendent Person, with an eternal "Thou."

> Every single You is a glimpse of that. Through every single You the basic word addresses the eternal You. The mediatorship of the You of all beings accounts for the fullness of our relationships to them—and for the lack of fulfilment. The innate You is actualized each time without ever being perfected. It attains perfection solely in the immediate relationship to the You that in accordance with its nature cannot become an It.[93]

This account, dependent on his Jewish conception of God, is part of an interesting reflection upon religion, influenced by his Hasidic experiences, in which, curiously, despite his external appearance as a master

---

92. Martin Buber, *Über Gemeinschaft und deren Verwirklichung* (Heidelberg: Verlag Lambert Schneider, 1985), 300–312. The relevance of otherness is also found in his dialogues on psychotherapy and the relationship between psychotherapist and patient or client. See also Carl Rogers, *Dialogues*, ed. H. Kirschenbaum and Valerie L. Henderson (London: Constable, 1990).

93. Buber, *I and Thou*, 123.

of mysticism and his enigmatic language, Buber supported a religion involved in reality and attached to everyday events, rejecting any enclosing of oneself in a Gnostic fashion, as well as opposing a conception of union with God which would mean loss of one's own identity as with mystics such as Meister Eckhart or, especially, Buddhism.[94]

3.2.3 | Emmanuel Lévinas

Emmanuel Lévinas (1906–95) is the last great representative of dialogical philosophy and is known worldwide for his beautiful theory about *the face of the other*, transformed, as an epiphany of interpersonality, into the starting point of philosophy and particularly of ethics. We can only deal partially here with this author of great richness and complexity, and for this reason we only point out that he began his work, negatively, with a criticism of idealism and of Heidegger, due to their neutral and impersonal vision of the being which does not give priority to the ethical *who*. "To affirm the priority of *Being* over *existents* is to already decide the essence of philosophy; it is to subordinate the relation with *someone*, who is an existent (the ethical relation) to a relation with the *Being of existents*, which, impersonal, permits the apprehension, the domination of existents (a relationship of knowing), subordinates justice to freedom."[95] Positively, he was inspired by Buber's discovery of interpersonality, from which he wished to extract all of its potentiality, bringing dialogical thought to its final consequences, which would mean, in Lévinas's thought, the priority of an interpersonal ethics.[96]

---

94. Martin Buber, *Eclipse of God: Studies in the Relationship between Religion and Philosophy*, 2nd ed. (Westport, Conn.: Greenwood Press, 1977), where he insists again on the real character of God against such positions as those of Heidegger and Sartre, which eliminate religion, or of Carl Jung, who classified it as a mere psychological activity.

95. Emmanuel Lévinas, *Totality and Infinity: An Essay on Exteriority*, trans. Alphonso Lingis (Pittsburgh, Pa.: Duquesne University Press, 1969), 45.

96. Despite being inspired by Buber, he made some criticisms of his theory of interpersonality: (1) it does not establish dissymmetry in the I-Thou relation, both being interchangeable; (2) he would give a certain ontological character to interpersonal relation

Lévinas's *cogito* is the presence of the face of the other, which, with its interlocutory force, presents itself as a principle of philosophy of an interpersonal sort. "The face, still a thing among things, breaks through the form that nevertheless delimits it. This means concretely: the face speaks to me and thereby invites me to a relation incommensurate with a power exercised, be it enjoyment or knowledge."[97] But this face, for Lévinas, does not present itself as a theoretical philosophical principle, but as an ethical interrogation which is radically unveiled before the possibility of homicide, which the Other makes possible by his radical otherness. "The Other is the sole being whom I can want to kill." And it is precisely there where ethics makes its appearance, where ethics is born, when the Other radically opposes murder, not by his power—fragile and limited—but with his transcendence. The Other "opposes to me not a greater force, an energy assessable and consequently presenting itself as though it were part of a whole, but the very transcendence of his being by relation to that whole; not some superlative of power, but precisely the infinity of his transcendence."[98]

Lévinas thus seeks to construct a philosophy that takes otherness to its ultimate consequences and which is capable of responding to the dramas of World War II and, especially, the Holocaust. As Karol Wojtyła affirms, "For [Lévinas] the face reveals the person. This *philosophy of the face* is also found in the Old Testament: in the Psalms, and in the writings of the prophets, there are frequent references to 'seeking God's face.'"[99] So then, for Lévinas the epiphany of the other as a principle of philosophy appears, above all, as an accusation against power and as an ethical call, and not as a purely theoretical principle. Thus does one of his most important philosophical presuppositions arise: "Preexisting

---

(the *between*); (3) saying-thou separated from giving-thou is ethereal (it lacks concretion and the ethical dimension). See Carlos Díaz, *El "nuevo pensamiento" de Franz Rosenzweig* (Salamanca: Fundación Emmanuel Mounier, 2008), 109–17. In this book the positions of Rosenzweig and Ebner on interpersonality are also compared.

97. Lévinas, *Totality and Infinity*, 198.
98. Ibid., 198–99.
99. John Paul II, *Crossing the Threshold of Hope*, 210.

the disclosure of being in general taken as basis of knowledge and as meaning of being is the relation with the existent that expresses himself; preexisting the plane of ontology is the ethical plane."[100]

3.3 | Romano Guardini

We shall close this section on personalism in the German language with Romano Guardini, one of its most distinguished and best known representatives.[101]

3.3.1 | Life

Guardini was born in Verona in 1885, but his family moved to Mainz (Germany) the following year and he remained in Germany until his death in 1968. His early education was based on a intertwining of Italian and German culture. At home he lived in an Italian atmosphere (it was there, for example, that he began to know and admire Dante's work), but outside the home (with friends, at school) the atmosphere was purely German. In this ambivalence of life and culture, Germany was always predominant; and when he had to decide between the two countries (for example, due to the outbreak of World War I or the return of his relatives to Italy), he always chose Germany. In fact, all his works were written in excellent German. His relations with his family were good but not excellent. He always maintained his discontent with the rather closed and rigid atmosphere of his home which reinforced his innately melancholic character.

He began university at Tübingen (1903), studying chemistry, but failed. Later, he studied political science in Munich, but his difficulties continued until he decided in 1905 to become a priest. He began to

---

100. Lévinas, *Totality and Infinity*, 201.
101. Hanna Barbara Gerl, *Romano Guardini (1885–1968), Leben und Werk* (Mainz: Grünewald, 1995).

study theology, first in Freiburg (1906–7) and then in Tübingen (1907–08) where he experienced some of the problems raised by the modernism then in vogue. His ordination to the priesthood took place in 1910. He then began his work as a young priest, and through this work, he approached two issues which would be important for the rest of his life. Above all, he became aware of the importance of the liturgy, which led him to collaborate with the liturgical movement, which was in its gestation during that period, by publishing a book that made him famous: *The Spirit of the Liturgy*.[102] Then, he also began educational and pedagogical work with youth which would later take on great importance. Also during these years he obtained his licentiate in theology with a study on St. Bonaventure.

By then it is reasonable to consider that his character was already formed. Guardini was shy, sickly, polite, spiritual, serious, and profound, but with a great capacity for oral and written communication and with a dynamic and attractive thought. He also had a certain organizational ability. His academic activities in the strict sense began in 1922 when he was appointed professor of dogmatic theology at Bonn after the defense of his thesis on Anselm of Canterbury. From this point on, his activities developed around two central elements: his work with young people at the Rothenfels am Main castle and his university teaching in Berlin.

The youth movement. At the turn of the century in Germany, there were many youth organizations, more or less Romantic in character. Some of them, such as the "Quickborn," were Catholic. This movement initially had a somewhat naive and utopian character (they were teetotalers) and did not ask much of their numerous members. Guardini made contact with the movement, and little by little he gave it form and content by motivating and forming the young with a core of innovative

---

102. See Romano Guardini, *The Spirit of the Liturgy*, trans. Ada Lane (New York: Sheed & Ward, 1935). Pope Benedict XVI has been strongly influenced by the theoretical and theological position of Guardini, in particular *The Spirit of the Liturgy*, writing a book with the same title.

ideas on subjects such as culture, aesthetics, authority and freedom, the Church, and so on. Thus, he gradually became its indisputable intellectual and religious leader.

In order to give strength and continuity to the movement, he organized youth encounters during the summer at Rothenfels, a castle situated on the banks of the Main. These encounters became very relevant, and many young people with religious and cultural sensibilities attended them (Josef Pieper, for example, was one of them).[103] The movement reached its peak around 1933. Later it began to slowly decline due to Nazi pressure, which culminated in the expropriation of the castle in 1939.

University Teaching in Berlin (1923–39). Guardini was a professor for many years at the most important university in Berlin, the Friedrich Wilhelm University, but in very singular circumstances because this university was in fact the ideological center of Protestantism; and the chair of Catholic *Weltanschauung* (worldview) which Guardini occupied for years was practically imposed on it by the Catholic politicians of the Center Party. In fact Guardini never became a full professor at the university, but his classes had a great reception and always had a full audience.

The chair he occupied was also peculiar because it was custom-made for him. He never felt himself to be either a philosopher or a theologian, but rather a Christian thinker who took from each one of these disciplines what interested him. In addition, he did not want to develop a task of scientific investigation in the academic sense of the word. His intention was to transmit a holistic vision of the world inspired by Catholicism; thus the name and the characteristics of his chair. Guardini elaborated his classes with this objective and divided them into three groups—(1) commentaries on the New Testament; (2) systematic arguments; and (3) commentaries on authors such as Dante, Montaigne, Pascal, Kierkegaard, Hölderlin, Rilke, and Dostoyevsky—showing in

---

103. Pieper later became a professor of philosophical anthropology at Münster. English translations of many of his books have been published by Faber, Ignatius Press, and St. Augustine's Press.

this choice of authors their particular sensibility for aesthetics. During this time he wrote one of his most important books, *The Lord*.[104]

The interruption of academic life caused by World War II (1939–45) gave him the opportunity to transform into written work much of the material which he had elaborated and thought about while teaching. Some of the more relevant texts are *The World and the Person* (1939), *Freedom, Grace and Destiny* (1943), and many commentaries on authors, such as Hölderlin (1939), Rilke (1941), and St. Augustine (1944). He also published numerous works of a spiritual nature: a way of the Cross, commentaries on the Rosary, on Christmas, faith, prayer, and so forth.

After the war he returned to teaching, first at Tübingen and then at Munich. During this period he wrote an important book, *The End of the Modern World* (1950), in which, to the surprise of many, and long before a similar analysis was performed by others, he predicted the theoretical exhaustion of modernity, in part, due to its disloyalty to the Christian spirit that had nurtured it.[105] In these years he gained international recognition, was awarded prizes, and became a renowned lecturer; and his books were translated into many languages. Later, with the arrival of the turbulent 1960s, his thought began to be forgotten; but it is currently being revived, his books are being translated and published, and he is becoming more and more influential. For instance, Pope Francis prominently cited Guardini's analysis of modernity in his encyclical *Laudato Si'*.[106]

3.3.2 | His Intellectual Position

The message. Guardini attempted above all to transmit a Christian vision of life with some special features: intellectual profundity, integrality (that is, embracing man in his fullness), and the ability to in-

---

104. See Romano Guardini, *The Lord*, trans. Elinor Briefs (Washington, D.C.: Regnery Publishing, 1954).
105. See Romano Guardini, *The End of the Modern World*, rev. ed. (1957; Wilmington, Del.: ISI Books, 1998).
106. See Pope Francis, *Laudato Si'* (2015), esp. nos. 105, 108, 115, 203, and 219.

fluence conduct and action. Guardini, in effect, was not interested in constructing a theoretical discourse that would be irreproachable from an academic point of view, but would be cold; rather, he wanted to offer a profound and warm message in which readers and hearers would recognize in some way their aspirations, their problems, and perhaps some of the solutions which they sought. He elaborated this message within two fundamental coordinates: (1) fidelity to the essence of the Christian tradition, which meant, more concretely, fidelity to the Magisterium of the Church, and a profound knowledge of Scripture and the patristic sources; and (2) a modern and renewed exposition, so that this message could raise its voice with authority in contemporary culture and would be attractive and understandable for those to whom it was directed.

Method. In the elaboration of this message, Guardini took a peculiar approach: a non-scientific *Weltanschauung* or worldview, with the intention that this would make the message more accessible to his readers and listeners. This basically meant two things. First, his writings are philosophical-theological, that is, there is no strict separation of philosophical and anthropological subjects from Christian and theological ones. Guardini considered that Christianity is a holistic proposal for the interpretation of reality and therefore it was unsatisfactory to present it in two separate and independent segments: philosophy and theology. Without devaluing these disciplines, he wished to present a message that would be simultaneously human and divine, like the Gospels.

Another unusual feature of his thought is the *method of opposites*. Guardini thought that many important dimensions of reality are structured into two antagonistic elements which complement and balance each other by contrast or "polar opposition."[107] For example, the structure or living form of the person (which remains constant) and freedom;[108] concept and intuition in cognitive activity, and many other examples.

---

107. This method has some similarities with Hegel's dialectic, but is different because it does not seek any element of synthesis and, above all, because it does not consider that all of reality is formed by these pairs of dimensions.

108. See Romano Guardini, *Persona e libertà. Saggi di fondazione della teoria pedagógica* (Brescia: La Scuola, 1987).

Personalist Anthropology. Guardini worked out his philosophical-theological position within a personalist framework which is manifest in many ways. He emphasized the centrality of person in his philosophical-theological proposal.[109] Like the philosophers of dialogue, he insisted on the radical distinction between persons and things, with the consequent need to rework some classical anthropological notions. He stressed the decisive importance of the relational dimension and the experiences which accompany it: encounter, dialogue, and so on.[110] He upheld the primacy of love and freedom over knowledge, and the value of the person's subjectivity and of the "I" without falling into subjectivism. Many of his analyses are close to the phenomenological approach, showing that he was influenced by Scheler). His idea of philosophy, like many personalists, was not that of an academic exercise but as a way of collaborating in the transformation of society.

4 | Personalism in Spain

The presence of personalism in Spain covers two rich and interconnected paths.[111] The first receives, principally, the influence of European personalism in Spain; and those who accept or depend on this path explicitly call themselves personalists (Carlos Díaz, Juan Manuel Burgos and, less so, Alfonso López Quintás). The second is a separate path which, via Miguel de Unamuno and José Ortega y Gasset, leads to a Spanish reflection on the person, also influenced but less intensely by foreign personalists. In this second group we find some of the most important names in contemporary Spanish philosophy: Xabier Zubiri, Julián Marías, Pedro Laín Entralgo. The two paths are not entirely inde-

---

109. See Guardini, *The World and the Person*, trans. Stella Lange (Chicago: Henry Regnery, 1965).
110. It seems that Guardini came to formulate these ideas independently of dialogical philosophy.
111. Latin American personalism, with names such as Ismael Quiles, Nicolás Derisi, Alberto Caturelli, and Agustín Basave Fernández del Valle, is not covered in this book. See Mondin, "I personalisti latino-americani," in *Da Kant ai giorni nostri*, 586–622.

pendent of each other; on the contrary, they cross and intermingle, thus multiplying the mutual influences and dependencies.

Because of the complexity and hermeneutical interest of this process, we shall begin our account with a brief historical overview.

4.1 | A Complex History

4.1.1 | The Beginnings: 1925–36

The history of personalism in Spain begins around 1930 in the context of a very active Spanish culture, already widely open to European events and currents thanks to the work of the entire group of "intellectuals of '98" and, in particular, to the educational and renewing work of Ortega. In this unsettled intellectual world, the most brilliant exponent of which was the College of Philosophy at the *Universidad Complutense* in Madrid which would give rise to the famous "school of Madrid," the influence of personalism, which was beginning to triumph in France, began to arouse echoes in Spain as well. The initial influence arrived in two forms: a very incipient dissemination by way of the branching out of groups of friends of *Esprit* which began to be formed in Spain, and by way of personalists previous to Mounier, basically, Maritain, Luigi Sturzo, and Marcel.

In particular, and with respect to Mounier, important events were the creation in Madrid in 1935 of a group of friends of *Esprit*, coordinated by a Madrid lawyer, José María Semprún Gurrea, who used the magazine *Cruz y Raya*, founded independently in the same year as *Esprit*, as a vehicle of communication, and the work of Maurici Serrahima in Catalonia, also linked to groups of friends of *Esprit*. In relation to Maritain the work of Alfredo Mendizábal was notable, and he spread and translated some of the Maritain's most important writings.

In fact, Spain came to play a relevant part in the gestation of Maritain's *Integral Humanism*, since its first edition arose from a series of conferences that Maritain gave in 1934 at the Summer University of Santander and which were later published as *Spiritual and Temporal Problems of a New Christendom*. Maritain's political theories had already influenced some political formations, such as the Popular Social Party and the Democratic Union of Catalonia.

These good relations between Spain and personalism were frustrated for a long time by the outbreak of the Spanish Civil War (1936–39). Besides the halt to intellectual life which the war imposed on all sides, the personalists' interventions during the war were creating an animadversion towards their thought which would last throughout the period of Francisco Franco's rule. Maritain's is an emblematic case. Although he did not explicitly declare himself in favor of either side—differently from other intellectuals—he rejected the use of the term "crusade" by the Nationals, and along with other personalists, he wrote manifestos in favor of the Basque nationalists, which automatically made him the target of the ideologues of the Nationals. A very striking case is that of Luis Legaz Lacambra, who had participated in the *Esprit* groups but, with the war, passed over to the positions of national-syndicalism.

> Lately, the theses of personalism received a valuable reinforcement from Maritain, the Catholic philosopher who has wonderfully fulfilled the function of winning Catholic adherents to the anti-Fascist cause, precisely in the name of Christian personalism. When in 1934 *Cruz y Raya* published the manifesto of the *Esprit* movement which Emmanuel Mounier leads in France, with its motto of the "personalist and communitarian revolution," the ground was being laid so that Catholics such as Semprún Gurrea and Alfredo Mendizábel might decidedly launch themselves on these paths, which lead to the "Third Spain" and "Christian Pacification."[112]

4.1.2 | Under Francisco Franco's Rule

Francisco Franco's victory consolidated a hardline orientation, but the failure of the Axis powers and Franco's Catholicism distanced him from

---

112. Luis Legaz Lacambra, "Sentido humanista del nacional-sindicalismo," *Jerarquía* 3 (1938): 99, cited in Benjamín Rivya, "Primera recepció i fracàs del personalisme a Espanya," in *Emmanuel Mounier i la tradició personalista*, ed. Agustí Colomer and August Monzón (Valencia: Universitat de Valencia, 2001), 56.

the totalitarian ideologies which had been imposed in Germany and Italy. Thus, the cultural influence of the *Falange*, the Fascist organization with which all the other National groups were united, was relatively weak; and from early on, the regime became orientated toward a strong identification with Catholicism, receiving notable social success and generating its most characteristic cultural product: National-Catholicism. Its fundamental theses were as follows: identity between the essence of the Spanish nation and Catholicism; the understanding of Catholic unity as a political unity; rejection of modernity and the European Enlightenment; exaltation of authoritarianism; and the re-proposal of sixteenth-century Spain as the model to be followed in the construction of a future Spain.[113]

In this context, logically, personalism was not viable despite its evident Christian roots, as was amply demonstrated by the rejection of the thought not only of Ortega, but also of irreproachable Catholics, such as Julián Marías and Maritain. Without going into these debates in detail now, it suffices to indicate that the philosophical atmosphere in Spanish universities was dominated by a very closed Thomism, from which any variation (even a Christian one) from strictly Thomistic principles spelled danger. Ortega evidently fitted this description, as did Marías, whose forced distance from Spanish universities was formalized in 1942 when, inexplicably, the examiners of his doctoral thesis failed it. A similar suspicion was directed at Maritain due to his open attitude, even though he was one of the great neo-Thomists of the twentieth century. The fundamental problem concerned his socio-political theses which, beginning with *Integral Humanism*, gradually led him to formulate a philosophy of democracy and a profound justification of the convergence between Catholicism and democracy. This position logically made him a natural enemy of Franco's dictatorial regime, a fact that the regime soon noticed, and his work was no longer published.

---

113. Franco's National-Catholicism did not attract prominent intellectuals, but rather promoted a pragmatic reworking, for that time, of the traditionalist Spanish thought of the nineteenth and twentieth centuries.

The panorama began to change in the early 1960s, as Spain began to modernize and Franco's regime started to weaken. Spaniards glimpsed the end of an age and, above all young people, urgently felt the need to form their minds with new ideas, different from those proposed by the outdated official channels. It was the time when personalism began to flow, by way of all its authors, especially Mounier. The first intellectual media which carried echoes of the personalists were some Catalan reviews, such as *El Ciervo* and *Serra d'Or*, and also *Cuadernos para el Diálogo*. Around this time the translation of the principal French and German personalist texts also began. Publishers, such as ZYX, Cristiandad (who translated Guardini, among others), Taurus (who translated Mounier), FAX (von Hildebrand), Guadiana, and many others, for the first time put some of the more relevant personalists at the disposition of the Spanish public. These were well received, as can be proved by the successive new editions of some of these works. Thus, late in the game, the assimilation of and debate about this philosophy began in Spain.

4.1.3 | The Transition

Thus began the 1970s which were very complex. Europe was swept by powerful currents of thought which significantly influenced the future ideological configuration of society. Marxism, while struggling politically, seemed to gain more strength from a cultural point of view, buoyed in part by the counter-cultural protests in May 1968 (across Europe but especially in France) that levied radical criticism of tradition. This attack on tradition was reinforced by the sexual revolution, which increasingly promoted a way of understanding and living sexuality that was very different from the traditional one. Rather than presenting a clear alternative to these trends, Catholicism after Vatican II was bitterly divided between a movement aimed at applying the council as written and another that claimed the "spirit" of Vatican II as an invitation to share in the culture's desire for a rupture with the past. These factors of turbulence made their way to Spain with greater force because the predicted change of regime accentuated interest in the innovations of an external world which had been inaccessible for decades, and because the official restrictions on philosophy had deprived Catholic intellectuals of critical elements for evaluating those new ideas.

In that period, when the ideological frontiers opened wide, and as one more element of this ideological tsunami, personalism entered Spain in a wider fashion. And this very specific context led it to an ephemeral triumph before it disappeared, because, as Javier Tusell has explained, personalism was

> a vehicle of ideological transition. This means that Maritain and, more so, Mounier were read, but without generating a stable personalist culture. Personalist literature was, at times, the object of infrequent interpretations in other cultural spheres and was immediately substituted by other, more radically leftist literature. Consequently, personalist authors played a very important part in those years, but, at the same time, and with some exceptions, they did not take root sufficiently so as to create a genuine personalism in Spain.[114]

In effect, from the 1960s on, interest in personalists in Spain grew, especially among Christian intellectuals anxious for new ideological instruments before the prospect of the regime change which was on its way. Thus, they particularly read the personalists who had something to say in this area, that is, Mounier and, to a much lesser extent, Maritain. It was fundamentally because Mounier was more radical than Maritain and closer to Marxism, and so was more attractive in a period in which socialist and communist ideology, having been repressed under Franco, was presented with great force and prestige to the new generations of Spaniards. In brief, reading and speaking about Mounier allowed many Catholics to present themselves well as progressives, radicals, and anxious for a political change, but from a Christian perspective.

So this was the period of the maximum influence of personalism in

---

114. Javier Tusell, *El personalismo en España* (Madrid: Fundación Humanismo y Democracia, 1985), 14.

Spain, which resulted in making it a compulsory subject in high school philosophy courses. But the descent was as rapid as the ascent. Being represented by its most radical, political, and combative aspect (that of Mounier, and, in addition, with an increasingly extremist interpretation) personalism quickly found itself on ambiguous ground, satisfying the interests of very few.[115] To moderates it appeared to be a radical ideology which could contribute little to a society such as the Spanish one, which only wanted a peaceful transition to a Western democracy. And, on the contrary, for more extremist groups, it constituted a lukewarm and irrelevant position: a bourgeois, Christian attempt to move closer to the Left.

Some Spanish Christian personalists tried to artificially maintain ground by radicalizing Mounier's original stance. Thus, Carlos Díaz sought to move it closer to anarchism, and Alfonso Comín to communism, entering into an intense dispute with each other, each in defense of his own interpretation.[116] But these attitudes constituted, at bottom, a move which, instead of resolving the problem, aggravated it, because from the perspective of a Christian approach, it was not possible to reach the ideological extremism of socialist or communist positions; one was always at a disadvantage. Therefore, the more coherent solution, for those who wanted to go to extremes, was to dispense with Christianity definitively and to anchor oneself in Marxism, a path which, in those years, not a few intellectuals took.[117]

---

115. One author who criticized Mounier was Manuel Zurdo, *La verdad sobre Emmanuel Mounier: De Mounier a la teología de la violencia* (Madrid: Iris de Paz, 1969). He criticized Mounier's ambivalence, considering that, although he was a coherent Christian to which no objection could be made from a theoretical point of view, his orientation as regards action, and especially that of his followers, is confused and excessively close to Marxism.

116. Later, Díaz honestly acknowledged that "in polemics with Comín, I exaggerated the libertarian strain in Mounier ... given the atmosphere of that period, not at all indifferent to theory, always ready to bring thinkers into one's own ambit, in the desire to support one's own opinions." Carlos Díaz, *Corriente arriba. Manifiesto personalista y comunitario* (Madrid: Encuentro, 1985), 39.

117. One of them was Gregorio Peces-Barba who, still considering himself to be Catholic, published one of the first studies of Maritain in Spain, *Persona, sociedad, estado* (Ma-

When the socialists came to power and gained an important cultural hegemony, this tendency was reinforced. Personalism disappeared from the ideological and political debate and lost influence at the individual level. The books which had reached several editions in the 1960s and 1970s began to go out of print, without being reprinted.

4.1.4 | From 1990 Onward

This situation lasted approximately until the 1990s. A first key factor in the change was the collapse of communism in 1989. In Spain, which had already been stabilized, there were no important political repercussions, but there were cultural ones, as in the rest of Europe. With the fall of the Berlin Wall, communism suddenly lost its ideological and cultural credibility. The disintegration of "real socialism" in the very countries which had created it (especially in Russia) meant that its cultural prestige, which had lasted for decades, suddenly dissolved. On the other hand, the radical culture of 1968 was also weakened, though for different reasons. Some of its ideas and demands, such as sexual liberation, had already been assimilated, while the merely rebellious dimension, parasitic to the struggle against an enemy that appeared to no longer exist, began to be wearying and obsolete. To this collapse of ideologies, postmodernism responded with its thesis of "weak thought" and with the prohibition of the formulation of "grand narratives," which would replace the old ones, because history had shown, not only that they were fictitious and fallacious, but also that they lead to totalitarian positions.

This intellectual setting, with its weakening of ideologies, is what, by contraposition, created a propitious atmosphere for the rebirth of personalism not only in Spain but also in Latin America. Since it is a phi-

---

drid: Cuadernos para el diálogo, 1972). José Luis López Aranguren approached Marxism during those years, but, contrary to Peces-Barba, he did not abandon Catholicism, although he maintained a critical position.

losophy without a highly consolidated formulation, it has, doubtless, benefited from not having to compete with ideological formulations as powerful as Marxism. But, on the other hand, having a strong vision of man, it competes positively with postmodernism among those who desire solid and meaningful narratives. In this group we find, naturally, Catholic intellectuals, many of whom have overcome the ideological traumas caused by the post-Vatican II conflicts, which some identified with personalism. In this sense, the papacy of John Paul II has been decisive both for the intellectual pacification of the Church, leading her along a path of progressive assimilation of Vatican II, and for dispersing doubts about the Catholic orthodoxy of personalist positions.

In these conditions, personalism has reappeared with notable force in Spanish culture as is shown by some objective indicators: the abundance of personalist publications (by classic and recent authors); the appearance of specifically personalist collections of philosophy, such as *Biblioteca Palabra* by Ediciones Palabra, the collection *Esprit* by Caparrós, and the collection *Persona* by the Instituto Emmanuel Mounier; the multiplication of doctoral theses on personalist authors, such as Stein, von Hildebrand, Marías, Wojtyła, and Marcel.[118] Related to all of this is, doubtless, the activity of the two personalist associations in Spain: the Instituto Emmanuel Mounier, founded by Carlos Díaz in 1984, and the Asociación Española de Personalismo, founded by us in 2003, who, more recently (July 2011), has founded the Asociación Iberoamericana de Personalismo, a federation of associations with representatives from Spain, Argentina, Chile, Mexico, Guatemala, Costa Rica, Colombia, and Ecuador.

---

118. As an anecdote, in the first version of this book published in 2000, I wrote, amazed and distressed, that "the existing bibliography on [Julián] Marías is surprisingly insufficient, something which clearly should be remedied. We can cite *three works*." Juan Manuel Burgos, *El personalismo: Autores y temas de una filosofía nueva* (Madrid: Palabra, 2000), 149. Today, 17 years later, the bibliography has increased notably and there are numerous doctoral theses completed and in progress.

4.2 | Spanish Personalist Philosophers

We now turn now, in the first place, to the great Spanish philosophers of the twentieth century (the golden age of Spanish philosophy) whose thought is close to personalist presuppositions but who, for historical or personal reasons, have not identified themselves with personalism. Miguel de Unamuno is certainly the starting point of this line of reflection in which he played a part similar to that of Kierkegaard in the general current of personalism. Unamuno, in effect, with his vindication of the individual, his peculiar existentialism, his emphasis on subjectivity, his theory of the "personal novel," and other aspects of his philosophy, created the bases for a new way of thinking in Spain in which the individual existence of a personal type was stressed in accordance with the characteristics of personalism. Ortega, from a more strictly philosophical perspective, took the next step by relaunching of a vitalistic and dynamic conception that sought to renew classical philosophical presuppositions from a modern perspective, aiming to integrate, in particular, the contributions of German philosophy, such as phenomenology and vitalism, and their thematic derivatives: subjectivity, dynamism, historicity, and so on.[119]

These two fundamental pillars, Unamuno and Ortega, along with individual access to the sources of European thought, are the bases for the philosophy of the great Spanish thinkers of a personalist orientation, namely, Marías, Zubiri, Laín Entralgo, and Leonardo Polo. All of them, as we shall see, constructed their anthropology around the notion of the person; and their anthropological concepts—corporeality, psyche, knowledge, freedom, interpersonality—are very similar to those of other European personalists.

---

119. Ortega shares some elements with personalists, but it appears that he cannot be included with them in any way, except through his important influence upon them. He can be assigned a role similar to Husserl's: the renovation of Spanish philosophy in a way compatible with personalism. But, because he did not employ the concept of person, he cannot be called a personalist.

4.2.1 | Xabier Zubiri, Pedro Laín Entralgo, and Leonardo Polo

Xabier Zubiri (1898–1983) is one of the most important Spanish thinkers of the twentieth century. He was influenced in his formation by Ortega and the School of Madrid, phenomenology and neo-Scholasticism. Upon these bases, Zubiri attempted to work out a new presentation of classical (Aristotelian) metaphysical thought and of anthropology which would take into account the contributions of modernity and move away from the dangers of substantialism and "thingism." This new construction can be difficult to approach, not only because its exposition is intrinsically difficult, but also because of the use of a terminology proper to Zubiri. It has nevertheless produced very interesting results. His realism, for example, is not limited to a factual statement of existing things, as in naive realism, but includes a consideration of man who thinks and acts upon reality; in other words, there is an integration of the "I" into the epistemological process. He rejected an intellectualism of an Aristotelian type and proposed a unitary conception of epistemological activity in which sensations and intelligence operate jointly: "sentient intelligence."[120] He transformed materiality into corporeality, like other personalists, and, above all, structured his entire reflection around the concept of the person, very aware that it is a Christian contribution unknown to the Greeks and which still has not been sufficiently taken up by philosophy.[121]

Pedro Laín Entralgo (1908–2001) has a complex biography because, from positions close to the *Falange* movement at the beginning of the Spanish Civil War, he evolved towards open and modern attitudes. His principal areas of interest are the history of the medical field, anthropology, and intellectual and literary criticism, with a preoccupation about

---

120. See Xabier Zubiri, *Inteligencia sentiente: Inteligencia y realidad* (Madrid: Alianza, 1984).

121. Greek metaphysics "has a fundamental and grave limitation, the complete absence of the concept and even of the word 'person.'" Xabier Zubiri, *El hombre y Dios* (Madrid: Alianza, 1984), 323.

Spain and its problems. In anthropology he adopted a personalist perspective influenced, among others, by Zubiri and Buber. His construction is somewhat fragmentary but original, and it stands out for its application of personalist concepts to the medical and clinical context, which he knew very well. From there, reflections arose on topics such as man as biography; the anthropology of indigence and limitation; the understanding of medicine as praxis and of the patient as a person who must be treated as a "who" and not at a "what"; a powerful anthropology of hope; a theory of the other as persons, object and neighbor; and so on. Because of all this Laín Entralgo is important for connecting traditional personalist anthropology with the recent problems which bioethics raises.

Among his works, *La espera y la esperanza* (*Waiting and Hope*, 1957) and *Teoría y realidad del otro* (*Theory and Reality of the Other*, 1961) stand out, and the latter is certainly a notable contribution to the study of interpersonal relations. In *Sobre la amistad* (*On Friendship*, 1986), we can find a detailed historical retrospective on this question in which the contribution of Christianity and the position of the principal philosophers is specified, along with reflections on different types of interpersonal relations, such as social sympathy; camaraderie (friendly attitude), regular informal meetings to discuss specific subjects; solidarity; and falling in love.

Also very close to personalism is the work of Leonardo Polo (1926–2013), who, in fact, expressly manifests his agreement with its general approach, although he has the understanding that the philosophical development which personalism has achieved is weak.[122] His general attitude toward metaphysics is similar to Zubiri's, since he attempts a reworking or, better, an amplification, in his case, in order to make metaphysics compatible with contemporary anthropology.[123] Polo proposes,

---

122. Leonardo Polo, *Antropología transcendental*, vol. 1, *La persona humana* (Pamplona: EUNSA, 1999), 22. It is a criticism similar to that of Ricoeur and Nédoncelle.

123. For Polo classical metaphysics is not wrong, but does not go far enough, above all in relation to the problem of analogy, thus making it necessary to amplify metaphysics with new transcendentals. Ibid., 31.

in particular, an amplification of the transcendentals made possible by abandoning the mental limit which basically consists of overcoming the elemental mode of cognitive actions. "If we deal with the limitation of the object, by abandoning the mental limit we become aware of transobjective questions; and if we detect the limitation of the operation, we reach transoperative questions. The former corresponds to metaphysics and the latter to anthropology."[124] The transobjective question leads to first principles (metaphysics); the transoperative question leads one to take into account the operations that are known in non-objective terms: there one would find anthropological transcendentality. From this original perspective, one enters into an anthropology, which is thematically and conceptually very close to personalism in which the person is the basic concept and the areas of interest are the well-known, including interpersonality (being as co-being), the relevance of freedom, the "I," the personal "who" as the ultimate and decisive nucleus of man, and knowing as personal action.

4.2.2 | Julián Marías (1914–2005)

Julián Marías's personalism. Marías's thinking[125] fundamentally depends upon Ortega, but he was also influenced by an important group of personalists: he knew the work of Maritain,[126] Landsberg,[127] and Scheler; he was a friend of Marcel,[128] and, above all, he was influence by Zubiri. But, despite this and despite the fact that, especially in the

---

124. Ibid., 26.
125. The richness of Marías's thought is immense but here we shall limit ourselves to his anthropology. For more on Marías, see Harold Raley, *Responsible Vision: The Philosophy of Julián Marías* (Clear Creek, Ind.: American Hispanist, 1980); Raley, *A Watch over Mortality: The Philosophical Story of Julián Marías* (Albany, N.Y.: State University of New York Press, 1997).
126. "I took Jacques Maritain's course, so acute and distinguished, on 'The spiritual and temporal problems of a new Christendom' (I did not see him again until 1949, in Paris)." Marías, *Una vida presente. Memorias* (Madrid: Páginas de Espuma, 2008), 112.
127. See ibid., 114.
128. See ibid., 333–37.

last stage of his philosophy, he centers on the concept of person, he never chose to identify himself with personalism, as we can read, for example, in *Mapa del mundo personal* (*Map of the Personal World*, 1993), where he makes a rare explicit mention of personalism that is rather negative. Marías considers, in effect, that "the philosophy of our century, which has investigated the reality of human life so accurately, although sometimes with inadequate words, has left relatively in the shade, relegated to a marginal position, the meaning of the *person*, and what has been called *personalism* is no exception."[129]

But if we turn to the contents, that is, to the anthropology, the perspective changes notably; although, to be able to nuance this assertion, it is necessary to clarify that his anthropology passes through three partially diverse phases. In the first, he took up, with hardly any modifications, Ortega's vitalism, which has as its starting point the individual life of the subject as the root of philosophy. In the second phase, he made his first important contribution with the description of the empirical structure of the subject in *Antropología metafísica* (*Metaphysical Anthropology*).[130] In the third and final phase, he published books with such significant titles as *Persona*, *Mapa del mundo personal*, and others.

So then, having in mind this periodization of his work, one may state that, in his first period, Marías was not a personalist, although his philosophical approaches are close to it. His vitalism, taken from Ortega, in effect, has results compatible with the positions of personalism, but we are dealing with two distinct philosophical approaches, with different traditions of reference and different conceptual structures. They are united by the desire to use direct analysis of experience, the profound awareness of the originality of human being and a dynamic anthropological structure that emphasizes freedom. The two approaches certainly have quite a lot in common, but not enough to be identified with one another. Now, Marías, in this first period, is essentially Orte-

---

129. Julián Marías, *Mapa del mundo personal* (Madrid: Alianza, 2006), 11–12.
130. See Julián Marías, *Antropología metafísica* (Madrid: Alianza, 1983). The first edition is from 1970.

gan, and thus, this evaluation, at bottom, can be taken as a judgment on the personalism of Ortega which, as we have already stated, is not really a personalism, although there are convergent elements.

A very different evaluation can be made of the first work of Marías's second and more original period, that of *Antropología metafísica*. Here the discussion clearly turns personalist with regard to the *perspective* and the *topics*. The awareness of the originality of the personal dimension of man is very acute, and the treatment of the irreducibility of personal reality is just like that of other personalists. The line which separates this period from a complete personalism is that the starting point is not person but life. His key anthropological concept is life as radical reality, from which arises man, understood as an empirical structure of life which, in turn, has a personal dimension which makes it a "who." But the personalist philosopher never "arrives" methodologically at the person, but rather sets out from the person because the person is the original and originating philosophical category.

A complete personalism is, however, taken up in the third phase. *Persona* (1996), for example, is not only thematically and conceptually personalist but *structurally* personalist. Everything focuses on the person who is presented no longer as a derived concept but as the central one. "The last remaining difficulty lies not in thinking about human life—this has been achieved with amazing perfection in our century—but about *the person who lives*."[131] Whether Marías makes this change with more or less formal perfection is another question. What is certain is that this new approach places Marías fully within the personalist line of reflection.[132]

---

131. Julián Marías, *Persona* (Madrid: Alianza, 1997), 134. This is a decisive text because it manifests a shift in the axis of Marías's anthropology *from life to the person*, something unthinkable in the first phase of his work.

132. See Juan Manuel Burgos, ¿*Es Julián Marías personalista?*, in *El vuelo del Alción. El pensamiento de Julián Marías*, ed. J. L. Cañas and J. M. Burgos (Madrid: Páginas de Espuma, 2009), 147–164. Some experts have defined his position as "vital personalism." Helio Carpintero, "La originalidad teórica del pensamiento de Marías," *Cuenta y Razón del pensamiento actual* 87 (1993): 91; and Rigobello, *Il personalismo*.

Anthropology. Marías's anthropology is particularly rich and thought-provoking, especially beginning with his central work, *Antropología metafísica.* As well as the ideas which have already been mentioned (relevance of the "who," thing-person distinction), he reflects, for example, on our bodily nature or corporeality understood as one of the radical forms of setting-up parallel worldliness. Opposed to reductive versions, such as "I am body" or "I have a body," he opts for an integral, harmonious, and structural vision: "I am installed in my body" or "I am in the world in a bodily manner," adding that the diverse modes in which this settlement can be suppressed, lead us to sleep, rest, absorption, and so forth.[133]

Man's vectored and futurized character (already partially present in Ortega's categories), united to the profound thinking about the "who" in Marías, leads to a *biographical or narrative* perspective lucidly emphasized. We cannot *define* any concrete person. To truly know who someone is, we can only narrate his history; and so we come closer to his specific individuality. This history, on the other hand, unfolds in time, but not as an agent or an external factor which slides over the surface of humanity, but as structural vector which configures personal identity. Man is, then, a temporal reality, with a fixed expiry date which leads to death, an essential element of life. And the whole man dies, not only the body. "It is not that you abandon corporeality like the skin of a reptile and escape intact into other worlds. On the contrary: the condition of the existence of death is that it occurs, that is, that it happens to *someone,* and this someone—*I, you*—effectively dies."[134]

Marías, like other personalists, also understands philosophy not as a merely academic task, but as a way of facing reality and aiming to modify it for the benefit of society, which he calls "responsible vision." "Philosophy has been thought of more as a science, as a construction

---

133. Marías, *Antropología metafísica*, 113. The parallel with writers such as Marcel, Mounier, and Wojtyła, is clear.

134. Ibid., 216.

of ideas, than as a human *doing*; and it cannot be forgotten that philosophy is something which man does, even if it later turns out that that which man does is a science."[135]

Finally, among many other topics that it be worth the effort to study, such as his perception of happiness as a necessary impossible, enthusiasm (*ilusión*, with its distinctive meaning in Spanish), affectivity, interpersonality,[136] and so on, we highlight his innovative reflections on sexuality and on man (*hombre*) as male (*varón*) and female which already appear in *Antropología metafísica*, and which make this work one of the first to develop a dual anthropology, understood as an anthropology in which "the" human person does not exist, but rather two concrete modes, different and complementary, of being a person: man and woman, a distinction which does not apply only to corporeality, but also affects the entire human structure.

> For many years, I have been using a linguistic distinction in Spanish which seems beautiful to me: the two adjectives "*sexual*" ["pertaining to sexual activity"] and "*sexuado*" ["having a sexual structure, as male or female"]. Sexual activity is a reduced province of our life, very important but limited, which does not begin with our birth and usually ends before our death, (but which is) founded on that condition of human life in general which consists of being either male or female and which affects human life in its entirety, at every moment and in all its dimensions.[137]

---

135. Julián Marías, *Introducción a la filosofía* (Madrid: Revista de Occidente, 1967), 71.

136. "Personal being is intrinsically *pluripersonal*.... To the person belongs this mode of reality which is designated by the pronoun *I*, but presupposes a *thou*; there is no *I* without *thou*. I say 'I' contrapuntally to a 'thou.' ... In summary, person means *persons*: if there is only one, it lacks meaning, as Unamuno saw," Julián Marías, *La felicidad humana* (Madrid: Alianza, 1994, 281–82). "*Ilusión*" in its philosophical sense means in Spanish "the projective actualization of desire with a plot," as defined by Marías in his *Breve tratado de la ilusión* (1984), where he explained that only in Spanish and only since the Romantic period did the old Latin word "*ilusio*," whose meaning was "delusion" or even "hallucination," start to have a positive meaning in relation with the futurizing capacity of the person. The Spanish "*ilusión*" is, according to Marías, a method of personal knowledge and a method also to improve one's happiness. (Contributed by Dr. Nieves Gómez and Prof. Harold Raley.)

137. Marías, *Antropología metafísica*, 120.

Upon this theoretical basis, Marías has worked out beautiful reflections on man and woman: their different intellectual structure, their different relation to the body and the world, their different manners of love and falling in love, and so forth.

4.3 | Spanish Personalists: Carlos Díaz, Juan Manuel Burgos, and Alfonso López Quintás

Finally we shall consider the Spanish philosophers who explicitly define themselves as personalists, especially Carlos Díaz, Juan Manuel Burgos, and Alfonso López Quintás.

Díaz (1944–) has been the principal promoter of Mounier's work in Spain and has worked tirelessly for the dissemination of communitarian personalism by means of the Instituto Emmanuel Mounier in Spain and in Latin American countries (Mexico, Paraguay, Argentina).

His philosophical output is enormous, with about two hundred books published on a near infinity of subjects, among which the most prominent are communitarian personalism and personalist anthropology but which also include anarchism, philosophy of religion, the history of philosophy, virtues, social analysis, and logotherapy. This huge output increases every year, making it difficult to determine which ones are his principal and mature ones, a problem to which is added a certain lack of elaboration in some of them. X. M. Domínguez has divided Díaz's work into six categories: essays of philosophical investigation, academic studies, essays on philosophical problems, provocative works to educate and promote militants, popular works for dissemination, and biographies.

In respect of his thinking it is necessary to note, above all, a fundamental periodization. His first phase was marked by an anarchist tendency and ended with *Contra Prometo* (*Against Prometheus*, 1980), in which, without completely renouncing anarchism, he takes a position regarding it and abandons it as his central line of thought. His second period, which follows this revision, is completely dedicated to communitarian personalism, understood in a very Mounierian way, as "a way of life whose meaning lies in centering the meaning of reality on the person, vindicating his absolute dignity in all spheres. This means living in a free commitment to that *ordo amoris* [order of love] which flows from personal being. This way of committed life leads to a prophetic and political militancy, to living a life exhausted for the other, to make love the motor of one's own life."[138]

This prophetic-militant attitude has not kept him from also making an effort to theoretically formulate this communitarian personalism in which we can distinguish works of theoretical foundation and specific studies such as those on sorrow, failure, guilt, and "warm" reason. In addition, personalism in Spanish is indebted to him for a splendid and enormous effort in translating authors such as Lacroix, Mounier, Landsberg, Stein, Buber, and Nédoncelle, as well as numerous biographies including Mounier, Buber, and Rosenzweig.

Juan Manuel Burgos (1961–), the author of this current work, has worked intensively on behalf of personalism, both on the personal level and on the institutional. He has founded the *Asociación Española de Personalismo* (2003), the *Asociación Iberoamericana de Personalismo* (2011), and the philosophical journal *Quién* (2015).[139] He has also successfully launched two collections of philosophical books on personalism, *Albatros* and *Biblioteca Palabra*, in which the Spanish version of Wojtyła's works is prominent.

His thought has been influenced mainly by Maritain, Guardini, Marías, and, above all, by Karol Wojtyła.[140] His work can be divided in three areas. The first area is the study of great personalist thinkers, mainly Maritain and Wojtyła, on whom he has published several essays. The second area is rooted in his conviction regarding the philosophical

---

138. Xosé Manuel Domínguez, "El personalismo comunitario de Carlos Díaz," *Persona* 9 (2008): 45–46.

139. Articles available at http://www.personalismo.org/revistaquien/.

140. See Juan Manuel Burgos, "The Method of Karol Wojtyła: A Way between Phenomenology, Personalism and Metaphysics," *Analecta husserliana* 104 (2009): 107–29; Burgos, *Para comprender a Karol Wojtyła*.

power of personalism, still to be developed. And to demonstrate this (and also to facilitate personalism's promotion and dissemination), he has been working on a project of unification and synthesis of personalist thought, starting from the idea that the philosophical foundations of many personalist thinkers are very similar. The first result of this project can be found in *El personalismo* (2000), where he was able to characterize the common traits which define personalism. Also from this period is *Antropología: una guía para la existencia* (2003; 6th ed., 2017), which offers a deep and well-structured personalist anthropology in a synthetic way that had not previously been achieved.

In the last few years, however, and without giving up completely this first project, he has changed his main line of work from the attempt to unify personalist thinking to the promotion of a new current of personalism, called modern ontological personalism, in which he develops his personal vision of personalism (see chap. 4, below). This new current is based on the anthropology of Karol Wojtyła, and its main objective is to achieve the goal proposed by that thinker: the fusion of the philosophy of being with the philosophy of consciousness. The main contribution of Burgos to this new current is the theory of personalism which supports it (lacking in Wojtyła), together with some anthropological research, such as his analysis of the concept of human nature (*Repensar la naturaleza humana*, 2007). Particularly important in the development of this new theory is the very recent proposal of a personalist philosophical methodology called *the integrated experience* (*La experiencia integral*, 2015), which differs significantly from both the phenomenological method and Thomistic epistemology. Burgos has also worked in several other fields, such as bioethics, psychology, and family, mainly trying to apply and develop the personalist ideas in these areas.

Finally, *Alfonso López Quintás* (1928) is the principal Spanish representative of dialogical thinking or dialogical personalism.[141] A great

---

141. In general, López Quintás has identified himself more strictly with dialogical philosophy, although in his most recent publications he has accentuated the personalist character of his philosophy. Two English translations of his books are *Signs of Admiration*

advocate of and expert on Guardini, of whom he was a disciple in Germany, he has developed an original philosophical perspective centered on the study of the most sublime and creative spheres of human experience, such as aesthetics, anthropology, metaphysics, and religion. This construction begins with a methodological clarification destined to resolve an important question: the equivocity of the term "objectivity," because objective knowledge, in effect, can be understood as a knowledge adequate to reality and also as a knowledge that is measurable, tangible, and subject to a universal verification. Now, this second type of knowledge, greatly valuable for specific regions of reality, is inadequate (and thus not objective) for reaching the higher spheres of human experience ruled by the creativity and richness of the personal. In *Metodología de lo suprasensible* (*Methodology of the Suprasensible*, 1963) López Quintás made an effort to overcome this difficulty and "to work out a theory of knowledge based on the ambiguous but very fruitful categories of *encounter, presence, ambit, amazement, distance of perspective,* and *reverence.*"[142] And, on these bases, he has tackled his investigations in aesthetics, creativity, and culture, and also other important work, such as his studies on the history of contemporary philosophy.

In recent decades, Professor Quintás's thought has reached an ever greater recognition and López Quintás chairs have been created in Latin America. The work of the *Escuela de Pensamiento y Creatividad* (School of Thought and Creativity), which he founded to spread his ideas, has certainly contributed to this recognition.

(United States: Qualfon University, 2014), and *The Knowledge of Values: A Methodological Introduction* (Lanham, Md.: University Press of America, 1989).

142. Alfonso López Quintás, *Filosofía española contemporánea* (Madrid: BAC, 1970), 361–62.

5 | British and American Personalism

5.1 | British Contributions to Personalist Philosophy

R. T. Allen

Although personalism, as a distinct philosophy or set of philosophies, is almost unknown in Great Britain, there have been significant contributions to personalist philosophy from the nineteenth century to today by a succession of philosophers and theologians, who, for the most part, have been seriously neglected ever since. Their history can be roughly divided into three phases.

5.1.1 | Beginnings

At the end of the eighteenth century some British philosophers, starting with the Scottish "Common Sense" school, reacted against the skepticism of David Hume, utilitarianism, and hedonism, associationism, "materialism" (that all reality is purely physical), and "naturalism" (that all reality can and should be interpreted within the concepts and categories of those for physical reality).[143] For alternatives, philosophers, such as Sir William Hamilton, S. T. Coleridge, H. Mansel, and John Grote (who explicitly referred to his philosophy as "personalism"), turned to Thomas Reid, the leading figure in the Scottish "Common Sense" school, Kant, and F. H. Jacobi, the founder, with Friedrich Schelling, of modern personalism. Later, several went to Göttingen and studied under Hermann Lotze, the climax of the movement of the personalist "speculative theism" stemming from Friedrich Jacobi.[144]

---

143. In Britain at this time, "Idealism" was used in a wider sense to mean any rejection of materialism and naturalism, whether or not it was "idealist" in the narrow sense of denying the reality of physical existence. Monist and pluralist, theist and nontheist, and intermediate forms of them, were to be found in both the wider and narrower groups. Consequently, it is very misleading simply to identify British personalist philosophers in those days with Idealism and equally important to ascertain just what version of Idealism any particular philosopher of this period espoused, and if and when he changed to another.

144. For a survey of the beginnings and developments of modern personalism, in

5.1.2 | The "Personal Idealists"

In 1865 H. Stirling's *The Secret of Hegel* inaugurated widespread British interest also in Hegel, in both more personalist versions and the impersonal monism of the Absolute Idealists. Having espoused, five years earlier, Johann Gottlieb Fichte and Hegel as the true development of Kant, Andrew Seth (1856–1931, and later A. S. Pringle-Pattison), began, and became the most prominent figure in, what was known as "Personal Idealism" which defended the reality and unique value of the finite person against the Absolutists, such as F. H. Bradley, Edward Caird, and especially Bernard Bosanquet.[145] Pringle-Pattison was somewhat hampered by his method of criticizing the work of others, which stunted the development of his own ideas. Hence he did not elaborate his insight that "ideas in themselves are nothing, and the analysis of knowledge can never give us reality," so that now *cogito ergo sum* should be replaced by *ago ergo sum*. Nor did he really break with Bernard Bosanquet's language of "wholes" and their "contents" of "ideas" for the structure of minds (never persons!). A more systematic "personal idealist," but not usually denoted as such, was his contemporary, W. R. Sorley (1855–1935).[146]

Britain, and in Germany and Sweden, see Jan Olof Bengtsson, *The Worldview of Personalism: Origins and Early Development* (Oxford: Oxford University Press, 2006). See also the *Dictionary of Nineteenth Century British Philosophers*, ed. W. J. Mander and Alan Sell (Bristol, UK: Thoemmes Press, 2002). Pages on British personalist philosophers are being added to www.britishpersonalistforum.org.uk, and articles on them in *Appraisal: The Journal of the British Personalist Forum*.

145. See Andrew S. Pringle-Pattison, *The Development from Kant to Hegel* (1882); and Pringle-Pattison, *Hegelianism and Personality* (Edinburgh: William D. Blackwood and Sons, 1887). His later principal publications are: *Man's Place in the Cosmos* (1902); *The Idea of God in the Light of Recent Philosophy* (1916, rev. ed. 1920); his contribution to "The Mode of Being of Finite Individuals," *Proceedings of the Aristotelian Society* 18 (1918), reprinted as *Life and Finite Individuality* (1918), the proceedings of a debate with Bernard Bosanquet which was the climax of the confrontation between the Personalists and the Absolutists; and *The Idea of Immortality* (1922).

146. See W. R. Sorley, *The Moral Life and Moral Worth* (1911); and Sorley, *Moral Values and the Idea of God* (1918, 3rd ed. 1935).

But opposition to Absolute Idealism somewhat deflected the Personal Idealists from the revival of naturalism and materialism on the basis of the growing successes of modern science, which has since been called "scientistic reduction" and now has affected our educational institutions and the general public and not just philosophers.

5.1.3 | After about 1925

In the 1920s interest in Idealism, in all senses, waned. The most original and creative philosopher of the inter-war years was R. G. Collingwood (1889–1943), who contributed to personalist philosophy with his philosophy of history, especially as the "re-enactment" of a person's thinking as enacted his actions, which unlike mere events need no further "explanation," and also his fiduciary philosophy.[147] After him three philosophers put the person at the center of their thinking, which although formed independently of the others, has significant overlaps: John Macmurray (1891–1956), Michael Polanyi (1891–1956), and Austin Farrer (1904–68).[148]

Austin Farrer distilled an empirical mandate from a conception of persons seeking explanations. Despite defending theism against Logical Positivism, he learned the empiricists' lesson, converting verificationism into a principle of "experienceable difference." This redeemed

---

147. See R. G. Collingwood, *The Idea of History* (Oxford: Oxford University Press, 1946; rev. ed. 1993), esp. pt. 4; "Reason Is Faith Cultivating Itself" (1927) and *Faith and Reason* (1928), both reprinted in *Faith and Reason: Essays in the Philosophy of Religion by R.G. Collingwood*, ed. Lionel Rubinoff (Chicago: Quadrangle, 1967); *Essay on Metaphysics* (Oxford: Oxford University Press, 1940; rev. ed. 1998).

148. Two others should be mentioned: Hywel D. Lewis (1910–92), especially his *The Elusive Mind* (London: Allen & Unwin, 1969), *The Self and Immortality* (London: Allen & Unwin, 1973), and *The Elusive Self* (London: Allen & Unwin, 1982); and Raymond Tallis (1946–), especially his trilogy: *The Hand: A Philosophical Inquiry into Human Being* (Edinburgh: Edinburgh University Press, 2003), *I Am: A Philosophical Inquiry into First Person Being* (Edinburgh: Edinburgh University Press, 2004), and *The Knowing Animal: A Philosophical Inquiry into Knowledge and Truth* (Edinburgh: Edinburgh University Press, 2005).

religion for empirical minds by reminding theology of its progenesis in the *praxis* of faith. Grounding theology in the pragmatics of personal becoming required the full-bodied redintegration of persons using the primary notion, "intelligent act." Applying the logic of intentionality, Farrer balanced precisely the cognitive and physical dimensions of this notion, reminding us that persons are, in essence, active agents. Physically instantiated, persons are also, therefore, socially and morally indemnified; the logic of intentionality demands an "overplus," an owner-I of acts intended. Analogically extended, the "owner-I" furnished the key to understanding the cosmological relation. Thus, Farrer purged theology of its old Aristotelian leaven, exchanging Being-just-being-itself, for "the God about whom we have something to do." Suitably refined, it also supplied a conception of real "being" as interactive. Echoing Einstein, action-concepts became Farrer's primary metaphysical category, *esse est operari*. Simultaneously, they became the grounds for a new epistemology. As real "being" is essentially interactive, so real knowledge of it is the product of deliberate interference with it.

Farrer's principal philosophical publications are *Finite and Infinite* (1943), *The Freedom of the Will* (1958), *Faith and Speculation* (1967), and *Reflective Faith* (1972).

John Macmurray's work focuses upon the person, the whole person, and distinguishes personal existence from both organic and merely physical existence to which it is often reduced. He reverses the intellectualism which has dominated much philosophy, especially from René Descartes onwards, and which has reflected upon the reflective self, withdrawn from action, and so assumes a pure subject facing a purely objective world. Hence arises the "problem of other minds," whereas in reality persons are persons only in relation to other persons, especially that of mother and child.[149] Likewise action is prior to knowledge, and

---

149. See John Macmurray, *Persons in Relation* (London: Faber, 1961), chaps. 2–4. For an introduction to Macmurray, see *The Personal World: John Macmurray*, ed. Philip Conford (Edinburgh: Floris Books, 1996). On pp. 19–20 he mentions an address given by Macmurray to the British Personalist Group.

belief is prior to doubt. For if I have no reason to question what I believe, I cannot doubt it; and knowledge must be someone's knowledge, that of someone who believes it.[150] Thus the self is the acting self and is subject only in and for itself as agent.[151] The acting self is the whole self: "Reason is the capacity to behave consciously ... in terms of the nature of the object,"[152] and thus emotion determines the "source and direction" of action, and thought its form and only partially.[153] Persons are agents first and knowers second: "All meaningful knowledge is for the sake of action, and all meaningful action for the sake of friendship."[154] The "form of the personal" he defines as that which contains its own negative.[155] Hence, "The functional life is *for* the personal; the personal life is *through* the functional life,"[156] and therefore persons require roles, functions, and "the devices of politics" to secure the free cooperation of individuals,[157] for we are fully persons only in friendship, which is the real meaning of "community."

Macmurray's principal philosophical publications are *Freedom in the Modern World* (1932), *Interpreting the Universe* (1933), *Reason and Emotion* (1935), *The Boundaries of Science: A Study in the Philosophy of Psychology* (1939), *The Conditions of Freedom* (1949), *The Self as Agent* (1957), and *Persons in Relation* (1961).

Michael Polanyi's target in his *magnum opus*, *Personal Knowledge*, is "Objectivism," the assumption that genuine knowledge can result only from an impersonal operation of exact and explicit rules upon data and a thorough testing of each stage, and that such knowledge is actually achieved in physics and chemistry, to which all other forms of

---

150. See Macmurray, *The Self as Agent* (London: Faber, 1957), 76–78.
151. See ibid., 100–102.
152. Macmurray, *Reason and Emotion* (London: Faber, 1935), 19.
153. Ibid., 26.
154. Macmurray, *The Self as Agent*, 98.
155. Ibid., 15.
156. Macmurray, "Persons and Functions" (1941), in *Selected Philosophical Writings*, ed. Esther McIntosh (Exeter, UK: Imprint Academic, 2004), 149.
157. Macmurray, *Persons in Relation*, chap. 9.

knowledge should be assimilated, so that whatever the individual himself puts into these processes must render the product "subjective." The skepticism and reductionism embodied in and following from these assumptions have corrupted our views of knowing ourselves, and the world, and have made it very difficult explicitly to uphold the intellectual, moral, and political ideals of human civilization. Hence his aim is to show that "into every act of knowing there enters a tacit and passionate contribution of the person knowing what is being known, and that this coefficient is no mere imperfection but a vital component of all knowledge,"[158] and to "restore to us once more the power for the deliberate holding of unproven beliefs."[159]

Polanyi seeks to do this by showing that natural science, which he knew from the inside as an internationally renowned physical chemist, itself does not and cannot meet the Objectivist ideal, for its rules and methods cannot be explicitly articulated and thus it necessarily requires the personal engagement and judgment of the scientist himself. Scientific research is an art, the deployment of skills, and so too are all our acts and forms of knowing. In the pivotal chapter 4 of *Personal Knowledge*, he demonstrates that skills are tacit integrations of subsidiary details into comprehensive and focal wholes, in which we attend *from* the latter and *to* the former. For the most part, we do not know the details in themselves but only as we *use* them to know the focal objects of our attention or to perform what we intend to do. Nor do we know *how* we integrate the details of the focal whole or complex performance into it. These tacit dimensions of all our knowing and action, he illustrates with homely examples, episodes from the history of science, his own earlier medical training, and the findings of empirical psychology. It follows that we can never completely test our knowledge, for in doing so we *a*critically rely upon our personal judgment and skills. Our relation

---

158. Michael Polanyi, *Personal Knowledge: Towards a Post-Critical Philosophy* (London: Routledge, 1958), 312.

159. Ibid., 268, 312.

to our minds and bodies is one of tacit *indwelling*, of normally attending from them and to what we know and do, and, we may add, of "reconstitutingly" indwelling the details and structures of objects of our focal attention. Thus we indwell the intellectual frameworks which we have tacitly built up and inherited, but also, by virtue of our tacit powers, we can adapt them to new realities which they could not otherwise assimilate. Hence, instead of the critical philosophy that has been dominant from Descartes onwards, Polanyi concludes that only a post-critical and fiduciary philosophy is self-coherent. This epistemology mirrors an ontology of levels, each with its own autonomous operational principles, the boundary conditions of which are determined by the principles of the next higher level, the highest of which is the person freely and responsibly exercising his own judgment.

In his later publications Polanyi developed and applied tacit integration to further topics in philosophy and new fields. Previously, in response to the political and economic problems of the twentieth century, he had developed his own fiscal proposals to ease the cycle of boom and slump and unemployment, and a strong defense of political and economic freedom centered upon devotion to "transcendent ideals" and "spontaneous orders" of free co-operation and mutual adjustment. Markets are not the model but a lower form of these orders, for they lack those ideals and serve them only indirectly. A free society is not an "open" one but one in which its members dedicate themselves to transcendent ideals.

Polanyi's principal philosophical publications include *Science, Faith and Society* (1946); *The Logic of Liberty* (1951), *Personal Knowledge* (1958), *The Study of Man* (1959), *The Tacit Dimension* (1966), *Knowing and Being*, edited by M. Gren (1969), and *Meaning*, with H. Prosch (1974).[160]

---

160. See also *Society, Economics and Philosophy: Selected Papers by Michael Polanyi*, ed. Richard T. Allen (Rutgers, N.J.: Transaction Publishers, 1997).

5.2 | North American Personalism

The main current of North American personalism originates in the nineteenth century, earlier than the self-identified personalists of Europe but like them, in reaction to earlier European philosophers, particularly Kant and Hegel. This current has an idealist orientation and has its origin in the influential Bostonian philosopher Border Parker Bowne.[161] Bowne's influence has been felt through generations of disciples that make up the "Boston school of personalism."

This current of personalism, very potent at its beginning, has progressively weakened, while the current that has continued and developed European realist personalism has grown. Among the philosophers of this second current, John F. Crosby stands out.

5.2.1 | The Idealistic Personalistic System of Border Parker Bowne (1847–1910)

The founder of North American personalism is Border Parker Bowne. He had an interesting biography; the son of farmers, he worked in various menial jobs prior to entering the academic world, and he later became a Methodist pastor. It would seem that he can be considered the first explicitly self-identified personalist in the history of philosophy, as he himself indicated in a letter to his wife, "I am a *Personalist*, the first of the clan in any thorough-going sense."[162] Well before Mounier, and also before Maritain and Marcel, his philosophical origins were also diverse and connected with those of British personalism, marked initially by German philosophy and the criticism against Hegel.[163] In particular,

---

161. See Bogumil Gacka, *American Personalism* (Lublin: Oficiyna Wydawnicza "Czas," 1995). See also *Bibliography of American Personalism*, ed. Bogumil Gacka (Lublin: Oficiyna Wydawnicza "Czas," 1994).

162. K. M. B., "An Intimate Portrait of Bowne," *The Personalist* 2 (1921): 10.

163. See Andrew (Seth) Pringle-Pattison, *Hegelianism and Personality* (Edinburgh: William Blackwood and Sons, 1887; London: Bibliolife, 2009). For a precise analysis of the origins of this type of personalism, see Jan Olof Bengtsson, *The Worldview of Personalism: Origins and Early Development* (Oxford: Oxford University Press, 2006).

Bowne was influenced by Lotze and Ulrici during his years of study in Europe at the universities of Gottingen, the Sorbonne, and Halle. After returning he worked briefly at New York University, but soon a door opened in the Department of Philosophy of Boston University, where he would remain until his death despite substantial offers from institutions as prestigious as Chicago, Yale, and Johns Hopkins.

His philosophy can be described as an *idealist personalist system* based on a complex web of philosophical *sources* that he himself described in the aforementioned letter to his wife:

> It is hard to classify me with accuracy. I am a theistic idealist, a *Personalist*, a transcendental empiricist, and idealistic realist, and a realistic idealist: but all these phrases need to be interpreted. They cannot well be made out from the dictionary. Neither can I well be called a disciple of anyone. I largely agree with Lotze, but I transcend him. I hold half of Kant's system but sharply dissent from the rest. There is a strong smack of Berkeley's philosophy, with a complete rejection of his theory of knowledge. I am a *Personalist*, the first of the clan in any thorough-going sense.[164]

Drawing on these sources Bowne constructed an original personalist system that included anthropology, metaphysics, ethics, and psychology. We will now examine some of his principal themes.

Above all, it should be noted that his position is strictly personalist. "Our first step toward the personal interpretation of experience consists in the insight that we are in a personal world from the start, and that the first, last, and only duty of philosophy is to interpret this world of personal life and relations."[165] But, in contrast to later European personalists, Bowne is avowedly an idealist, with strong Kantian tones. He held, like Wojtyła, that the mission of philosophy is to analyze the contents of experience, but experience according to Bowne is solely subjective: "we speak of a world of experience instead of a world of things."[166] More concretely, experience is understood as a flux of sensations struc-

---

164. K. M. B., "An Intimate Portrait of Bowne," 10.
165. Borden Parker Bowne, *Personalism* (1908; Miami: Hard Press, 2013), 53.
166. Ibid., 26.

tured by the immanent principles of an active intelligence, such that "no one can ever perceive any world but the one he makes."[167] And if it is true that knowledge requires an epistemic dualism, that is to say, the relation between subject-knower and object-known, the primacy in this relation belongs to the subject in whose active intelligence the object of thought is "constructed."

Bowne, however, disagreed with Kant about the structure of the ego or self because "where there is not perceiving subject there can be no phenomena; and when we put the subject among the phenomena, the doctrine itself disappears."[168] The ego is real (noumenal) and knowledge of it is more secure than anything; a way of thinking that makes easier to overcome the well-known solipsistic problem of idealism: if others are *only* phenomena that I know, then they do not have their own proper existence, they are *only* an aspect of myself. Positively, he understood the self as "a living conscious unity, which is one in its manifoldness and manifold in oneness."[169] And he held that the global awareness of itself on the part of the self gives rise to personality, whose essential significance "is selfhood, self-consciousness, self-control, and the power to know."[170]

The *metaphysics* of Bowne can be understood, in large part, as a critical response to Hegel, whose thought was still very prominent at the end of the nineteenth century. Its principal features are: (1) Individuality: He deals with what really exists, the individual, against the fallacy of the Hegelian universal. (2) Unity: All reality is conceived in terms of spirit, and one of the objectives of personalism should consist in demonstrating this thesis. (3) Activity: Reality consists of being able to act. Within thought we distinguish being from acting, but in reality they are united. Being, on the other hand, is not pure rationality as Hegel would say. On the contrary, life is richer than speculation.

---

167. Ibid., 71.
168. Ibid., 88.
169. Ibid., 262.
170. Ibid., 266.

In this sense, the "activist" is a realist, but only in this sense, because Bowne held openly the *phenomenality of matter*. "The world of things can be defined and understood only as we give up the notion of an extra-mental reality altogether, and make the entire world a thought world; that is, a world that exists only through and in relation to intelligence."[171] This does not mean, however, that he identifies "thought" things with "real" things since these latter are given in experience and the former "exist" only in thought detached from experience. And "if we will ask for the place of the world, we must say the Divine Intelligence is that place."[172]

In line with other personalists, he warns of problems related to the classic concept of cause, proposing an interesting distinction between what he calls natural causality and free causality. The latter, which consists in "the mystery of self-determination," is the most relevant and the only thing which permits one to escape the infinite chain of causes.

Finally, with respect to *ethics*, Bowne adopted many Kantian elements, such as his view of practical reason, but he integrated specifically personalist elements as well:[173] 1) a theistic perspective with God as supreme Person, (2) the sanctity of the human person, (3) the absolute value of the law of free will, (4) that the social order be administered impartially, (5) "in reducing principles to practice we must be on guard against an abstract and impracticable idealism ... [for] the abstract ethics of the closet must be replaced by the ethics of life."[174]

5.2.2 | The School of Boston

The disciples of Bowne formed what became known as the School of Boston, among whom we will highlight the following figures.

---

171. Borden Parker Bowne, *Metaphysics*, rev. ed. (New York: Harper and Brother Publishers, 1898), 422.
172. Bowne, *Personalism*, 143.
173. Gacka, *American Personalism*, 68–69.
174. Borden Parker Bowne, *The Principle of Ethics* (New York: Harper & Brothers, 1892), 309.

Edgar Sheffield Brightman (1884–1953) was a direct disciple of Bowne and taught at Boston University, where he directed the philosophy department from 1919 until 1953. Like his teacher he was an idealist, and according to Buford, "he defined Personalism as the hypothesis that all being is either a personal experience (a complex unity of consciousness) or some phase or aspect of one or more such experience. Nature is an order generated by the mind of Cosmic Person. Finite persons are created and grounded by the uncreated God, and as such possess free will. Reality is a society of persons."[175] Among his original contributions can be identified a moral theory developed in *Moral Laws* (1933) and a revision of theism that came to affirm the existence of certain defects or limited evil in God (the Given) as a way of explaining the presence of evil in the world.

Albert Cornelius Knudson (1873–1954), for his part, focused on rethinking theology along the lines of personalist philosophy. He taught in the Divinity School of Boston University, and his most well-known work is *The Philosophy of Personalism* (1927).[176] Peter Anthony Bertocci (1910–1989) was the disciple of Brightman and thus constituted the third generation of the school. For him, person "is a self-identifying, being-becoming agent who, maturing and learning as he interacts with the environment, develops a more or less systematic, learned unity of expression and adaptation that we may call his personality."[177] He worked in the area of psychology, maintaining contact with Gordon Allport of Harvard. He rejected the notion of substance in order to explain the person and, alternatively, he thought temporality constituted the essence of man.[178] These three, Brightman, Knudson, and Bertocci, were interested in the question of God and tried to elaborate a personal concept of divinity deduced from their vision of personalism.

175. Thomas O. Buford, "Personalism," in *Internet Encyclopedia of Philosophy*, http://www.iep.utm.edu/personal/.
176. Albert Cornelius Knudson, *The Philosophy of Personalism* (New York: The Abingdon Press, 1927).
177. Peter A. Bertocci, "Why Personalistic Idealism?" *Idealistic Studies* 10, no. 3 (1980): 181–198.
178. Peter A. Bertocci, "The Essence of a Person," *The Monist* 671, no. 1: 28–41.

One other figure, Ralph Tyler Flewelling (1871–1960) deserves mention in this context, although some histories consider him part of a separate school of personalism, known as "the California school" and associated with George Holmes Howison (1834–1916). Flewelling did however, study with Bowne, and thus it seems questionable to consider his work a truly separate strand. Flewelling took personalism to the University of Southern California, where he founded the journal *The Personalist* (1920–1979). Flewelling was especially interested in applying personalist principles in political life, under the heading of Personalistic Democracy. For him, "the only abiding basis for democracy is respect for the sanctity of the person. This does not mean respect for some persons but for those possibilities which reside in varying degree in *every* person ... For this reason democracy will seek to provide the circumstances in education and freedom and work under which each person may best realize his own and the common good."[179] He emphasized that this democratic freedom would only be successful if matched by self-restraint on the part of free citizens.

If Flewelling sought to apply personalist principles to the political sphere, no one proved this project more fruitful than Martin Luther King Jr. (1929–1968), who despite not being a systematic philosopher, deserves a special mention. Dr. King studied at Boston University with Brightman and received a PhD in philosophy. He applied the personalist principles to his famous struggle for the civil rights of African Americans in the United States and wrote in 1958, "This personalism remains today my basic philosophical position. Personalism's insistence that personality—finite and infinite—is ultimately real strengthened me in two convictions: it gave me a metaphysical and philosophical grounding for the idea of a personal God, and it gave me a metaphysical basis for the dignity and worth of all human personality."[180]

179. Ralph. T. Flewelling, "Personalism," in *Twentieth Century Philosophy: Living Schools of Thought*, ed. D. R. Runes (New York: Philosophical Library, 1943), 341.
180. Martin Luther King Jr., "My Pilgrimage to Nonviolence," *Fellowship* (September 1, 1958): 480.

Among philosophers, the work of the Boston school has been carried forward by Thomas O. Buford, who graduated with his PhD from Boston University in 1963. Buford founded the Personalist Forum and co-founded the International Conference on Persons, which organizes an international congress every other year.

5.2.3 | The Continuers of European Realist Personalism: John F. Crosby

North American idealist personalism has gradually lost weight and influence in parallel with the general weakening of idealist philosophy throughout the twentieth century. And that space has been occupied by a new generation of North American personalists who follow the European personalist philosophers of a realist orientation. Among them, John F. Crosby stands out.

John F. Crosby (1944–) attended Georgetown University and received his doctorate in philosophy from the University of Salzburg. Later, he taught at the University of Dallas (1970–87) and at the International Academy of Philosophy in Liechtenstein (1987–90); since then, he has worked at the Franciscan University of Steubenville, where he has occupied several different positions, directing, among other activities, the M.A. program in philosophy.

Well versed in the thought of Thomas Aquinas and the classical tradition (Plato, Aristotle, Augustine), he has perceived the need for a structural change in the *philosophia perennis* with a personalist orientation, thus taking on positions close to the current known as modern ontological personalism (see chap. 4, sec. 2.2), although his thought is also strongly influenced by realist phenomenology. His principal personalist sources are John Henry Newman, Max Scheler, Karol Wojtyła, and Dietrich von Hildebrand. On these thinkers he has written several works, such as *Personalist Papers*[181] and, more recently, *The Person-*

---

181. See John F. Crosby, *Personalist Papers* (Washington, D.C.: The Catholic University of American Press, 2003).

alism of John Henry Newman.[182] Standing out among his works is his investigation on the nucleus of personal reality, *The Selfhood of the Human Person*,[183] in which, from the starting point of Karol Wojtyła's anthropology in *The Acting Person*, he has explored the ultimate characteristics of personal reality (incommunicability, unrepeatability, subjectivity, dignity), granting them ontological priority over the relation. The I-Thou relationship, in effect, as important as it may be in the constitution of the person, is only possible if an *I* and a *Thou* exist who have been previously endowed with an unrepeatable personal nucleus, capable of self-possession and self-communication.

Along the lines of Crosby, one may also mention Adrian Reimers (University of Notre Dame), who has completed important studies on Karol Wojtyła;[184] and John Henry Crosby, the son of John F. Crosby, who is contributing a great deal to the dissemination of personalism and, in particular, of the work of Dietrich von Hildebrand, through the Hildebrand Legacy Project.[185]

---

182. See John F. Crosby, *The Personalism of John Henry Newman* (Washington, D.C.: The Catholic University of American Press, 2014).

183. John F. Crosby, *The Selfhood of the Human Person* (Washington, D.C.: The Catholic University of American Press, 1996).

184. See M. Acosta and A. Reimers, *Karol Wojtyla's Personalist Philosophy: Understanding Person and Act* (Washington, D.C.: The Catholic University of America Press, 2016); and Adrien Reimers, *Truth about the Good: Moral Norms in the Thought of John Paul II* (Ave Maria, Fla.: Sapientia Press, 2011).

185. See http://www.hildebrandproject.org/.

CHAPTER FOUR | **Personalist Philosophy**

A Proposal

Now that we have finished our survey of personalist thinkers, it is time to make an evaluation and reach some conclusions. What have we learned from this journey? Certainly, the knowledge that allows us to affirm the existence of an important philosophical movement, extended over many countries, of a notable substance and originality and with a body of similar principles, easily verifiable by the resemblance of the subjects treated, the methodology used, the common philosophical sources, and the many and continuous mutual interactions. Nevertheless, far from negligible difficulties have also appeared, regarding the identity and consistency of this intellectual movement. A recurrent objection has been the conceptual weakness of personalism. Also, the possibility of bringing such diverse writers together can be questioned. Does the unitary character of this group of philosophers really respond to objective data or is that unitary character just a forced strategy? Finally, it seems that some prominent personalists, including Emmanuel Mounier, lacked a definite idea of the contents and structure of personalism, which they thought of as a common matrix that could nourish very diverse principles and ideas.

This complex panorama manifests the need to resolve, as profoundly as possible, whether personalism can really be considered a unitary philosophy or not, a question which, apart from its undoubted theoretical interest, has a great practical importance. If it is accepted that personalism consists of a diffuse social and ideological movement which contributed original ideas in the middle of the twentieth century but which cannot demonstrate that it has a solid and common body of principles and ideas, we would have to conclude that this movement has spent its energy and that this book has become simply a study in the history of philosophy. If, on the contrary, we conclude that personalism has all the elements necessary to become a sound philosophy, this volume acquires a very different character: the presentation of a philosophy which, already having influenced history, still has much to contribute.

The principal difficulty in definitively resolving this dilemma is that a certain degree of interpretation is inevitable because of the relative diversity of the points of departure. In other currents of thought, interpretation—inevitable in philosophy—is bound by the privileged status of one of its constituents or of its founder (Kant, Hegel, Thomas Aquinas). In personalism, for better or worse, this is not so. Mounier does not have this central position, and for that reason, the possible paths are multiplied. There is, therefore, no ready-made synthesis, interpretation, or neutral summary. One cannot claim an uncontested "center" of personalism since the importance conferred on the factors that compose personalism varies according to whether one is a follower of Karol Wojtyła, Martin Buber, Mounier, or one of the others. Nevertheless, the synthesis and resolution of the difficulties posed is still urgent if, as we said, we do not wish that personalism should become a page of the history of philosophy already written and finished.

What follows in this chapter is intended to avoid this premature eulogy on personalism by proposing a synthetic perspective which, in the author's opinion, reflects the nucleus of the thought of the authors surveyed above and, in addition, can ensure the future and fruitfulness of this philosophy. In my first publications I proposed a similar version, although less elaborated, with the conviction, then apparent to me, that it was the one, true, *authentic* personalism.[1] In this book I prefer to clarify that it is *one* personal view, which is no obstacle to the intention to remain as close as possible to the inspiring idea of the great masters. But it is, one must acknowledge, a personal version, because the selection, structuring, and importance given to the elements of the system are the author's decision.

This proposal must begin, logically, by analyzing the philosophical character of personalism, a question raised by Mounier himself.

1 | Is Personalism a Philosophy?

1.1 | Personalism as a Movement of Social Transformation: Emmanuel Mounier

Emmanuel Mounier, the founder or principal representative of personalism, had, nevertheless, a fluctuating and evolving vision of what should be understood as personalism. We have already mentioned this question, but we shall deal with it now in more detail, because, as is evident, it carries a great deal of importance.

In his *Manifeste au service du personnalisme* (1936), Mounier presented in some detail his first formulations on what should be understood as personalism. In previous publications there were some topics with this inspiration, but he did not seem to have a precise idea of how or where to integrate this set of ideas.[2] However, in this work, now more mature, positions of some substance appear which defend a very broad and diffuse view of personalism. In particular, Mounier begins this work with a presentation of personalism which we will quote almost in its entirety because of its importance:

---

1. Principally, Juan Manuel Burgos, *El personalismo: Autores y temas de una filosofía nueva* (Madrid: Palabra, 2000).
2. Neither is the fact itself surprising. Really, for any interpretation of Mounier, account has to be taken of his precocity, which compelled him to propose ideas without the degree of elaboration that only can be produced with time.

We call personalist any doctrine, any civilization that affirms the primacy of the human person over material necessities and the collective mechanisms that sustain its development.... For us personalism is not more than a code word, a convenient collective designation for different doctrines that, in the historical situation in which we are inserted, can coincide in the basic physical and metaphysical conditions of a new civilization. Personalism does not announce, then, the creation of a school, the opening of a chapel, the invention of a closed system. It testifies to a convergence of wills, and it places itself at its service, without affecting its diversity, in order to seek the means to effectively influence history. We should, therefore, speak in the plural, of "personalisms."[3]

And, a little later, he ends his pronouncement with a reference to the origin and substance of the ideas which he is propagating: "The foundational truths on which we will build our conclusions and our action were not invented yesterday. Only their historical insertion, founded on new data, can and should be new. We attribute to the search, still hesitant, of that historical appearance, as a sign of union, the singular name of personalism."[4]

Personalism appears, therefore, for Mounier, in one of his principal publications, not as a philosophical system or a school of thought, but as a movement or attitude of revindicating the person, in contrast to fascism and communism, which seeks to group under that banner all who fight in the same direction; a fight which, from the point of view of the contents, would not be particularly original since it would be based on conclusions and ideas already current since antiquity. Its originality would lie in a revolutionary but nonviolent radicalism.

Mounier held this thesis for many years. In fact, as late as 1947 in the book *What Is Personalism?*, we find no significant changes of orientation. He continues to call personalism an inspirational movement and pricker of consciences which could or even should disappear when it had

---

3. Emmanuel Mounier, *Manifeste au service du personnalisme*, in Mounier, *Oeuvres*, vol. 1, *1931–1939* (Paris: Éditions du Seuil, 1961), 483.
4. Ibid.

achieved its objective. "The best future one could wish for personalism is that it should so awaken in every man the sense of the whole meaning of man, that it could disappear without trace, having become the general climate of our days."[5] And, again, he does not understand personalism as a philosophy or as a school. "What makes personalism very difficult for some to understand is that they are trying to find a system, whereas personalism is perspective, method, and exigency,"[6] which lead to a "revolutionary" action since "it is not sufficient to say: person, community, total man, in order to insert personalism into the historic drama of our age. We must also say: end of Western bourgeois society, introduction of socialist structures, the proletarian role of initiative."[7]

Now, shortly afterwards, in one of his most philosophical works, *Existentialist Philosophies: An Introduction*, there is an important shift because Mounier presents personalism for the first time as a *philosophical school* in the context of other schools of philosophy, such as existentialism or phenomenology. And the expression "personalist philosophy" also appears, perhaps for the first time, in comparing personalism and existentialism.[8] This tendency is confirmed in his mature work, *Personalism* (1949), where we find statements that could be considered antithetical to some of his previous pronouncements. The key passage is the following:

> Personalism is a philosophy, it is not merely an attitude. It is a philosophy but not a system. Not that it fears systematization. For order is necessary

---

5. Mounier, "What Is Personalism?" in *Be Not Afraid* (London, Rockcliff, 1951; New York, Sheed and Ward, 1962), 111–112 ("Author's Introduction").

6. Ibid., 193.

7. Ibid., 186.

8. "Existential Philosophy is a personal[ist] philosophy; the subject of enquiry is the human person.' The existent [person] is presented in the terms of a being in collision with the inertia or impersonality of the thing. Existentialists are unanimous on this point. They have sounded the call to a revival of Personalism in contemporary thought. That is to say, in general terms, Existentialism presents a picture of a kind of intensified Personalism." Mounier, *Introduction to the Existentialisms*, trans. Philip Mairet (London: Methuen, 1948), 50, quoting Berdyaev.

in thinking: concepts, logic, schemes of unification are not only of use to fix and communicate a thought which would otherwise dissolve into obscure and isolated intuitions; they are instruments of discovery as well as of exposition. Since it defines certain positions, personalism is a philosophy and not only an attitude.[9]

This idea, nevertheless, is diluted a little later by Mounier when it is placed in the context of a reflection in which he again takes up the idea of "the personalisms," although with less intensity than in previous writings.

The conclusions that can be inferred from these passages are sufficiently clear but not simple. For the greater part of his intellectual and philosophical work, virtually up to three years before his death, Mounier understood personalism as a movement of social and intellectual action motivated by some principal ideas about the person which demanded radical changes in society on a revolutionary scale.[10] Such a movement was not supposed to be a system or a philosophy, but an attitude, a perspective, and a demand which required personal commitment. Therefore, personalism not only could but *would have to* include within itself all those principles, ideas, and movements which join together in those ideals. Only in the last years of his life—still a period of intellectual youth, since he was not yet even forty-five years old—Mounier began to evolve towards a conception of personalism as philosophy and systematic reflection. Therefore—and this is our central conclusion—with respect to greater part of Mounier's work, it is completely proper to describe or define personalism as an attitude or movement of which the strong point is the vindication of the person against his many enemies and the correlative transformation of society in this direction, but not as a philosophy with a solid conceptual apparatus for interpreting and understanding reality.

---

9. Mounier, *Personalism*, trans. Philip Mairet (London: Routledge and Kegan Paul, 1952), vii–viii.

10. In the peculiar sense in which Mounier used this term.

1.2 | Personalism as Anti-Ideology: Jean Lacroix, Jacques Maritain

The predominant perspective in Mounier is the same perspective that Maritain and Lacroix adopted, although with different emphases. In particular, Maritain, in a well-known passage, stated:

> Yet nothing can be more remote from the facts than the belief that "personalism" is one school or doctrine. It is rather a phenomenon of reaction against two opposite errors, which inevitably contains elements of very unequal merits. Not a personalist doctrine, but personalist aspirations confront us. There are, at least, a dozen personalist doctrines, which, at times, have nothing more in common than the term "person." Some of them incline variously to one or the other of the contrary errors between which they take their stand. Some contemporary personalisms are Nietzschean in slant, others Proudhonian; some tend toward dictatorship, while others toward anarchy. A principle concern of Thomistic personalism is to avoid both excesses.[11]

Maritain was doubtless exaggerating, since it certainly appears excessive to speak of Nietzschean personalisms, but he has in his favor that his position differs little from that maintained by Mounier to legitimize the convergence in personalism of any current that would reasonably vindicate the dignity of the person.

This is also the position of Jean Lacroix. For this direct disciple of Mounier, personalism is not, in any way, a particular philosophy but an anti-ideology.[12] By this expression he means that personalism is not a philosophy but neither is it an ideology in any of the meanings that this word is given. It is simply a type of inspiration or faith which can feed all of them. And precisely thus does it receive its (valuable) anti-ideological character.

---

11. Jacques Maritain, *The Person and the Common Good*, trans. John Fitzgerald (Notre Dame, Ind.: University of Notre Dame Press, 1966), 12–13.

12. See Jean Lacroix, *El personalismo como anti-ideología*, trans. Evandro Botto (Madrid: Guadiana, 1973), Originally published as *Le personnalisme comme anti-idéologie* (Paris: P.U.F., 1972).

In particular, Lacroix understands that an ideology can be of three types: (a) neutral, constructed from an attitude of respect towards reality; (b) negative, the result of a theoretical crystallization of a false or erroneous conscience; and (c) positive, a vision capable of becoming a cultural influence in defense of man. Now, since all of them imply *a definite vision of man and the world*, personalism cannot be identified with any of them. And neither can it be classified or described as philosophy. In the first place, because "Mounier's end has never been to work out a philosophy but rather a 'philosophical matrix.' He has not created personalism. Like many others, he had inherited it."[13] Second, and above all, because it turns out to be intrinsically unviable and unsustainable. For,

> There are many personalisms: idealist like Kant's; realistic like Laberthonière, existentialist like Gabriel Marcel or Berdyaev, individualist like Renouvier, even Communist and above all personalist anarchists. If we were to call personalism what these (or other) doctrines have in common, we would end up in total confusion like "eclecticism" or "spiritualism," and that is simply the negation of any sort of philosophy. This mistake explains the discredit that has befallen personalism in the view of philosophers.[14]

Lacroix strongly insists on this, perhaps too strongly, even if one takes Mounier as the sole point of reference.

> There is not, nor has there ever been, any such philosophy as personalism. There are definitely philosophies more directly inspired by personalism. Each can be studied in and for itself. But what is studied is an intellectual construction, different in every case, and not what inspires them. Does it follow that personalism can be only an ideology? The paradox, if you like—it is really a truism—consists in holding that it is less than an ideology but is an anti-ideology *par excellence*. Really, everyone explicitly or implicitly recognizes this. Personalism is neither an ideology nor a philosophy. It bases itself on more fundamental, primordial, and profound concepts, those of faith and rational beliefs.[15]

---

13. Lacroix, *El personalismo como anti-ideología*, 193.
14. Ibid., 65.
15. Ibid., 30.

For Lacroix, then, personalism is neither a philosophy nor an ideology, but only a principle of inspiration, a belief or faith, able to nourish and motivate very diverse systems of thought, such as Marxism and anarchism although from some perspectives, not from all.

> It is a form of totality that keeps itself from any partiality and from any "partisanism." Its totality, nevertheless, is not that of worldviews, but comes from its direct relationship to the whole of humanity, which differs by nature from concrete societies and from separate individuals. Personalism contemplates the universal, in each man and in humanity (which does not occur in any ideology). In itself, then, it does not form a system and rather distrusts any systemization that would run the risk of threatening the person.[16]

1.3 | The Battle of the Concept: Paul Ricoeur's Criticism

Paul Ricoeur has written on this perspective in two important publications thirty years apart.[17] The first, "Une philosophie personaliste," was written soon after the death of Mounier and contributes an overall evaluation of his philosophy. It is a brilliant essay which, in only a few pages, admirably condenses Mounier's principal theses, and which can be summarized as follows: Mounier, more than a philosopher, was a teacher, the *"educator* of a generation."[18] His objective was not to develop a philosophy but to transmit a set of foundational ideas capable of transforming a society in crisis. "Its main contribution to contemporary

---

16. Ibid., 64–65.
17. See Paul Ricoeur, "Une philosophie personnaliste." *Esprit* 174, no. 12 (1950): 860–87, translated by Charles A. Kelbley as "Emmanuel Mounier: A Personalist Philosopher," in *History and Truth* (Evanston, Ill.: Northwestern University Press, 1965), 133–61; Ricoeur, "Meurt le personnalisme, revient la personne," *Esprit* 73, no. 1 (1983), 113–19, translated as "Muere el personalismo, vuelve la persona," in *Amor y justicia*, trans. Tomás Domingo Moratalla (Madrid: Caparrós, 1993), 95–104; parts in Ricoeur, "Self as Ipse," in *Freedom and Interpretation*, ed. Barbara Johnson (New York: Basic Books, 1993), 103–19; and parts in Ricoeur, *Figuring the Sacred: Religion, Narrative and Imagination*, trans. David Pellauer, ed. Mark I. Wallace (Minneapolis: Fortress Press, 1995).
18. Ricoeur, "Emmanuel Mounier: A Personalist Philosopher," 135.

thought has been to offer a *philosophical matrix* to professional philosophers, to propose tonalities to them, theoretical and practical holding notes containing one or several philosophies, pregnant with one or several philosophical systemizations."[19]

Ricoeur also notices Mounier's final philosophical turn but evaluates it with severity. He thinks that Mounier does not intend to develop a personalist philosophy but only "a 'personalist' interpretation of philosophies of existence"[20] and that, in any case, the result of this project is deficient because the attitude which informs it is not really philosophical:

> Person and existence refer primarily to two orders of concern which are not exactly co-extensive: on the one hand, there is an ethico-political concern, a "pedagogical" intention in touch with a crisis of civilization; on the other hand, there is a critical and ontological reflection in contact with classical "philosophical" tradition.
>
> Second, the word person is a way of designating one of the interpretations of existence, once one is situated on the strictly critical and ontological level of the philosophies of existence. Thus, the word stresses certain aspects of existence which are contained explicitly in the pedagogical intention personalism: these are the ones which we earlier emphasized in connection with the material conditions for the realization of human existence, the communal path of this realization, its orientation through values, and its foundation in being which is more interior to it than itself.[21]

In conclusion, although Ricoeur praises the educational attitude of Mounier, his evaluation of him as a philosopher is stark. Mounier appears not to have done real philosophy even when he attempted to, in his last years. And part of the problem, according to Ricoeur, was created by the very concept of person, philosophically inferior to that of existence, to the point that the concept of existence has the critical and

---

19. Ibid., 136.
20. Ibid.
21. Ibid., 160–61.

philosophical priority, although the former would have in its favor the moral-political priority.

In a certain sense it can be said that the circle of Ricoeur's thought closes, more than thirty years later, with the writing, in 1983, of a famous article "Meurt le personnalisme, revient la personne" ("Personalism is dead, the person returns"). At this time, the disciples of Mounier, who kept his flame alive for many years, had died out, and the intellectual project of the Mounierian movement appeared definitely exhausted. Ricoeur understands that it is the moment to evaluate and diagnose this great project, and he expresses his conclusions in this article.

First of all, as a marginal note, he deplores "the unfortunate choice" of an "ism" which has contributed to the confusion, in such a way that personalism "has never stopped fighting with its own devils,"[22] understanding by this the equivocations tied to the literal meaning of a term which obstructs its comprehension. But afterwards, going to the heart of the question, he indicates that the principal problem of personalism is that "it was insufficiently competitive to win the battle of the concept"[23] against the other "isms" of the time: Marxism and existentialism. Ricoeur refers to the years after World War II, the time of the expansion of personalism, in which it entered into a face to face confrontation with the other two great philosophies of the time, Marxism and existentialism.

Ricoeur's thesis is that in the confrontation with those two formidable philosophies, personalism easily succumbed because it did not deploy conceptual instruments for maintaining a substantial fight. In the intellectual confrontation between a movement or inspiration and two philosophies, the result was foreseeable, although later, in the 1960s, the winners were themselves defeated by structuralism and a new Nietzschean current which would modify the principal parameters of European culture.

---

22. Ricoeur, "Muere el personalismo, vuelve la persona," 98.
23. Ibid., 96.

In this context, perhaps modifying his previous theses slightly, Ricoeur announced the end of personalism and proposed as an alternative the fruitfulness of the concept of the person, which he considered capable of prevailing over those of consciousness, subject. and "I." Then he asked: how can we speak of the person without the aid of personalism? In effect, every concept requires behind it an intellectual project that moves and promotes it. If there are no thinkers who reflect upon the person, this concept will become stale and weak in time. And, if personalism has died, who will support the concept of the person?

Ricoeur believed that this was possible by means of the *person-attitude*, which would consist of always keeping this category in mind in the development of one's own intellectual and philosophical system, in such a way that it would give it form and make it fruitful in this way. Ricoeur was able to recognize that the concept of "person-attitude" is somewhat ambiguous, but considered that this problem could be overcome by giving it an epistemological status which would consist of establishing a precomprehension which would determine the orientation of the investigations. It would be the "focus of an 'attitude' to which many and very different 'categories' can correspond, depending on the conception one has of what can really be called philosophy."[24] The point would be, in conclusion, to address the notion of person not from a substantive and specific philosophy, but from different premises which would be distinctive for each investigator, which should certainly have the common features proper to the focus that delimits the person-attitude and which, according to Ricoeur, would be governed by two criteria: crisis and commitment, and by three corollaries: time, difference, and the horizon of an integral historical vision.

---

24. Ibid., 101.

1.4 | Personalism as Philosophy

The ideas that we have just expressed pose, from the point of view of several different relevant sources, acute criticisms about the possibility of considering personalism a philosophy. There are three principal objections: (1) personalism is not a formal philosophy; therefore, (2) it lacks definition and depth; and (3) as a cause or consequence of the above, it includes excessively disparate philosophies or movements.

We shall attempt respond to these objections in what follows.

1.4.1 | Mounier's Personalism

Both the criticisms and the evaluations considered above start from a central presupposition, made explicitly or implicitly: the identification of personalism with Mounier's thought. So, everything that is affirmed about Mounier is automatically ascribed to personalism as a doctrine, current, philosophy, or movement. We shall discuss this presupposition later, but now we shall evaluate Mounier's position.

From this perspective, we must agree with those who have emphasized the philosophical weakness of Mounier's thought. We have looked at this difficulty above (see chap. 2, sec. 3, above), and the list of philosophers who hold a similar position can be lengthened considerably. Mounier's books lack the formal rigor needed to give his thought greater depth and, as Ricoeur said, to fight the battle of the concept. And this lack of formal rigor was the cause of a failure evidenced in personalism's loss of intellectual credibility, about which well-known personalists such as Maurice Nédoncelle bitterly complained:

> Personalism or, if you prefer, interpersonalism, has gained an enviable place in the parliament of contemporary philosophies, but its success has cost it dear. It has become nauseatingly vague and commercial. It has become caught up in a well-thinking politics whose intentions are respectable, but which has nothing to do with philosophical investigation. In it, the spirit of investigation is dead: it is no more than a slogan. An atrocious

desire to renounce such a disappointing label takes hold of me, and thus to remain alone.[25]

Now, we have to quickly add that this is *only a failure in a certain sense*, because, in philosophy, not everything depends upon formal rigor. Intuition also has its role and can be more important than formalization. And, on this point, Mounier was brilliant. He intuited significant innovations and presented them in an attractive and lucid way, and thus his books became very influential; and, in a certain sense, that influence is still alive in the intellectual subsoil and mental roots of individuals, institutions, and traditions based on Mounier's thought.[26] For all these reasons, Ricoeur's judgment seems to us to be lucid, but excessively severe. Mounier was not only an educator, but also an intellectual, and even more than that, a philosopher, who—with all his limits—was capable of generating an influential current of thought, something that is given to very few.

We now turn to his conception of personalism. We have already confirmed that he understood it fundamentally as a movement for transforming society inspired by some key ideas, but not a philosophy. Thus, if personalism is identified with Mounier, we can say that the theses of Maritain, Lacroix, and Ricoeur are valid. Personalism would be constitutively too diffuse to be able to accommodate a solid, rigorous, and formal philosophy which the present age appears to need. And, since the movement inspired by Mounier only continues to be active in small groups, it seems that one would have to validate the death certificate issued by Ricoeur or, at least, acknowledge personalism's very precarious state of health.

---

25. Nédoncelle, *Persona humana y naturaleza. Estudio lógico y metafísico*, trans. Carlos Díaz (Salamanca: Fundación Emmanuel Mounier, 2005), 18.
26. In this sense, Coll's evaluation also seems to fall a little short: "Mounier's genius did not consist so much of creating a new philosophy, communitarian personalism, as of making the living synthesis of the intuitions of other personalists or of bringing to a full development what others offered him." Josep Maria Coll, "Mounier i els corrents personalistes," in Coll and others, *Emmanuel Mounier i el personalisme* (Barcelona: Crüilla, 2002). 76.

One may object that, in his last years, Mounier began to turn to more philosophical positions. Certainly, this is a pertinent observation which indicates the possibility—intuited by Mounier himself—that personalism could in fact be transformed into a philosophy. This is the thesis that we shall maintain in what follows, and its potential support in Mounier is important, but one must recognize that this direct assistance is weak because it relies only on fragmentary support from his later writings. Therefore, we conclude that one who wishes to maintain that Mounier's personalism is not a philosophy but an intellectual movement for transforming society would be fully justified in doing so.

1.4.2 | Beyond Mounier

Now, is the fundamental presumption that sustains the above judgment correct? That is, is it correct to affirm that personalism is identical with Mounier's proposal? Doubtless, Mounier had the merit of giving life and relevance to the personalist movement as such, but this does not mean that he has been the only one to formulate a personalist type of philosophy. As we have shown, many other philosophers in the twentieth century formulated a philosophy with similar presuppositions and orientations. And it seems clear, in the light of the cumulative impression of the theories and philosophies surveyed above, that the combined work of these thinkers contains a wealth that is more than abundant for the construction of an authentic philosophy capable of winning the conceptual battles being fought today.

Up to now, however, very few studies have appeared which have aimed at specifying the central elements and characteristics of this philosophy, which, to a degree, is easy to understand because of the many difficulties involved. Their relative diversity is one of the principal obstacles. To extract apparently common elements from so great a number of philosophers, to structure them and make them compatible with others that come from diverse conceptual schemes is a difficult and demanding task. In addition, this diversity imposes an inevitable degree of interpretation and innovation to which we have already alluded: in the determination of what is common or diverse, in the weight to be given to the different versions of personalism, in the way of resolving or "filling" the gaps present in this reconstruction of personalism, in the choice of a more activist or more philosophical version of this same personalism, in the determination of its relation with other similar theoretical perspectives, etc.

At the same time, this is a necessary task for the future of this philosophy. If personalism appears as a core of more or less homogenous principles and ideas, but one difficult to articulate in its essential insights, its development will be very limited. First, it will pose an enormous difficulty for future generations to reach the nucleus of this doctrine—especially taking into account that the strictly Mounierian perspective could today be considered somewhat obsolete. Second, there will be obstacles for a minimally coordinated and homogenous development of this philosophy.[27] Moreover, the difficulties in relation to knowledge and dissemination are not to be underestimated. If personalism does not present a moderately unitary profile, but only a myriad of relatively disparate authors, every one of whom fights on his one account, then there will be a danger that none of them has sufficient strength to make himself heard in the coming decades.

Fully aware of this situation, I have been working for some years on the development of such a synthesis, which I now present in a more mature and complex version. It is a personal integration or systematization of ideas and concepts dispersed throughout the personalist authors in different degrees of development, and which also includes theoretical contributions, categorizations, and systematizations made by the author. This presentation of personalism, which simultaneously reunites the features of synthesis and proposal for the future, is framed within the current which we have named "modern ontological personalism"

---

27. In particular, in attempts to apply these fundamentals to new spheres, such as education, psychology, ethics, etc.

(see below sec. 2.2),[28] but we understand that, in its essential features, it can be accepted, or at least this has been our intent, by all versions of personalism.[29]

2 | Concepts, Definitions, and Classifications

2.1 | A Few Clarifications

2.1.1 | Personalism or Personalist Philosophy

With the terms personalism or personalist philosophy we mean the philosophical current or currents born in the twentieth century which have the following characteristics: (1) they are structured around a modern concept of the person; (2) the modern concept of the person is understood to be the anthropological perspective which chooses as emphases or areas of study some or all of the following elements: the person as "I" and "who"; affectivity and subjectivity; interpersonality and the communitarian aspect; corporeality; the distinction in the person of three basic dimensions or levels: bodily, psychological, and spiritual; the person as male or female; the primacy of love; freedom as self-determination; the narrative character of human existence; transcendence as the relationship with a Thou; and (3) some of the principal philosophers of reference include: Mounier, Maritain, Nédoncelle, Scheler, von Hildebrand, Stein, Buber, Wojtyła, Guardini, Marcel, Marías, and Zubiri.

The use of the terms "personalism" or "personalist philosophy" is, for us, equivalent, though one may distinguish some interesting nuances. The expression "personalist philosophy" has the advantage of

---

28. For a general overview, see Juan Manuel Burgos, "El personalismo ontológico moderno. I. Arquitectónica," *Quién* 1 (2015): 9–29; and "El personalismo ontológico moderno. II. Claves antropológicas," *Quién* 2 (2015): 7–32.

29. The ideas that we present would normally require a more detailed exposition, but that would defeat the introductory character of this volume. In any case, such an exposition can be found in the authors from whom the majority of these ideas originate, and those of a more methodical character, in several of the author's investigations which we shall quote later.

announcing straight away that the *set* of principles and ideas which it encompasses is a philosophy (not a movement of some type), and, furthermore, it indicates that it is not limited only to Mounier (from whom it fundamentally derives), but extends to all personalist thinkers. Likewise, it helps us to avoid the "ism" which some (Marcel, Marías) would tend to reject, although it does not appear that this can be considered to be a serious problem (think, for example, of "Hinduism" or "Buddhism").[30] In the opposite direction, we notice that the term "personalism" is the more common and customary and, in addition, connects directly with the thinkers who have created, used, and disseminated it and from whom it would not make sense to distance this philosophy. Therefore, it does not seem viable, desirable, or possible to relinquish it. So, our understanding is that it is best to use the one or the other of these concepts according to taste or context, while taking their content to be identical.[31]

2.1.2 | Personalism and Humanism

The concept of humanism is complex and has a long history in which we should distinguish between historiographical humanism, which appears in the Renaissance (associated with names such as Erasmus, Thomas More, and Luis Vives), and philosophical humanism. The latter also arises, in some sense, in the Renaissance; but, understood as a philosophical perspective which values the importance of the human being, it was generalized and took root above all in the nineteenth century and especially the twentieth. Given the ambiguity of this conception, it is easy to understand that "humanisms" can be very different

---

30. The author uses *"cristianismo"* which does not translate into an "ism" in English.—Trans.

31. The use of the expression "personalist philosophy" instead of "personalism" is sufficiently equivalent to Marcel's proposal to substitute "existentialism" for "existentialist philosophy." This proposition, which was based on justified theoretical bases, had, however, scarce reception since the habitual way of referring to existentialism (even in academic circles) continues to be this one, not that of "existentialist philosophy."

among each other. In fact, it initially appeared as an anti-religious theory which sought to promote man against a God who, supposedly, alienates him. The rejection of this thesis generated, in turn, the concept of Christian humanism, which vindicated the positive and humanist character of Christianity.[32]

But, aside from these historical questions, if we understand humanism to be any intellectual conception which values and gives importance to human being, *personalism must be understood as a particular type of humanism*. And, in particular, as *one of the possible versions of Christian or Judeo-Christian humanism*, since, with reference to philosophical premises, which are what is important here, both substantially coincide.

2.1.3 | Personalism and Philosophy of the Person

Philosophy of the person is any philosophy, past or present, which gives attention to man as a personal being. This expression, consequently, includes numerous philosophical schools, diverse in character and era: from some Fathers of the Church, such as St. Augustine,[33] to Boethius to St. Thomas Aquinas, St. Bonaventure, and other medievals, to Neo-Thomism to the different personalist philosophers to the humanist psychologies of Carl Rogers[34] to Abraham Maslow and Viktor Frankl, and so on.

---

32. See Henri de Lubac, *The Drama of Atheist Humanism*, trans. Edith M. Riley, Anne Englund Nash, and Mark Sebanc (London: Sheed and Ward, 1949); Hans Urs von Balthasar, *The God Question and Modern Man*, trans. Hilda Graef (New York: Seabury Press, 1956); Martin Heidegger, "Letter on Humanism," in *Martin Heidegger: Basic Writings*, ed. David F. Krell (New York: Harper and Row, 1977); Ludwig Feuerbach, *The Essence of Christianity*, trans. George Eliot (Amherst, N.Y.: Prometheus, 1989).

33. "Wherefore each individual man ... according to the mind alone, is one person and is the image of the Trinity in his mind." *De Trinitate*, bk. 15, chap. 7, no. 11, translated by Stephen McKenna, C.Ss.R., as *The Trinity* (Washington, D.C.: The Catholic University of America Press, 1963).

34. See Carl Rogers, *On Becoming a Person: A Therapist's View of Psychotherapy* (London: Constable, 1961).

The expression "philosophy of the person" is adequate for reflecting the importance of the person in philosophy and, more generally, in anthropology, but it is ambiguous from a technical point of view. It is easy to note, in effect, that the theories which we have mentioned have very diverse theoretical presuppositions, so that a serious, collective grouping of them is impossible; only a comprehension and a profound analysis of each of them in the framework of the philosophical or intellectual current to which it belongs is possible. In this sense, our understanding is that personalism constitutes *one of the possible philosophies of the person*, but others exist and have existed;[35] and so it would be a mistake and counterproductive to identify personalism and philosophy of the person, since it would only serve to create confusion and, moreover, contribute to diluting the identity of personalism since it could be identified with any philosophy throughout history which has discussed the person.

2.1.4 | Personalism as a Particular School of Philosophy

Personalism should be understood as a particular school of philosophy, and not as a contemporary version of what is called the *philosophia perennis*. A contrasting position is that maintained by Josef Seifert: "True personalism is not a philosophical school of recent decades, restricted to a small number of adherents, but in reality another form of what is called the *philosophia perennis*, understood in the best and broadest sense of the term, which includes all the genuine contributions to philosophy, but only insofar as they are true. The *philosophia perennis* and an adequate personalism are not, of course, *particular schools* of philosophy."[36]

Nonetheless, in our judgment, the concept of the *philosophia per-*

---

35. Many contemporary thinkers who have worked with this perspective can be found in *Enciclopedia della persona nel XX secolo*, ed. Antonio Pavan (Naples: ESI, 2008).

36. Josef Seifert, "El concepto de persona en la renovación de la Teología Moral," in *El primado de la persona en la moral contemporáneo* (Pamplona: EUNSA, 1997), 35.

ennis is not technically operative. It is rather like that of philosophy of the person. They are terms so broad that they inevitably become vague and diffuse beyond the proposal or promotion of certain general values of the person. But personalism is, in fact, a particular school of philosophy similar to others, such as Aristotelianism, Thomism, Kantianism, or empiricism. All of these schools *qua* schools, are partial, but, precisely for this reason, they have been able to propose theses which have modified the history of philosophy. The same happens with personalism: it is a particular vision of man, born in the twentieth century, which has been able to propose original philosophical ideas but which neither deals nor can deal with everything concerning the human being nor employs every possible perspective.

2.1.5 | The Historical Origin of Personalism

Personalism, therefore, has a definite historical origin: the twentieth century. It is not a philosophical theory which connects with the beginnings of human reflection on the person in the earliest Christian writings.[37] It can and must connect from an historical perspective with that tradition—another name for *philosophia perennis*—but with the clear awareness that this is so tenuous and diverse that it cannot show a substantial philosophical continuity because it is constituted by all the intellectuals who have reflected in the broad common framework of Judeo-Christian humanism. But, as is evident, from this framework there can arise and in fact there have arisen very diverse philosophies which even have generated reasonable (and sometimes bitter) confrontations which provide evidence, if necessary, that these differences may be profound.

Therefore, personalism, although it fits, with all rights and privileges, within that tradition, constitutes a specific form of thought which

---

37. This thesis is presented by José Luis Cañas, "¿Renacimiento del personalismo?" *Anales del Seminario de Historia de la filosofía* 18 (2001): 151–76.

originated in the twentieth century and which has certain particular qualities which make it distinct.

2.1.6 | Personalism and the Defense of the Dignity of the Person

Personalism, logically, defends the dignity of the person, but this does not mean that any theory which defends the dignity of the person can automatically be called personalism. That requires much more: that the theory accept, in one way or another, the theoretical postulates of the builders of personalism (see above sec. 2.1.(a)). A generic defense of the dignity of the person can be made on the basis of many philosophies (for example, Kant's), and from another perspective, it simply reflects a central thesis of Christianity, although formulated in a language which has adopted both personalist and Enlightenment presuppositions.

2.1.7 | "Authentic" Personalism and "Broad" Personalism

Some authors have come up with a distinction between personalism in a broad or generic sense and authentic personalism or personalism in a strict sense. By the former is understood any version of philosophy which gives importance to the person (philosophies of the person) while personalism in the strict sense would be twentieth-century personalism.[38] In our opinion this terminology is somewhat inaccurate and anachronistic because it uses a concept which has appeared in the twentieth century to describe philosophies (or theologies) from distant times. Personalism, simply, arose in the twentieth century. It is another question whether there are other theological or philosophical systems which have also employed the concept of person.

---

38. Josef Seifert draws a similar distinction between adequate personalism (equivalent to strict personalism) and imperfect personalism (equivalent to broad personalism), in which he includes, for example, St. Thomas. See Seifert, "El concepto de persona en la renovación de la Teología Moral," 35.

2.2 | Personalist Currents

Within personalism, diverse currents coexist, which it is well to bring to light, both for information's sake and also because knowledge of them can assist in the process of clarification of concepts and positions which we are attempting to carry out. We shall briefly present them, since they have already been described by way of their principal representatives.

2.2.1 | Principal Currents

(1) *Anglo-American personalism* is the first systematic personalistic proposal. Its main representative is Borden Parker Bowne, and the most characteristic feature is idealism: only human persons and the Divine Person exist.

(2) *Phenomenological personalism* is composed of the philosophers who followed the first phenomenologist Edmund Husserl and developed a realistic phenomenology based on the person. Max Scheler and Dietrich Von Hildebrand belong to this group.

(3) *Communitarian personalism* is fundamentally governed by the postulates and attitudes of Emmanuel Mounier. It is thus characterized by: (a) a stress on action and social transformation; (b) not stressing the strictly academic and philosophical aspect of personalism; and (c) having Mounier as the principal ideological inspiration.

(4) *Dialogical personalism* refers principally to the philosophers of dialogue and, therefore, places special emphasis on interpersonality as a key element in the development and interpretation of philosophical anthropology. Its most emblematic philosopher is Martin Buber.

(5) *Classical ontological personalism* is that version of personalism which takes many elements from classical philosophy and particularly from Thomism, although it shapes them with personalist contributions. Maritain could be the principal philosopher.

(6) *Modern ontological personalism or neo-personalism*: this version of personalism, which is the one that we propose, has the understanding that: (a) the construction of an adequate contemporary personalism requires the integration of classical and modern concepts in a new synthesis which would go beyond both; (b) currently, the priority is the technical formulation of personalism; and (c) it seeks to influence society principally in a cultural and intellectual way. Wojtyła is the principal representative of this perspective.

The differences between these forms of personalism are significant but secondary, so that, if they do not go to extremes, they can coexist perfectly well. In fact, within each version, the basic principles of the others are generally accepted, within the common framework of personalism. Thus, for example, it is normal for a neo-personalist to acknowledge the great importance of Mounier or the relevance of the principle of interpersonality. Likewise, there are communitarian personalists with a solid grounding in philosophy who actively work in this field. But each version tends to emphasize the aspect which identifies it. Yet this harmonious coexistence can be complicated when some group claims its principal feature as exclusively its own or that of personalism.

2.2.2 | Debates among the Currents

We shall now examine some important debates among the versions of personalism, the solution of which would be of great interest.

Dialogical personalism, like all personalism, stresses interpersonality by means of the idea of the constitution of the "I" via the "thou," but it highlights this concept with a particular insistence which, in some authors such as Lévinas, could give the impression that the "I" only exists in the relation, a thesis which ontological personalists do not share with some dialogical authors because the former give priority to the subject, as we see, for example, in Wojtyła. The theoretical resolution of the problem is as complex as it is interesting, since relation has entered forcefully into the constitution of the person, which impedes simple and easy responses. Now, it should be debated with passion but not heatedly, leaving space for all the positions within the common framework of personalism.[39]

Classical ontological personalism and modern ontological personalism (neo-personalism) differ regarding the changes that have to be made in the framework of classical philosophy. Maritain and Wojtyła would be the points of reference. Maritain perceived essential points of personalism, but remained a Thomist because, for him, Aquinas's philosophy supplied the adequate structures for interpreting reality. Wojtyła, however, perceived that a new anthropological synthesis was needed, which would fuse classical and modern philosophy, the philosophy of being and of consciousness.[40] In this way, although the superficial formulation of these two positions can be very similar, the profound structure is different because it employs different concepts for constructing anthropology and ethics (substance, nature, soul, in the one case; identity, "who," "I," consciousness, psyche, spirit, in the other).

---

39. The radicalization of this debate can become paradoxical. Coll, a great expert on interpersonality, affirms that "this mutual constitution between the 'I' and the 'thou' is the most characteristic feature of *personalism* and which must thus form part of its definition. Consequently, any personalism, as such, must be *dialogical* or *communitarian* personalism, while the other currents of more or less personalist inspiration are classed as *philosophies of the person*, among which one may doubtless include Maritain's Thomism and that of Pope Wojtyła" (Coll, "Mounier i els corrents personalists," 52). Apart from the fact that Maritain coined the expression "communitarian personalism," that Wojtyła is not a Thomist and speaks of the constitution of the "I" in the "thou," although not on an ontological level, it seems on the contrary that, as the very name indicates, the central feature of any personalism must be the person, and that those approaches that wish to structurally prioritize the relation should be called dialogical philosophies, communitarianism, relationalism, etc. And not the other way around.

40. "This presentation of the problem, completely new in relation to traditional philosophy (and by traditional philosophy we understand here the pre-Cartesian philosophy and above all the heritage of Aristotle, and, among the Catholic schools of thought, of St. Thomas Aquinas) has provoked me to undertake an attempt at reinterpreting certain formulations proper to this whole philosophy." Karol Wojtyła, *The Acting Person*, trans. Anna-Teresa Tymieniecka (Dordrecht: D. Reidel Pub. Co, 1979), xiii.

3 | Structural Features of Personalism

Now we shall survey the structural—not the thematic—characteristics of personalist philosophy which, as in this entire chapter, are presented as the result of a personal synthesis, rationalization, and formalization of visions and proposals which can be found in different degrees of elaboration in the great personalists.

3.1 | The Structural Centrality of the Person

The decisive and foremost feature which characterizes any personalist philosophy is the structural centrality of the person in its conceptual architecture. This means not only that it values the person or takes the person into account in one way or another in its anthropology, since this feature is also present in many philosophies inspired by Christianity or in the philosophies of the person, but also that the concept of the person is the key to or hinge of anthropology and ethics.

It is common knowledge that the concept of person, as such, is an invention of Christianity, since Greek philosophy did not employ this concept but the more general concept of man.[41] Christianity had to formulate its conviction of the equal dignity of every man and woman independently of their race or condition, its tri-personal conception of the divinity, and the co-existence of two modes of being in Christ. This formulation took centuries, but, after a long and difficult process, it reached the brilliant distinction between nature and person as the way to formulate the answer. In summary: the person corresponded to the subsistent *who*, and nature, to the *what*. In God there are three *whos*, in Christ two *whats*, and every man is a *who*.

However, this powerful distinction historically remained in a theo-

---

41. See Maurice Nédoncelle, "Prosopon et persona dans l'antiquité classique. Essai de bilan linguistic," *Revue des Sciences Religieuses* 22, no. 3–4 (1948): 277–99; Onorato Bucci, "La formazione del concetto di persona nel cristianesimo delle origini: 'Avventura semantica' e itinerario storico," *Lateranum N.S.* 2 (1988): 383–450.

logical context. The Fathers of the Church did not produce formal philosophies, and when, in the Middle Ages, these began to develop, the irruption of Aristotle's philosophy tipped the balance in favor of Greek thought, since his powerful philosophy imposed its perception over the perception which could have been derived from the insufficiently developed idea of the person. And so, although Aquinas used and valued the notion of person, in his anthropology it plays a secondary role. The primary role in Aquinas's thought is played instead by Aristotle's concept of substance through the use of Boethius's famous definition: the person is "an individual substance of a rational nature."[42]

Julián Marías clarified it thus:

> When, within Scholastic philosophy, attempts were made to think philosophically about the person, the notions which were decisive were not those that proceeded from these contexts, but those of "property" and "substance" (*hypostasis*). Boethius's famous definition, so influential—*persona est rationalis naturae individua substantia*—had as its starting point Aristotle's notion of *ousía* or *substantia*, conceived primarily to talk about "things," always explained using the eternal examples of the statue and the bed, based on the old Greek ideal of the "independent" or [self-]sufficient, of the "separable" (*khoriston*). That this substance or thing that we call "person" be rational, would certainly be important, but not sufficiently so as to rework this character of *ousía* and modify its mode of being, its manner of reality. The person is a *hypostasis* or *suppositum* like the rest; just that it is of a rational nature.[43]

---

42. Aquinas gave many definitions of the person, some original: "'Person' signifies what is most perfect in all nature—that is, a subsistent individual of a rational nature" (*Summa theologiae*, trans. Fathers of the English Dominican Province [London: Burns Oates and Washbourne, 1920], I., q. 29, a. 3, c); "a distinct subsistence in rational nature" (*In Sententiarum*, 1, d. 23, q. 4); "a distinct subsistence in human nature" (*Quaestiones disputatae de potentia Dei*, translated by the English Dominican Fathers as *Disputed Questions on the Power of God* [Westminster, Md.: The Newman Press, 1952], q. 9, a. 4). But when he wants to give an "official" definition, he always returns to that of Boethius.

43. Marías, *Antropología metafísica* (Madrid: Alianza, 1970), 41.

Thus, surprising though it may be, it was not until the twentieth century that we find philosophical anthropologies based upon the concept of person. These are the personalist anthropologies, and we have described them in the preceding chapters. They have rediscovered the potentiality of the concept of person in philosophy and have tried to make the maximum use of it, which has required, in addition to *a reconstruction of anthropology* on the basis of the concept of person, a *reconstruction* and reformulation *of the very concept of person* upon new philosophical bases; a reconstruction which, in the case of modern ontological personalism, has explicitly opted for a fusion of classical and modern elements. Personalism, therefore, is characterized by being structured around a *modern* concept of person.

3.2 | Personalist Categories

The reconstruction of the concept of person represents only the tip of the iceberg of this intellectual project, since, in a similar way, the remaining anthropological and ethical concepts have to be reconstructed and reformulated with two objectives: (1) to reflect what is specifically personal, overcoming the Greek ballast; and (2) to incorporate anthropological topics and concepts which originated in modernity. By the "Greek ballast" we mean the tendency, originating in Greek philosophy, to describe man by using philosophical notions developed to explain things or animals, applying minor modifications to them, with the result that what is specifically human, what constitutes man as person, is obscured or even disappears, when one thinks about man as a thing or an animal, just with some special characteristics.[44] We have already posed this problem for the person, but it appears in many contexts. If, for example, we develop the category of appetite or tendency to explain the dynamism of the animal and vegetable world, and *we then apply it to man*, the peculiar

---

44. See Burgos, *Repensar la naturaleza humana* (Pamplona: EUNSA, 2007), 58–64, "The Greek Ballast and the Problem of Extension."

characteristics of human freedom are obscured. Freedom is *not* a tendency, it is a response, freely caused by a man capable of self-determination and of generating an irreducible and unique decision. Nothing of this appears in the concept of tendency. Goodness, similarly, does not exist in the vegetable or animal world. The only goodness (or evil) deserving of the name is that which lies in the human heart.

This analytical deficit has its origin in the fact that, for the Greeks, man was one more thing within the world of nature—special, certainly, but one among others—while in the West, through the influence of Christianity, man emerges forcefully from that world as radically distinct. This emergence, which establishes an insuperable separation between mankind and the rest of the beings, has some structural consequences which were not sufficiently valued by a classical philosophy too dependent on Greek metaphysical postulates. Consequently, the theory of being and its categories came first, and afterwards, by means of the application of analogy, it managed to reach man.[45] But this trajectory is too long and difficult, and man ends up being analyzed by means of general and abstract categories which hide some of his special features, such as subjectivity, intimacy, and relationality.

The acknowledgement of this problem and the need to resolve it have induced personalists to a *direct analysis* of the person, which, without conceptual intermediaries taken from other contexts, leads to the formulation of *specifically personalist categories*, that is, of *categories exclusive to the human person*, which adequately reflect the features which univocally characterize the person.[46] This approach facilitates, furthermore, the incorporation, from a realist perspective, of some anthropological categories originating in modernity, such as subjectivity.

---

45. The perception of the problem is generalized among personalists. For the author's own treatment of this issue, see Juan Manuel Burgos, *La experiencia integral: un método para el personalismo* (Madrid: Palabra, 2015), 243–67.

46. This integrating perspective is not always easy to reach with sufficient depth. For example, Frankl, whose perspective is typically personalist, seems, however, not to have achieved it completely. See Viktor Frankl, *Psychotherapy and Existentialism* (New York: Washington Square Press Books, 1985).

3.3 | The Personalist Method

Personalism, due to its origin as a movement in Mounier, its open attitude, and its rejection of system in the Hegelian sense, has directed little attention to methodological questions. In fact, we find some references to method in Nédoncelle, Marcel, Wojtyła, and little more. However, the philosophical procedure followed by the majority of personalists has been, in practice, fairly similar.

Avoiding a metaphysical perspective of a downward flow, which consists of applying transcendental categories to things in general, then to living beings, and so on, and finally to the person, personalism has moved to a direct experiential analysis of the human being, similar to the phenomenological method. This similarity is so great that it has led some to affirm that personalists use this method; but, in the strict sense, this is not so. There are great similarities but also important differences. One of the principal differences, if not the fundamental one, is that none of them use Husserl's *epoché*.[47]

In general terms, and following Wojtyła on this point, it could be said that the personalist method is an ontological analysis of reality based on an integral concept of experience which includes, simultaneously, objective and subjective elements. The objective ones come from knowledge and perception of the world external to the subject (which includes some aspects of the perception of one's own body); and the subjective ones are present in the experience of one's own, intimate world, entirely nontransferable to what is exterior in objective terms. Wojtyła's understanding is that both elements are always present at the same time, since, "Man's experience of anything outside of himself is always associated with the experience of himself, and he never experiences anything external without having at the same time the experience of himself."[48] And, consequently, it is methodologically feasible to

---

47. The methodological approach that puts the existence of the world into brackets, without taking an explicit position about this question. See chap. 1, sec. 4.3, above.
48. Wojtyła, *The Acting Person*, 3. For a detailed account, see Juan Manuel Burgos,

integrate, from the beginning, philosophy of being, centered on objectivity, and philosophy of consciousness, which has subjectivity as its starting point. Very recently I have developed this idea proposing a specifically personalist methodology called *integral experience*.[49]

3.4 | Personalism and Modernity

Personalism places itself before modernity as a contemporary philosophy, and thus chronologically later. And its approach to modernity is that of selective integration. For some time, the problem of modern philosophy has been a Gordian knot for a philosophy inspired by Christianity because, due to the prevalence of a certain traditionalism, modernity has been understood as a total rupture with philosophical realism and the Christian worldview: a cultural rupture since the Renaissance and a philosophical one since Descartes. And so, in some contexts, it has been rejected as a whole.

This attitude has the understanding that Descartes, via the *cogito*, introduced a transcendental turn in philosophy, leading it from the realism in which it had operated since its beginnings in Greece, towards a subjectivism which progressively developed into distinct forms of idealism (Kant, Hegel) and finally became atheist in the twentieth century (Sartre, Marx, and so on), as shown by the progressive secularization and de-Christianization of Western society which still continues to advance today.[50]

"The Method of Karol Wojtyła: A Way between Phenomenology, Personalism and Metaphysics," *Analecta husserliana* 104 (2009): 107–29.

49. See Burgos, *Experiencia integral*; and a short exposition in Juan Manuel Burgos, "Integral Experience: A New Proposal on the Beginning of Knowledge," in *In the Sphere of the Personal: New Perspectives in the Philosophy of Persons*, ed. James Beauregard and Simon Smith (Wilmington, Del.: Vernon Press, 2016), 41–59.

50. See *The Decline of Christendom in Western Europe (1750–2000)*, ed. Hugh McLeod and Werner Ustorf (Cambridge: Cambridge University Press, 2003); Mariano Fazio, *Historia de las ideas contemporáneas: una lectura del proceso de secularización* (Madrid: Rialp, 2006); Jürgen Habermas and Joseph Ratzinger, *The Dialectics of Secularization: On Reason and Religion*, trans. Brian McNeil, ed. Florian Schuller (San Francisco: Ignatius Press, 2006).

This diagnosis certainly has many valid elements, but, for personalist thought, it is too one-sided. Although it cannot be denied that idealism has generated a solipsistic and subjectivistic thought, harmful for European culture, it also has to be acknowledged that within its framework there have been decisive philosophical advances which should be taken up—in one way or another—by any later philosophy. It is not possible to erase seven centuries of the history of philosophy and to stop the clock at the thirteenth century as if nothing has happened since then. It is necessary to take into account the philosophy produced in this long period and move ahead.

The conclusions which some personalist thinkers have made have led them, on the one hand, to reject the basic approach of idealism and, on the other, to try to take up some of the fundamental concepts of modernity—subjectivity, consciousness, "I," etc.—reformulated or modified as necessary.[51] In addition, one may recognize that some of these concepts could—or even should—have been developed in a Christian philosophical framework since, in reality, they reflect secularized versions of originally Christian concepts. For example, Ferdinand Ebner held that, "the 'I' is a late discovery of the human spirit which reflects upon itself and reveals itself to itself in the form of an idea. Ancient philosophy knew nothing of this. Because it was due to the spirit of Christianity—that is, due to the religious dimension—that for the first time man discovered the awareness of himself."[52] And the same could be said for the vindication of freedom or subjectivity and, in social and political contexts, of pluralism, as Maritain already affirmed in *Integral Humanism*.

---

51. As remarked in chap. 1, above, this is a project whose necessity has been seen by many Christian philosophers and not just the personalists.

52. Ferdinand Ebner, *La palabra y las realidades espirituales*, trans. José M. Garrido Páginas (Madrid: Caparrós, 1995), 25. Originally published as *Das Wort und die geistigen Realitäten: Pneumatologische Fragmente. Die Geschichte der Fragmente*, ed. Richard Hörmann (Berlin: LIT-Verlag, 2009). Translated by Harold Johnson Green as *The Word and the Spiritual Realities: A Translation of and Critical Introduction to Ferdinand Ebner's "Das Wort und die geistigen Realitäten" and a Comparison with Martin Buber's "Ich und Du"* (Evanston, Ill.: Northwestern University, 1980).

3.5 | Personalism and Metaphysics

Of the many ways that metaphysics can be understood, there are two that are especially important for personalism. The first conceives metaphysics, in a broad sense, as *an ultimate, radical and fundamental knowledge,* or as the search for ultimate and substantial certainties which are above the fluctuations of time and history, or as that field of knowledge which goes beyond what sensations and isolated experiences reveal, and tries to reach an essential comprehension of beings which arrives at their ultimate nucleus. In all these meanings, which it would be well to define more precisely, personalism is presented as a philosophy with a metaphysical or ontological orientation, with the aspiration of reaching ultimate truths.

The second meaning of metaphysics, which is frequently and imperceptibly identified with the first, consists of formulating these ultimate truths by means of *the philosophy of being in one of its Aristotelian or scholastic versions.* And, in this case, the question of metaphysics poses a different and complex situation which we may schematically divide into two aspects. Generally, personalism has no problem in taking up a philosophy of being as the final principle for explaining reality,[53] but the same is not true of the Aristotelian categories understood as transcendental or of a "deductivist" explanation of reality.[54] The concept or notion of being seems unavoidable for explaining the essential structure of what is real. But it is a very different question whether the Aristo-

---

53. This is clear in all those who have a certain link with the Thomistic tradition. For others, it should be clarified. Some have not considered this problem with much interest because they focus on anthropology or because their tradition of reference—in the case of the philosophers of dialogue, for example—does not raise this sort of question.

54. For example, A. González Álvarez first defines the general characteristics of an entity (*ens*) and then "contracts them to its inferiors." See *Tratado de Metafísica,* vol. 1, *Ontología* (Madrid: Gredos, 1967). This deductivism varies with each author, but it is a characteristic tendency of this type of thought, as shown in Stephen Brock's study of action in which, first, he analyzes action "in general" and, then studies a particular case, "human" action. See *Action and Conduct: Thomas Aquinas and the Theory of Action* (Edinburgh: T. & T. Clark, 1988).

telian categories can assist in interpreting *all* reality. In fact, it is not so. As we have mentioned in speaking of method, beings, and particularly man, are so different as to require their own exclusive categories. The indiscriminate application of some general concepts—such as the four causes, substance, or accidents—to *any type of being* is an unjustifiable simplification because of the complexity of existence.

Moreover, this approach inverts the adequate methodological itinerary. In order to determine the ontological configuration of the world, it starts with the abstract entity (*ens*) (which does not exist) and deductively applies its categories to different ontological strata: things, organisms, plants, and so on. But this method curiously proceeds from the least perfect to the most perfect, so that the categories of the most perfect (the person) are determined by the imperfect. An adequate ontology, on the contrary, must restate *the primacy of personal being as the paradigm, the principal analogue, of any categorization of being*.[55]

3.6 | Personalism and the Transformation of Society

In our society, philosophy tends ever more to retreat into academic ivory towers, producing erudite and precise texts which do not try to have any influence on society or, even less so, to contribute to the construction of a worldview. These works are, most of the time, narcissistic intellectual games destined to fascinate the reader, colleague, or audience. This conception or exercise of philosophy is probably one of the reasons for its limited success nowadays and is diametrically distant from the approach practiced by personalists, who have always seen philosophy as a means for interacting with reality and transforming it.

---

55. In this sense, Stefanini stated, "Being is personal and everything which is not personal in being is the result of the person's productivity, as a means for the manifestation of the person and for communication between persons" (Luigi Stefanini, *Personalismo sociale*, 2nd ed. [Rome: Studium, 1979], 7). This attempt to rework metaphysics in a personalist way is also found in Zubiri, Polo, Marcel, and others.

Every human being is called, by means of his action, to influence and modify the world which surrounds him; and he can achieve this with special efficacy through those instruments whose use he masters particularly well. For the philosopher, those instruments are the theoretical constructions which he can evaluate, analyze, or create. With them he can and should try to influence the world. If, furthermore, as in the case of personalism, he promotes a philosophy that vindicates the very special dignity of the person with respect to everything that exists, one may understand that the personalist philosopher feels particularly called and committed to engage himself in those public affairs in which the dignity of the person is involved or questioned.[56] And, in fact, this has been the attitude of the majority of the great personalist philosophers, although with different emphases. Mounier and the communitarian personalists tend to exercise very direct social and cultural action. Other personalists (ontological personalism in general) prefer more academic action because they consider that this is the sphere in which their influence can be truly effective.

3.7 | Personalism and Christianity

The great majority of the great personalists have been convinced and committed Christians, including several converts (Edith Stein, Jacques Maritain, Gabriel Marcel, Dietrich von Hildebrand) and, so far, two saints, Edith Stein and Karol Wojtyła (Pope John Paul II). And the Jewish personalists, such as Buber and Rosenzweig, also had an intense religious life. This explains why transcendence has so much force in personalism. If we attend, however, to the theoretical aspect, what matters is to explain how their beliefs influenced their philosophy; and, in my judgment, the correct way of expressing it is through the concept of

---

56. On this topic, important in much European personalism, see Paul Landsberg, "Reflexiones sobre el compromiso personal," in *Problemas del personalismo* (Salamanca: Fundación Emmanuel Mounier, 2006), 23–35. [N.B.: "*Compromiso*" means "commitment," "engagement," "taking part."—Trans.]

a hermeneutic circle, or, in personalist terms, of the feedback between experience and reflection.

In the first place, we need to state that, for the unitary anthropology of personalism, it is not only problematic but inadequate to establish very strict separations between terms such as faith and reason, intellect and will, nature and grace, because these faculties, structures, or dimensions are not autonomous entities. "The" reason or "the" faith does not exist, but a *man* who believes and who reasons. In the same way, "the" intellect does not know nor does "the" will want, but rather the *person* does these things. Thus, the point of departure in this area must be the process of overcoming these dichotomies that were especially reinforced during the period of rationalism. But union or integration is not equivalent to confusion, and so, while artificial separations must be avoided, it is necessary to reflect in some way the fact that there are different dimensions and, in the matter at hand, that reason and faith, philosophy and theology are distinct forms of knowledge and distinct sciences.

Personalists have, *de facto*, resolved this problem in the following way.[57] The starting point of their reflection has been their integral human experience which, logically, includes religious elements which can be either direct (religious experience) or apprehended/transmitted by means of an institution (such as the Catholic Church or Judaism). And on the basis of this experience they have formulated their *strictly rational philosophy*, although impregnated in various ways by the conceptions, experiences, rites, and cultural traditions specific to each religion. This impregnation, as contemporary hermeneutics has emphasized, is completely inevitable. We can only think within the context of our cultural and life framework, whether we like it or not. There is no

---

57. What I would like to express is that not all, not even the majority, have formulated a theory on the relations between faith and reason or between philosophy and theology, but, as a matter of fact, they have worked out a philosophy inspired by Christian sources as set out here. Only some of them have tackled the subject explicitly, such as Maritain in *De la philosophie chrétienne* (1933), *Science et sagesse* (1934), and other books.

absolutely neutral position, as rationalism naively believed. Personalists have not only been fully aware of this fact, but, with their religious sensibility, they have perceived it as something positive, with the understanding that religion (Christian or Jewish) could be a powerful source of inspiration for the construction of the new anthropology in which they were involved.[58]

The Christian personalists, in particular, have intuited that the philosophical potentiality of Christianity had not been sufficiently exploited and, approaching the message of the Gospels with a renewed look, have extracted new ideas, whose origin is easily traceable, in concepts such as the primacy of love, the "incarnation" in Mounier, and Karol Wojtyła's personalist norm, among others. These concepts, in turn, to now close the hermeneutic circle, have subsequently allowed for a deepening of Christian anthropological understanding.

The same has happened with the philosophers of dialogue, as Pope John Paul II remarked on, wondering about the origins of the idea of interpersonality.

> Where did the philosophers of dialogue learn this? Foremost, they learned it from their experience of the Bible. The *sphere of the everyday* man's entire life is one of "coexistence": "thou" and "I"—and also in the *sphere of the absolute and the definitive*: "I" and "THOU." The biblical tradition revolves around this "THOU," who is first the God of Abraham, Isaac, and Jacob, the God of the Fathers, and then the God of Jesus Christ and the apostles, the God of our faith.
>
> *Our faith is profoundly anthropological*, rooted constitutively in coex-

---

58. Perhaps it would be convenient to remark that it is *only* a source of inspiration, both because of the philosophical framework of their thought and because of their awareness that Christianity can inspire, and has in fact inspired, different philosophies. In this sense, it is interesting to read Mounier's preliminary observation in the 1946 republishing of his *Personalisme et christianisme*: "This study, prepared in December 1939, of which the original, in English, was published in the Collection of the Catholic University of Washington, was titled, *Personalisme catholique*. That risked giving a personal study an impression of orthodoxy which the author lacks the authority to confer. Thus we prefer a more modest title." *Oeuvres*, vol. 1, *1931–1939*, 728.

istence, in the community of God's people, and *in communion with this eternal "THOU."* Such coexistence is essential to our Judeo-Christian tradition and comes from God's initiative. This initiative is connected with and leads to creation, and is at the same time—as Saint Paul teaches—
"the eternal election of man in the Word who is the Son" (cf. Eph 1:4).[59]

4 | Personalism as a Realist Philosophy

We shall now present the essential contents of personalism from a thematic point of view in two phases. In the first one we shall succinctly describe some basic features which permit personalism to be identified as a realist philosophy. Then, in the following section, we shall describe those aspects of personalism which are particularly new and original. We call attention, in any case, to the special way in which personalism belongs to the realist tradition, in the sense that it takes up the great principles of realism with a new perspective which we shall try to make explicit. In other words, the newness of personalism is also made manifest in its characterization as a realist philosophy.[60]

4.1 | An Ontological or Metaphysical Vision of the World

Personalism has an *ontological or metaphysical vision of the world*, that is, it intends to "transcend empirical data in order to attain something absolute, ultimate, and foundational in its search for truth."[61] Without, at this point, entering into the very complex problem of establishing the precise meaning of ontology or metaphysics—which varies from author to author—a feature common to all personalist philosophers is the search for an ultimate explanation which transcends the empirical data understood in a merely scientific or empiricist sense. For personalism,

---

59. Pope John Paul II, *Crossing the Threshold of Hope* (New York: Knopf, 1995), 36.
60. In the previous historical chapters, the origin of the ideas which are set in what follows has already been mentioned.
61. John Paul II, *Fides et ratio*, no. 83.

reality has ontological density, and the key elements of its structure can be grasped intellectually. The objective of personalist philosophy is the understanding of these structures, especially the anthropological ones, which are given to the person through experience.[62]

4.2 | Person: Identity and Subsistence

The ontological density of reality culminates in the person, who is not a mere succession of experiences or a pure stream of consciousness, but a subsistent (substantial) subject who maintains his identity through changes. It is true that man changes profoundly, but not completely.[63] There is a *something*: the "I," the *suppositum*, the subsistent "who, the substance, that remains invariable and enables us to establish and found the identity and continuity of persons. Every person is the same person that he was ten, twenty, or forty years ago, because his "I," his substrate, his substance in Aristotelian language, prevents his basic identity from being altered by the changes.[64]

On this classic topic of realism, the personalist innovation appears by way of a certain rejection of the concept of substance, which had already been explained through the thought of Julián Marías, and which affects the Aristotelian *concept*, not the idea that the concept tries to formulate, that is, the permanence of the subject or person through time, since, if this were rejected, the person, the key concept of personalism, would be watered down to nothing and disappear. Why, then,

---

62. We are not referring to scientific experience, but rather to integral experience, as in Wojtyła, Marcel, etc., from which *all* knowledge comes.

63. "My [infancy] is long since dead, yet I still live." Augustine, *Confessions*, trans. Vernon J. Rourke (Washington, D.C.: The Catholic University of America Press, 1953), bk. I, chap. 6. (Rourke has "babyhood" for "infancy.")

64. Some of the most powerful research which has tried to identify the characteristics of this "I" or "Self" has been developed by John F. Crosby through his notion of "selfhood," which, being fully personalist, he believes compatible with the Aristotelian notion of substance. See *The Selfhood of the Human Person* (Washington, D.C.: The Catholic University of America Press, 1996), esp. 124–144.

this rejection of the concept of substance? Because the description of man based in the categories of substance and accidents is difficult to integrate into a contemporary anthropology.[65] This is the limit which the majority of personalists see in the notion of substance and the reason for their reticence about using it or for why they have attempted to work out other ways of solving the problem.[66]

4.3 | Human Nature

Personalism holds that there exists *a human nature*, that is, that all human beings are essentially similar. Mounier has expressed it very clearly:

> There is a *world* of persons. If they formed an absolute plurality, it would be impossible for one among them, you or I, to think them all at once, to apply the common name of person to them. There must be some common factor. Contemporary thought is repudiating the idea of an abiding human nature, since it is becoming aware of still unexplored possibilities in our condition. It rejects the conception of "human nature" as a prejudice that would limit these possibilities in advance. And indeed, they are often so astonishing that we ought not to ascribe limits to them without the greatest reserve. But it is one thing to reject the tyranny of formal definitions and quite another to deny, as existentialism sometimes does, that man has any one essence or constitution. If every man is nothing but what he *makes himself*, there can be no humanity, no history, and no community (which indeed is the conclusion that certain existentialists end by accepting).
>
> *Personalism therefore includes among its leading ideas, the affirmation of the unity of mankind, both in space and time*, which was foreshadowed by certain schools of thought in the latter days of antiquity and confirmed in the Judeo-Christian tradition.[67]

---

65. See Stefanini, *Personalismo sociale*, 46.
66. As Zubiri, through his concept of substantivity. See *Sobre la esencia*, 4th ed. (Madrid: Alianza, 1972), 125, 157; and *El hombre y Dios* (Madrid: Alianza-Fundación Xavier Zubiri, 1984).
67. Mounier, *Personalism*, 29–30, emphasis added.

Here again, though, we find problems similar to those related to substance. Personalists are reluctant to use the term "nature," but not because they reject a basic identity among all men, but because a conceptual identification of human nature with the *Aristotelian concept of nature* is almost inevitable. Now, this Aristotelian concept of nature, like that of substance, by remaining within an exclusively Greek framework, presents problems, because it incorporates a teleological scheme which is very suitable for things and animals, but too rigid and static to integrate human freedom. In fact, today, the most common meaning of "nature" refers to that which is untouched by man and unrelated to him, "vegetable and animal nature" unaffected by human action. Thus is it easy to understand that applying the same term to man can be equivocal.

4.4 | A Realist Epistemology

As for knowledge, personalism adheres to a realist epistemology, that is, it affirms the human ability to know an objective reality that exists independently of him. And, likewise, it rejects idealism in any of its multiple modalities. For personalism, in accord with the realist tradition, man has a spiritual faculty which allows him to make the world his own without thereby ceasing to be himself different from the world. This process is objective in the sense that man is capable of reaching the world as it is, without essentially deforming it, a fact that is confirmed by the phenomenon of intersubjectivity, inasmuch as we can compare our knowledge with other people and construct with them a common knowledge.

The innovative aspect of personalist epistemology is rooted in its positioning midway between an extreme objectivism (active in some versions of the realist tradition and in rationalism), and subjectivist or idealist theories. For extreme objectivism, the person would be a mere mirror reflecting reality, so that everyone's knowledge would be the same. But this thesis is simplistic and reductive, because it does not account for subjectivity, nor for the fact that knowing is an action of the whole person, nor for the fact that knowledge is framed in the context of an intellectual and even epistemological tradition.[68] Therefore, since persons differ in their intellectual capacities, interests, sensibilities, means, culture, and tradition, so also does their way of accessing reality. Furthermore, as Marías noticed, we should not understand "reality" in an excessively simplistic manner, since "reality is 'what I find, just as I find it'. This means, in turn, that I am an ingredient of reality, that it is chimerical to omit the 'I' surreptitiously when speaking of reality."[69]

In conclusion, personalism considers that knowledge is objective in the sense that with it we reach a reality independent of the one who knows it, but personalism also acknowledges that there is a subjective part, both in the process of knowing and in the content of reality to which one approaches. Likewise, contrary to Enlightenment rationalism, for which the "goddess reason" was capable of examining any obscurity, personalism acknowledges that there are aspects which escape the human mind because of its limitations, which leaves open the gate to *mystery* and to transcendence.[70]

4.5 | Human Freedom

Another key principle of personalism (and of realism) is the recognition of human freedom, which is stoutly affirmed against any sort of determinism, whether biological, psychological, sociological, historical, or otherwise. Man is not subject to determinism, but has the ability to choose and freely to respond or not to his natural impulses. It is true that external circumstances and the real possibilities of action limit and

---

68. See Alasdair MacIntyre, *Three Rival Versions of Moral Enquiry* (London: Duckworth, 1990).

69. Marías, *Antropología metafísica*, 151.

70. See Marcel, "Concrete Approaches to Investigating the Ontological Mystery," in Marcel, *Gabriel Marcel's Perspectives on the Broken World*, trans. Katharine Rose Hanley (Chicago: Marquette University Press, 1998), 172–209.

condition him, but the final word is always his own. In this radical power we glimpse the absolute character of human dignity.

But, for personalism, freedom is not situated only on the level of action, as the classical tradition has believed, but rather freedom occupies a more essential and radical place which affects the essential structure of the person. Freedom, as Wojtyła has forcefully remarked, is not only or even principally choice; it is a *self-determination* which is based on the dominion of the person over himself. "Every authentically human 'I will' is an act of self-determination; ... and it presupposes structural self-possession. For only the things that are man's actual possessions can be determined by him; they can be determined only by the one who actually possesses them. Being in possession of himself man can determine himself."[71]

In other words, to be free consists not so much in choosing but in the capacity to construct ourselves by means of choices, in being able to decide not only what we want to be, but *who we want to be* through each of our actions. In this, personalism connects with existentialism, with its constructive vision of human existence, but starting from a concept of nature which limits the extent of self-determination, and establishing the starting point: not Sartre's vacuum, but the person who already exists.

4.6 | Good and Evil

The recognition of *good and evil* as an identifying and peculiar datum regarding the person is a characteristic of all realist philosophy: man encounters the good and the evil, actions that he knows with certainty he should not perform and actions that his heart judges to be right. There have been philosophies that have denied the validity of this fact, and have reduced it to an emotion (Ayer), to an introjection of social pressure (Freud) or to other factors, but it is, definitely, a feature which identifies the human being as such and infinitely distances him from animals.

---

71. Wojtyła, *The Acting Person*, 106.

Personalism takes up with conviction the centrality of this feature in the constitution of man and his existence, but presents it in a self-referential way (accepting some Kantian intuitions). The norms of morality do not appear, therefore, as rules which an external authority—parents, society, the Church, God—imposes from outside, but as the expression of the person's being in his dynamic aspect. "I should do the good," because to do what is good perfects and enriches me, fulfils me as a person. "I must avoid evil" because it harms me and others. As we saw in the Lublin School, and also in Scheler and Guardini from another perspective, personalism fully adopts the basic presuppositions of realist ethics, but insists on their foundation in the person, on their recognition through moral experience and on their motivating character, which should present the good in such a way that the person, in spite of the difficulties which always accompany its realization, decides to carry it out.

4.7 | Transcendence

Finally we shall mention the *religious dimension*. The perfection of man contrasts paradoxically with the prominence of his limits, with illness, finitude, and ignorance. The human mind, despite its greatness, is faced with questions which it cannot resolve by its own means: the ultimate meaning of life, the justification of the existence of suffering, the meaning of death and the mystery of the hereafter, the identity of God. These *ultimate questions*, as well as the very structure of the person, which man does not give to himself but finds in his own being, postulate and require the existence of a superior Being who makes understandable the existence of human nature and those ultimate questions as basic as they are irresolvable.[72] And, since the human being is a person, such a

---

72. It is a concept similar to Jaspers's limit situations: "situations which we cannot get out of and which we cannot change." K. Jaspers, *La filosofía desde el punto de vista de la existencia*, trans. José Gaos (Mexico: Fondo De Cultura Economica, 1953), 17. Originally published as *Einführung in di Philosophie*. See also Karl Jaspers, *Philosophy*, trans. E. B. Ashton (Chicago: University of Chicago Press, 1969–71), sec. 3, chap. 7, "The Limit-Situations."

superior being cannot simply be an unmoved mover, a Being infinitely perfect and Omnipotent but impersonal and anonymous; it must also, in some way difficult to know and grasp, be a Person, similar to the human person, but infinitely perfect.[73] As Jacques Grevillot said,

> according to personalism, God is essentially *person*. He is, as Marcel likes to say, a "Thou." I am not facing him "like one thing facing another, more powerful and grandiose thing, but as a person in the presence of another person." In other words, being is essentially personal. The person is not a quality of being which appears at the terminus of a long evolution, like a complement of substances which would constitute the solid structure of the real. God is the person who creates other persons and maintains with them, by means of the world which reveals him and which he has created for them, personal relations. Here is the final word which explains everything.[74]

5 | Personalism as a New Philosophy

To conclude, we shall set out some of the more innovative features of personalism. The difference from the previous section is that these features are not only original modifications of traditional subjects (such as freedom or the good), but rather new subjects which, for that very reason, demonstrate the conceptual and philosophical originality of personalism.

5.1 | From the "What" to the "Who": The Personalist Turn

One of the essential features of modern philosophy is that it has impressed on Western philosophy the anthropological turn which made man the center of philosophical reflection. Abandoning the theocentric

---

73. See Josef Seifert, *Erkenntnis der Vollkommenen: Wege der Vernunft zu Gott* (Bonn: Lepanto Verlag, 2010); and Harry R. Klockre, "The Personal God of John Henry Newman," *Pacific Philosophical Quarterly* 57, no. 2 (1976): 145–81.

74. Jacques Grevillot, *Las grandes corrientes del pensamiento contemporáneo: existencialismo, marxismo, personalismo cristiano* (Madrid: Rodas, 1973), 254.

stance of the Middle Ages, man became the axis of philosophy and the point of departure for Descartes, Kant, and others.

This new perspective, however, only touched upon the person superficially. Descartes's *cogito*, the Transcendental Ego of Kant or Husserl, the Marxist man, Hegel's system, and Nietzsche's Superman, all converge negatively in not having used the concept of person in a decisive way. But, in addition and above all, these theories did not take into account the decisive aspect which one only discovers when one values each woman and each man *individually*: the presence of an ultimate, irreducible, unrepeatable dimension, which turns each subject of the human species into a unique *who*, that is, into a person.[75]

The road to this conviction was long and complex, and only in the twentieth century was a full philosophical awareness of it reached. Kierkegaard opened a breach which led to the rebellion against Hegel's system; the realist phenomenologists and some existentialists contributed to it in a very significant way; and finally personalist philosophy led to it in full. And thus was the anonymous individual of the Enlightenment finally transformed into a personal "I" who achieves the integration into his structure of an essential community of nature with the rest of mankind and a difference so profound that we can state with Luigi Pareyson, that, in the case of man, "every individual is, to say it in some way, unique in his species."[76] This intellectual process which has transformed the anonymous rationalist subject into a singular and unrepeatable person, and converted a *what* with a human nature into a personal and irreducible *who*, can be described as *the personalist turn of contemporary philosophy*,[77] to which practically all the personalist philosophers have contributed: Marías, Wojtyła, Marcel, Guardini, Polo, Zubiri, Mounier, and so on.

---

75. See Robert Spaemann, *Persons: The Difference between "Someone" and "Something,"* trans. Oliver O'Donovan (Oxford: Oxford University Press, 2006).
76. Pareyson, *Esistenza e persona* (Genoa: Il Melangolo, 1985), 176.
77. See Juan Manuel Burgos, ed., *El giro personalista: del qué al quién* (Salamanca: Fundación Emmanuel Mounier, 2011).

5.2 | The "Three-Dimensional" Structure of the Person

Classical philosophy insisted upon the integral unity of man in terms of body and soul. The paradigm is St. Thomas Aquinas, who, with his description of the soul as the substantial form of the body, integrated the Platonic and Aristotelian traditions in search of unity: a subsistent soul which is also functionally and operatively related to a body.

The brilliance of this development is well known, but we may ask ourselves if this approach fully achieved its objective, above all on an *operative* level, because, despite the existence of this unity formally *de jure*, it could fall victim to a certain *de facto* dualism, as seen in the tendency—almost inevitable due to the bi-partition of the person—to assign each of the human qualities, structures or dimensions to the body *or* to the soul; to think of man as a composite of body *and of* soul, and, in this sense, to operationally perpetuate a dualism, despite the intention, in theory, to eliminate it. On the other hand, this division leaves in no man's land some structures which do not fit well with either of the two dimensions, such as the structures related with levels of not entirely lucid consciousness, for example, sleep, some imaginative processes, the unconscious, and so on. And it is also very complex to deal with everything related to subjectivity as an experience.

While not ignoring that these processes, structures, or faculties can be tackled from the classical perspective, it seems better and closer to anthropological experience to distinguish *three levels in the person*: the somatic, the psychological, and the spiritual.[78] This approach achieves two very important objectives. It avoids any possible operative dualism, incompatible with a triple system. And it opens up a more sophisticated anthropological structure which permits a more detailed and complete analysis of psychological, emotional, experiential, and similar concepts.

---

78. This structure can be found in Wojtyła and Frankl *inter alia*.

5.3 | Affectivity and Subjectivity

Dietrich von Hildebrand is one of the personalists who has most forcefully argued for the centrality of affectivity and the heart, but, in one way or another, all of them have sought to overcome an anthropology which has emphasized the intellect and will to the detriment of affectivity because of its presumed irrationality and non-spiritual character. Affectivity, in effect, has been presented as a secondary and destabilizing feature, as an unstable impulse closely connected to the body, and capable of infecting the purity of the operations of the intellect and will. It is true that occasionally it has been noted that affectivity, passion, contributes a force which, when correctly managed, adds to the efficacy of action, but even from this positive perspective it is usually presented as a secondary force always undermined by the danger of sentimentalism.

To overcome this vision of things—a process which is indispensable for achieving an integral anthropology—it is necessary to affirm two theses. The first is the *originality* of affectivity, that is, its radical difference from knowledge and from human dynamism. To this end, affectivity must be understood as an "experience of oneself," as the way in which the subject is aware before himself of what he experiences, knows, and lives. Feeling is neither knowing nor wanting. Feeling is feeling, like seeing is seeing. It is an original anthropological dimension. In the second place, it is necessary to realize that this anthropological feature extends to the threefold structure of the person: body, psyche, and spirit. There is a bodily affectivity: the way in which we feel the body; there is a psychological affectivity: the emotions; and there is a spiritual affectivity which, in addition, gives account of some of our most profound personal experiences, the relations of affection and of love with our loved ones.

Affectivity is also framed in the context of subjectivity and consciousness. To experience oneself, to have a unique and unrepeatable personal world, is an essential feature of the human being which, in addition, is exactly what makes him a "who." Attention to subjectivity is, therefore, wholly decisive in the construction of an integral anthropology, since if there is no subjectivity there is no subject and thus no person.

Finally, it is very important to stress explicitly that subjectivity and subjectivism are two very different concepts. Subjectivism is a relativistic epistemological attitude. Subjectivity is an anthropological datum. Man poses subjectivity as a matter of fact, and thus one must affirm, in Wojtyła's terms, that subjectivity is an objective reality and, consequently, that any realist philosophy must give an account of it if it wishes to live up to its name.[79]

5.4 | Interpersonality

The centrality of interpersonality has already been emphasized, particularly in the treatment of philosophy of dialogue. Man is born of a relationship between two parents, and just after being born, he establishes with them—especially with the mother—a very intense bond which decisively affects his future. Likewise, relations with friends, education, and culture influence the construction of his identity. Moreover, interpersonal relations are not passive, they are not limited to the influences that the person receives, but rather they are the anthropological environment for his self-realization by means of self-giving: "Man, who is the only creature on earth which God willed for itself, cannot fully find himself except through a sincere gift of himself."[80] The person must give himself in relation in order to construct himself in a paradoxical process that transforms the process of going out of oneself into an enrichment and strengthening of one's own identity.

Personalism has typically expressed this process by means of the beautiful formula of the constitution of the "I" through the "Thou,"

---

79. "To discriminate clearly between man's 'subjectivity'—which we are here considering together with the analysis of consciousness—and 'subjectivism' as a mental attitude. To have shown the subjectivity of the human person is fundamental for the realistic position of this study." Wojtyła, *The Acting Person*, 56–57.

80. Vatican Council II, *Gaudium et spes* (December 7, 1965), no. 24.

which emphasizes the decisive importance of the Other in the constitution of personal identity. The beauty of this discovery has led some to a kind of mysticism of the relation, which so exalts the substance and relevance of interpersonal structures that it can endanger personal identity. In this context, it seems to us that we must be attentive to the precise content of these theses, since, in our judgment, if an ontological primacy of the relation is coherently upheld, it would in practice incur in an anti-personalist theory proximate to a group collectivism. The person would cease to be an end in himself and become a means for the relation. In fact, great personalists such as Nédoncelle, Guardini, and even Buber himself have taken care to stress the importance of "distance" in theories of relation in order not to lose the personal substrate.

This tendency, in some Catholic positions, manifests itself in an overvaluation of the analogy between man and the Trinitarian God, applying to the former the model of divine relationality, that is, seeing man as relation: with other humans or with God. Certainly, the Trinitarian conception of God is an unsurpassable call regarding the relevance of this dimension *in man*, a point which Christian philosophy was unable to recognize for centuries. Thomas Aquinas, for example, had no problem defining a divine Person as a subsistent relation,[81] but on the anthropological level, he tended to understand man as a substance, in which relation played an accidental role (along the lines of Aristotle). Twentieth-century Catholic philosophy and theology overcame this limit, recognizing the possibility of applying the relational character of God to the human person, on the basis of the *imago Dei*. But the application of this new perspective should be done with moderation, since man is *not* God, and concretely, a *direct and automatic* application of divine relationality could generate the dissolution of man as a subsistent being. The human person is an individual being who enters into relation,[82] but not a subsistent, personal relation. Adam and Eve were created as

---

81. "Persona igitur divina significat relationem ut subsistentem." Thomas Aquinas, *Summa theologiae* I, q. 29, a. 4, c.

82. See John Macmurray, *Persons in Relation* (London: Faber, 1961).

independent beings, although in relation, as John Paul II's theology of the body has brilliantly shown. To transform them into a subsistent relation would be equivalent to dissolving them into nothingness, since relation, in the world of humans, is only viable from individual persons. Without human persons, there is no relation.

5.5 | The Primacy of Action and Love

Personalism has decisively opted to overcome Aristotle's intellectualism under the direct inspiration of Christianity, which not only upholds the primacy of charity, as St. Paul affirmed: "So abideth faith, hope, charity, these three; but the greatest of these is charity" (1 Cor 13:13 AV). But a much more amazing and extraordinary saying is, "God is love" (1 Jn 4:16). In fact, one of the reasons that led Aristotle to maintain the primacy of the intellect was the theoretical impossibility of applying action to the divinity because that would mean admitting necessity into it. "Still, every one supposes that they (the gods) live and therefore that they are active; we cannot suppose them to sleep like Endymion. Now if you take away from a living being action, and still more production, what is left but contemplation?"[83] Christianity radically resolved this problem by conceiving of God who loves, and still more, a God who is love. And the personalists applied themselves to extracting the philosophical and anthropological consequences.

One of the consequences is the revaluation of will, action, and praxis. Will, taken to be self-determining freedom, is, from this perspective, ontologically superior to purely intellectual activity. And thus a change in the philosophical focus occurs. The primacy of intellect led during many centuries to a disproportionate increase in epistemological sub-departments such as logic, critique, and gnoseology (the theory of

---

83. Aristotle, *Nicomachean Ethics*, bk. 10, chap. 7 (1178b5–25), in *The Complete Works of Aristotle: The Revised Oxford Translation*, vol. 2, ed. Jonathan Barnes (Princeton, N.J.: Princeton University Press, 1984).

exact knowledge), along with a parallel neglect of action. Now, the practical aspect, praxis in its multiple dimensions, becomes decisive in as much as it is the medium in which man expresses and transforms himself; and finally one becomes aware that, to understand man, one has to understand the many dimensions of his activity. This orientation has made it possible for personalism to begin to tackle many spheres which the realist tradition, and scholasticism in particular, had only outlined: work, aesthetics, economics, social philosophy, politics, and so on.

Moreover, as a particularly decisive element, personalism emphasizes the primacy of love as the guiding factor in human activity and as a decisive thematic action, which gives meaning to life in the context of interpersonal relations.[84] A human life without love, in which someone had not been loved or had not been able to love, would certainly be an inhuman and radically incomplete life.[85]

5.6 | Corporeality. Sexuality. Man as Male and Female

Corporeality appears in personalism as a personal reality, that is, as the overcoming of a merely biological vision of the body on which the spirit would exert influence. The body is the somatic dimension *of the person*, and, in this sense, it is inseparable from him. *There is not a body without a person.*

To correctly set out this conception, it is necessary to stress the bodily-psychological-spiritual unity which allows the person, present

---

84. Love should not be understood as a "generic act of the will," a concept that is far too abstract and confusing, but as a unique type of interpersonal relation. "Genuine love only exists between persons. We refer only to this love." Jean Mouroux, *Sentido cristiano del hombre*, trans. Mateo de Torre (Madrid: Palabra, 2001), 265, originally published as *Sens chrétien de l'homme* (Paris: Aubier, 1945).

85. See Jean Guitton, *Essay on Human Love* (London: Rockcliff, 1951); Maurice Nédoncelle, *Love and the Person*, trans. Sr. Ruth Adelaide (New York: Sheed and Ward 1966); Denis de Rougemont, *Passion and Society*, 2nd. ed., trans. Montgomery Belgion (London: Faber, 1956); C. S. Lewis, *The Four Loves* (London: Fount Paperbacks, 1977); Vladimir Solovyov, *The Meaning of Love*, trans. Thomas R. Beyer Jr. (London: Steiner Books, 1985); Juan José Pérez-Soba, *El amor: introducción a un misterio* (Madrid: BAC, 2011).

in all three dimensions or, better still, who unfolds and is structured through these dimensions, to manifest himself as a person in and through his body. This is not to say that there is no strictly biological part of man, but that corporeality is more than biology or, if you like, is personalized biology. Marcel, Stein, and many others have tried to express this idea in formulae which show the non-instrumental character of corporeality.

Going further, sexuality can then be understood, as Marías and Wojtyła did, as a particular dimension of being a person, rooted in biology, but transcending it and affecting the very constitution of the subject. The person, in effect, not only has a masculine or feminine biology but *is* man or woman; is a masculine person or a feminine person, because having a sexual identity affects, configures, and modulates all human structures, as neurology is currently demonstrating in an undeniable way.[86]

Finally, we can also note that personalism has the instruments to formulate a *philosophy of the family* thanks to its integral theory of the person, corporeality, sexuality, interpersonality, man as male and female, and love. It must be pointed out, however, that this philosophy, to a great extent, has yet to be constructed, since it must tackle the specific subjects pertaining to the family: paternity, maternity, filiation, fraternity—a ground where almost everything remains to be done.[87] What personalism has already worked out is a very original and powerful theory of marriage, whose most decisive influence can be found in the transfiguration of the Catholic theology of marriage which led to the personalist approaches present in the Second Vatican Council's Pastoral Constitution on the Church in the Modern World *Gaudium et Spes*.[88]

---

86. See Louann Brizendine, *The Female Brain* (London: Bantam Books, 2007); Giulia Paola di Nicola, *La reciprocità uomo-donna* (Rome: Città Nuova, 1988); Natalia Lopéz Moratalla, *Cerebro de mujer y cerebro de varón* (Madrid: Rialp, 2007).

87. See also Rocco Buttiglione, *L'uomo e la familia* (Rome: Dino Editore, 1991).

88. As is well known, Cardinal Wojtyła intervened very decisively in the composition of this document. Wojtyła had been thinking deeply about love and marriage in response to questions from and discussion with young people, and it was just prior to the council

5.7 | Communitarian Personalism

The personalist understanding of community and society has already been described in some detail in the introduction and in the exposition of the thought of Mounier and Maritain. Therefore we shall briefly state now that personalism anchors itself between the extremes of liberal individualism and the collectivisms, with the objective of avoiding both the risk of making the individual a mere appendix of the social body (collectivism) and that of making him an active and relevant being but lacking in solidarity and seeking only his own good, disinterested in his fellow citizens (liberal individualism).

The sociopolitical influence of personalism has been great, especially in the decades after World War II. The moral shock that followed the experience of the horrors of the war generated a very strong conviction that every means must be taken to prevent anything like it from happening again. In this context, personalism appeared as a suitable and opportune instrument to give shape to this moral impulse on a sociopolitical level. In this way, important leaders and even entire political groups were inspired by its principles, and, by their many actions, personalism came to influence such important events as the working out of some national constitutions (Germany, Italy and, later, Spain) and the Universal Declaration of Human Rights (1948), proclaimed by United Nations, in which Jacques Maritain played a notable part.[89]

(1960) that his book *Miłość i odpowiedzialność* (*Love and Responsibility*) had been published. See *Karol Wojtyla: Un estilo conciliar. Las intervenciones de Karol Wojtyla en el Concilio Vaticano II*, ed. Gabriel Richi Alberti (Madrid: Publicaciones San Dámaso, 2010).

89. This influence is still current, as can be seen in "Du personnalisme à l'action politique" [Grandes Conférences Catholiques], *Notes et Documents* (Institut International Jacques Maritain) 34 (December 2009): 36–40, by the first permanent president of the European Union, Herman van Rompuy.

5.8 | Further Expansions

As a final reflection, we shall point out that personalism is initiating a process of expansion by which it seeks to apply its anthropological principles to new spheres. This task is not straightforward since, to reach substantive results in a particular area and not just general indications, there is a need for people who are experts both in personalist anthropology and in the specific area of expansion, and this is not easy to find.

Probably the sphere in which most progress has been made so far is that of personalist bioethics, thanks to the proposals made in this subject over the course of many years by Elio Sgreccia and his work group, who have given rise to the FIBIP (International Federation of Bioethics Centers of Personalist Inspiration).[90] It is easy to see that personalist anthropology can contribute a sound philosophical basis to a bioethics in defense of the dignity of the person, at the same time as it offers interesting conceptual instruments for analyzing the interpersonal relations which are established between medical personnel and patients as well as their relatives and friends.

Also, an interesting dialogue is being opened between personalism and contemporary communitarianism—as represented by Alasdair MacIntyre, Charles Taylor, Amitai Etzioni, Michael Sandel, and Michael Walzer, among others[91]—based on the intuition that communitarianism could be the link between interpersonal relations and political philosophy, a link which is lacking in personalist anthropologies, which have focused almost exclusively on the person and interpersonal relations and dealt only sporadically with simple social structures (groups,

---

90. See Elio Sgreccia, *Personalist Bioethics: Foundations and Applications*, trans. John A. Camillo and Michael J. Miller (Philadelphia: The National Catholic Bioethics Center, 2012); James Beauregard, "Personalism and Global Bioethics: The Contribution of the Modern Ontological Personalism of J. M. Burgos," *Quien* 2 (2015): 77–89.

91. See Stephen Mulhall and Adam Swift, *Liberals and Communitarians* (Oxford: Blackwell, 1992).

neighborhoods, and informal support systems) and still less with the more complex ones.

A nascent, but very promising, sphere are the studies on personalist psychology which aim, in the first place, to establish a systematic dialogue with the humanistic psychology of Carl Rogers, Abraham Maslow, and others, and, in particular, with the logo-therapy of Viktor Frankl, since his anthropological presuppositions are personalist; and, secondly, toward the possible formulation of a specifically personalist psychology, on which X. M. Domínguez[92] and J. L. Cañas[93] are working in Spain and Rosa Zapién in Mexico through her project on "Integrative Personalist Psychology."[94] Also, it appears possible to apply personalism to economics,[95] especially in the areas directly related to personnel management, to education, and to some areas of jurisprudence and philosophy of law.

It should be acknowledged, in any case, that in almost all these matters, this sort of thinking is still incipient even though a promising future can be glimpsed, since the perception of the potentiality of personalism continues to increase, as does the number of interested persons.

---

92. See Xosé Manuel Domínguez, *Psicología de la persona* (Madrid: Palabra, 2012).

93. See José Luis Cañas, *Antropología de las adicciones: psicoterapia y rehumanización* (Madrid: Dykinson, 2014).

94. See Rosa Zapién, "La psicología integrativa personalista: hacia un nuevo paradigm de intervención clínica, Quién," *Revista de filosofía personalista* 4 (2016): 113–135.

95. See Gloria L. Zuñiga, "What Is Economic Personalism? A Phenomenological Analysis," *Journal of Markets & Morality* 4, no. 2 (2001): 151–75; Domènec Melé, "Integrating Personalism into Virtue-based Business Ethics: The Personalist and the Common Good Principles," *Journal of Business Ethics* 88, no. 1 (2009): 227–44. And Richard T. Allen, "Personalism and the Free Market," *Appraisal* 9, no. 4 (October 2013): 33–51.

Bibliography

Spanish-language materials or translations are frequently featured due to the author's composing the original book in Spanish. English-language versions are also provided when available.

Acosta, Miguel, and Adrian Reimers. *Karol Wojtyla's Personalist Philosophy: Understanding Person and Act.* Washington, D.C.: The Catholic University of America Press, 2016.

Allen, Richard T. "Personalism and the Free Market." *Appraisal* 9, no. 4 (October 2013): 33–51.

Amato, Joseph. *Mounier and Maritain. A French Catholic Understanding of the Modern World.* Tuscaloosa, Ala.: University of Alabama Press, 1975.

Aristotle. *Nicomachean Ethics.* In *The Complete Works of Aristotle: The Revised Oxford Translation*, vol. 2. Edited by Jonathan Barnes. Princeton, N.J.: Princeton University Press, 1984.

Augustine of Hippo. *Confessions.* Translated by Vernon J. Rourke. Fathers of the Church 21. Washington, D.C.: The Catholic University of America Press, 1953.

———. *De Trinitate.* Translated by Stephen McKenna, C.Ss.R., as *The Trinity*, The Fathers of the Church 45 (Washington, D.C.: The Catholic University of America Press, 1963).

Balboni, Paolo E. "Annotazioni storico-guiridiche." In Balboni, *Mounier trent'anni dopo: Atti del Convegno di studio dell'università cattolica.* Milan: Vita e Pensiero, 1981.

Barré, Jean Luc. *Jacques et Raïssa Maritain: Les mendiantes du ciel.* Paris: Stock, 1995. Translated by Bernard Doering as *Jacques and Raïssa Maritain: Beggars for Heaven* (South Bend, Ind.: University of Notre Dame Press, 2005).

Bartnik, Czesław. *Oeuvres rassemblées,* vol. 16, *Le Phénomène de la nation.* Lublin: Standruk, 2005.

———. *Studies in Personalist System.* Lublin: KUL, 2007.

Beauregard, James. "Personalism and Global Bioethics: The Contribution of the Modern Ontological Personalism of J. M. Burgos." *Quien* 2 (2015): 77–89.

Bengtsson, Jan Olof. *The Worldview of Personalism: Origins and Early Development.* Oxford: Oxford University Press, 2006.

Bertocci, Peter A. *Introduction to the Philosophy of Religion.* New York: Prentice-Hall, 1951.

———. "The Essence of a Person." *The Monist* 671, no. 1 (1978): 28–41.

———. "Why Personalistic Idealism?" *Idealistic Studies* 10, no. 3 (1980): 181–98.

Bombaci, Nunzio. *Emmanuel Mounier: Una vida, un testimonio.* Translated by Carlos Diaz. Persona 4. Salamanca: Fundación Emmanuel Mounier, 2002.

Bowne, Borden P. *The Principle of Ethics.* New York: Harper & Brothers, 1892.

———. *Metaphysics.* Rev. ed. New York: Harper and Brothers, 1898.

———. *Personalism.* 1908. Reprint, Miami: Hard Press, 2013.

Brightman, Edgar S. *Person and Reality.* Edited by Peter A. Bertocci, Janette E. Newhall, and Robert S. Brightman. New York: Ronald Press, 1958.

Brizendine, Louann. *The Female Brain.* London: Bantam Books, 2007.

Brock, Stephen L. *Action and Conduct: Thomas Aquinas and the Theory of Action.* Edinburgh: T&T Clark, 1988.

Bubbio, Paolo D., ed. *Luigi Pareyson: Existence, Interpretation, Freedom: Selected Writings.* Translated by Anna Mattei. Aurora, Colo.: The Davies Group, 2009.

Buber, Martin. *I and Thou.* Translated by Walter Kaufmann. New York: Scribner's Sons, 1970.

———. *Eclipse of God: Studies in the Relationship between Religion and Philosophy.* Westport, Conn.: Greenwood Press, 1977.

———. *¿Qué es el hombre?* Translated by Eugenio Imaz. Mexico: FCE, 1984. Translated by Ronald Gregor-Smith as "What Is Man?" in *Between Man and Man* (New York: Routledge, 2002).

———. *Über Gemeinschaft und deren Verwirklichung.* Heidelberg: Verlag Lambert Schneider, 1985.

———. *Paths in Utopia*. Translated by R. F. Hull. Syracuse, N.Y.: Syracuse University Press, 1996.

———. *The Knowledge of Man: Selected Essays*. Translated by Maurice Friedman and Ronald Gregor-Smith. Amherst, N.Y.: Prometheus Books, 1998.

———. *Gog and Magog: A Novel*. Translated by Ludwig Lewisohn. Syracuse, N.Y.: Syracuse University Press, 1999.

———. *Between Man and Man*. Translated by Ronald Gregor-Smith. Syracuse, N.Y.: Routledge, 2002.

Bucci, Onorato. "La formazione del concetto di persona nel cristianesimo delle origini: 'avventura semantica' e itinerario storico." *Lateranum N.S.* 2 (1988): 383–450.

Buckham, J. W., and G. M. Stratton, eds. *George Holmes Howison, Philosopher and Teacher*. Berkeley, CA: University of California Press, 1934.

Burgos, Juan Manuel. *La inteligencia ética. La propuesta de Jacques Maritain*. Bern: Peter Lang, 1995.

———. *El personalismo: Autores y temas de una filosofía nueva*. Madrid: Palabra, 2000.

———. *Para comprender a Jacques Maritain*. Salamanca: Fundación Emmanuel Mounier, 2005.

———. *Repensar la naturaleza humana*. Pamplona: EUNSA, 2007.

———. "The Method of Karol Wojtyła: A Way between Phenomenology, Personalism and Metaphysics." *Analecta husserliana* 104 (2009): 107–29.

———, ed. *El giro personalista: del qué al quién*. Salamanca: Fundación Emmanuel Mounier, 2011.

———. *Antropología: una guía para la existencia*, 6th ed. Madrid: Palabra, 2017.

———. *Para comprender a Karol Wojtyła: Una introducción a su filosofía*. Madrid, BAC, 2014.

———. "El personalismo ontológico moderno. I. Arquitectónica," *Quién* 1 (2015): 9–29.

———. "El personalismo ontológico moderno. II. Claves antropológicas," *Quién* 2 (2015): 7–32.

———. *La experiencia integral: un método para el personalismo*. Madrid: Palabra, 2015.

———. "Integral Experience: A New Proposal on the Beginning of Knowledge." In *The Sphere of the Personal: New Perspectives in the Philosophy of Persons*, edited by James Beauregard and Simon Smith, 41–59. Wilmington, Del.: Vernon Press, 2016.

Burrows, Rufus. *Personalism: A Critical Introduction*. St. Louis, Mo.: The Chalice Press, 1999.

Busch, Thomas W., ed. *The Participant Perspective: A Gabriel Marcel Reader*. Lanham, Md.: University Press of America, 1987.

Buttiglione, Rocco. *Karol Wojtyła: The Thought of the Man Who Became Pope John Paul II*. Translated by Paolo Guietti and Francesca Murphy. Grand Rapids, Mich.: Wm. B. Eerdmans Publishing Co., 1997.

———. *L'uomo e la familia*. Rome: Dino Editore, 1991. Translated by Antonio Esquivias as *La persona y la familia* (Madrid: Palabra, 1999).

Campoamor, Ramón de. *El personalismo: Apuntes para una filosofía*. Madrid: M. Rivadeneyra, 1855.

Cañas, José Luis. "¿Renacimiento del personalismo?" *Anales del Seminario de Historia de la filosofía* 18 (2001): 151–76.

———. *Antropología de las adicciones: psicoterapia y rehumanización*. Madrid: Dykinson, 2014.

Carpintero, Helio. "La originalidad teórica del pensamiento de Marías." *Cuenta y Razón del pensamiento actual* 87 (1993): 89–91.

Colomer, Agustì, and August Monzón, eds. *Emmanuel Mounier i la tradició personalista*. Valencia: Universitat de Valencia Press, 2001.

Coll, Josep Maria. "Mounier i els corrents personalistes." In Coll and others, *Emmanuel Mounier i el personalisme*, 51–77. Barcelona: Cruïlla, 2002.

Collingwood, Robin G. *The Idea of History*. Oxford: Oxford University Press, 1946. Revised edition 1993.

———. *Faith and Reason: Essays in the Philosophy of Religion by R.G. Collingwood*. Edited by Lionel Rubinoff. Chicago: Quadrangle, 1967.

———. *Essay on Metaphysics*. Oxford: Oxford University Press, 1940. Revised edition 1998.

Conford, Philips, ed. *The Personal World: John Macmurray*. Edinburgh: Floris Books, 1996.

Copleston, Frederick. *A History of Philosophy*, vol. 9, *Modern Philosophy*. London: Search Press, 1975.

Crosby, John F. *The Selfhood of the Human Person*. Washington, D.C.: The Catholic University of America Press, 1996.

———. *Personalist Papers*. Washington, D.C.: The Catholic University of American Press, 2003.

———. *The Personalism of John Henry Newman*. Washington, D.C.: The Catholic University of America Press, 2014.

Dahl, Robert A. *On Democracy*. New Haven, Conn.: Yale University Press, 2000.

Deats, Paul, and Carol Robb, eds. *The Boston Personalist Tradition in Philosophy, Social Ethics, and Theology*. Macon, Ga.: Mercer University Press, 1986.

Díaz, Carlos. *Corriente arriba: Manifiesto personalista y comunitario*. Madrid: Encuentro, 1985.

———. *¿Qué es el personalismo communitario?* Salamanca: Fundación Emmanuel Mounier, 2002.

———. *El "nuevo pensamiento" de Franz Rosenzweig*. Salamanca: Fundación Emmanuel Mounier, 2008.

Doménach, Jean-Marie. *Dimensiones del personalismo*. Barcelona: Nova Terra, 1969.

———. "La presenza di Mounier nella cultura europea del dopoguerra." In *Mounier trent'anni dopo. Atti del Convegno di studio dell'università cattolica*. Milano: Vita e Pensiero, 1981.

Domingo Moratalla, Agustín. *Un humanismo del siglo XX: el personalismo*. Madrid: Pedagógicas, 1985.

Domínguez, Xosé Manuel. "El personalismo comunitario de Carlos Díaz." *Persona* 9 (2008): 45–46.

———. *Psicología de la persona*. Madrid: Palabra, 2012.

Ebner, Ferdinand. *The Word and the Spiritual Realities: A Translation of and Critical Introduction to Ferdinand Ebner's "Das Wort und die geistigen Realitäten" and a Comparison with Martin Buber's "Ich und Du."* Translated by Harold Johnson Green. Evanston, Ill.: Northwestern University, 1980. Originally published as *Das Wort und die geistigen Realitäten: Pneumatologische Fragmente. Die Geschichte der Fragmente*, ed. Richard Hörmann (Berlin: LIT-Verlag, 2009).

Etzioni, Amitai. *My Brother's Keeper: A Memoir and a Message*. Lanham, Md.: Rowman and Littlefield, 2003.

Farrer, Austin. *Finite and Infinite*. Westminster: Dacre Press, 1943.

———. *The Freedom of the Will*. London: A. & C. Black, 1958.

———. *Faith and Speculation*. London: A. & C. Black, 1967.

———. *Reflective Faith*. London: SPCK, 1972.

Fazio, Mariano. *Historia de las ideas contemporáneas: una lectura del proceso de secularización*. Madrid: Rialp, 2006.

———. *Cristianos en la encrucijada: Los intelectuales cristianos en el período de entreguerras*. Madrid: Rialp, 2008.

Fazio, Mariano, and Francisco Fernández Labastida. *Historia de la filosofía*, vol. 4, *Filosofía contemporánea*, 2nd ed. Madrid: Palabra, 2009.

Ferre, Fredrick. *Living and Value: Toward a Constructive Postmodern Ethics*. Albany, N.Y.: The State University of New York Press, 2001.

Feuerbach, Ludwig. *The Essence of Christianity*. Translated by George Eliot. Originally published in 1841. Amherst, NY: Prometheus, 1989.

Flewelling, Ralph Tyler. "Personalism." In *Twentieth Century Philosophy: Living Schools of Thought*, ed. D. R. Runes, 321–341. New York: Philosophical Library, 1943.

———. *The Person; or The Significance of Man*. Los Angeles: The Ward Ritchie Press, 1952.

Frankl, Viktor. *Psychotherapy and Existentialism*. New York: Washington Square Press Books, 1985.

Francis, Pope. *Laudato Si'*. Encyclical letter. May 24, 2015. http://w2.vatican.va/content/francesco/en/encyclicals/documents/papa-francesco_20150524_enciclica-laudato-si.html.

Frings, Manfred. *The Mind of Max Scheler*. Milwaukee, Wis.: Marquette University Press, 1997.

Gacka, Bogumil. *American Personalism*. Lublin: Oficiyna Wydawnicza "Czas," 1995.

———, ed. *Bibliography of American Personalism*. Lublin: Wydawnicza Czas, 1994.

Gerl, Hanna Barbara. *Romano Guardini (1885–1968), Leben und Werk*. Mainz: Grünewald, 1985.

Gilson, Étienne. *Le réalisme méthodique*. Paris: Pierre Téqui, 1935. Translated by Philip Trower as *Methodical Realism* (Front Royal, Va.: Christendom Press, 1990).

———. *Por un orden católico*. Translated by J. A. Maravall. Madrid: Cruz y Raya, 1936.

———. *History of Christian Philosophy in the Middle Ages*. London: Sheed and Ward, 1955.

González Álvarez, Angel. *Tratado de Metafísica*, vol. 1, *Ontología*. Madrid: Gredos, 1967.

Granat, Wincenty. *Osoba ludzka* [The Human Person]. Sandomierz: Wydawnictwo Diecezjalne, 1961. Reprinted Lublin: Wydawnictwo KUL, 2006.

Grevillot, Jacques. *Las grandes corrientes del pensamiento contemporáneo: existencialismo, marxismo, personalismo cristiano*. Madrid: Rodas, 1973.

Guardini, Romano. *The Spirit of the Liturgy*. Translated by Ada Lane. New York: Sheed & Ward, 1935.

———. *The End of the Modern World*. London: Sheed & Ward, 1957. Revised edition, Wilmington, Del.: ISI Books, 1998.

———. *The World and the Person*. Translated by Stella Lange. Chicago: Henry Regnery, 1965.

———. *Persona e libertà. Saggi di fondazione della teoria pedagógica*. Brescia: La Scuola, 1987.

———. *The Lord*. Translated by Elinor Briefs. Washington, D.C.: Regnery Publishing, 1996.

———. "El salvador en el mito, la religión y la política." In Romano Guardini, *Escritos políticos*, translated by José Mardomingo, 27–88. Palabra: Madrid, 2010.

Guena, Sylvain. *Correspondence Jacques Maritain et Emmanuel Mounier (1929–49)*. Paris: Desclée de Brouwer, 2016.

Guitton, Jean. *Essay on Human Love*. London: Rockcliff, 1951.

Guzowski, Krzysztof. "Different Personalities, One Person? Wincenty Granat's Proposal Concerning Personalism." *Appraisal* 6, no. 1 (March 2006): 28–32.

———. "Bartnik, Czeslaw." In *Enciclopedia della persona nel XX secolo*, edited by Antonio Pavan, 85–90. Naples: ESI, 2008.

———. "Granat, Wincenty." In *Enciclopedia della persona nel XX secolo*, edited by Antonio Pavan, 407–9. Naples: ESI, 2008.

Habermas, Jürgen, and Ratzinger, Joseph. *The Dialectics of Secularization: On Reason and Religion*. Translated by Brian McNeil, edited by Florian Schuller. San Francisco: Ignatius Press, 2006.

Heidegger, Martin. "Letter on Humanism." In *Martin Heidegger: Basic Writings*, edited by David F. Krell. New York: Harper and Row, 1977.

Hellman, John. *Emmanuel Mounier and the New Catholic Left 1930–1950*. Toronto: University of Toronto Press, 1981.

Howie, John. "W. E. Hocking's Transfigured Naturalism." In *A William Ernest*

Hocking Reader with Commentary, edited by John Lachs and D. Micah Hester. Nashville, Tenn.: Vanderbilt University Press, 2004.

Husserl, Edmund. *Logical Investigations*. Translated by J. N. Findlay. London: Routledge, 1973.

———. *Ideas Pertaining to a Pure Phenomenology and to a Phenomenological Philosophy, Book I*. Translated by Fred Kersten. The Hague: Nijhoff, 1989.

James, William. *The Will to Believe and Other Essays in Popular Philosophy*. New York: Dover, 1956.

Jaspers, Karl. *La filosofía desde el punto de vista de la existencia*. Translated by José Gaos. Mexico: Fondo De Cultura Economica, 1953.

———. *Philosophy*. Translated by E. B. Ashton. 3 vols. Chicago and London: University of Chicago Press, 1969–71.

John Paul II, Pope. "Lettera al 'Convegno promosso nel centenario della nascita di Jacques Maritain,' 5-VIII-1982." In *Jacques Maritain oggi*, edited by V. Possenti, 17–22. Milan: Vita e Pensiero, 1983.

———. *Crossing the Threshold of Hope*. Translated by Jenny McPhee and Martha McPhee. New York: Knopf, 1995.

———. *Gift and Mystery*. New York: Doubleday, 1996.

———. *Fides et Ratio*. Encyclical letter. September 14, 1998.

———. *Man and Woman He Created Them: A Theology of the Body*. Translated by Michael Waldstein. Boston: Pauline Books & Media, 2006.

———. *Memory and Identity: Conversations at the Dawn of a Millenium*. New York: Rizzoli, 2005.

John Paul II, with André Frossard. *Be Not Afraid*. Translated by J. R. Foster. London: Rockcliff, 1984.

Kant, Immanuel. *The Moral Law: Kant's Groundwork of the Metaphysics of Morals*. Translated by H. J. Paton. London: Hutchinson, 1948.

Kierkegaard, Sören. *Diary*, vol. 11. 1854. Edited by Cornelio Fabro. Brescia: Morcelliana, 1982.

Kitching, Gavin. *Karl Marx and the Philosophy of Praxis*. London: Routledge, 1988.

Klockre, Harry R. "The Personal God of John Henry Newman." *Pacific Philosophical Quarterly* 57, no. 2 (1976): 145–181.

K. M. B. "An Intimate Portrait of Bowne." *The Personalist* 2 (1921): 5–15.

Knudson, Albert Cornelius. *The Philosophy of Personalism*. New York: The Abingdon Press, 1927.

Koninck, Charles de. *De la primauté du bien commun contre les personalistes.* 1943. Montreal: Éditions de l'Université Laval, 1952.
Kuhn, Thomas. *The Structure of Scientific Revolutions*, 3rd ed. Chicago: University of Chicago Press, 1996.
Lacroix, Jean. *El personalismo como anti-ideología.* Translated by Evandro Botto. Madrid: Guadiana, 1973. Originally published as *Le personnalisme comme anti-idéologie* (Paris: P.U.F., 1972).
Landsberg, Paul. *Problemas del personalismo.* 1937. Salamanca: Fundación Emmanuel Mounier, 2006.
Lazea, Dan. "The Ontological Personalism of Luigi Pareyson: From Existentialism to the Ontology of Liberty." *Appraisal* 6, no. 1 (March 2006): 7–16.
Legaz Lacambra, Luis. "Sentido humanista del nacional-sindicalismo." *Jerarquía* 3 (1938): 94–112.
Leo XIII, Pope. *Aeterni Patris.* Encyclical letter. August 4, 1879. https://w2.vatican.va/content/leo-xiii/en/encyclicals/documents/hf_l-xiii_enc_04081879_aeterni-patris.html.
Lévinas, Emmanuel. *Totality and Infinity: An Essay on Exteriority.* Translated by Alphonso Lingis. Pittsburgh, Pa.: Duquesne University Press, 1969.
Lewis, C. S. *The Four Loves.* London: Fount Paperbacks, 1977.
Lewis, Hywel D. *The Elusive Mind.* London: Allen & Unwin, 1969.
———. *The Self and Immortality.* London: Allen & Unwin, 1973.
———. *The Elusive Self.* London: Allen & Unwin, 1982.
Lopéz Moratalla, Natalia. *Cerebro de mujer y cerebro de varón.* Madrid: Rialp, 2007.
López Quintás, Alfonso. *Pensadores cristianos contemporáneos.* Madrid: BAC, 1968.
———. *Filosofía española contemporánea.* Madrid: BAC, 1970.
———. *The Knowledge of Values: A Methodological Introduction.* Lanham, Md.: University Press of America, 1989.
———. *Signs of Admiration.* United States: Qualfon University, 2014.
Lorda, Juan Luis. *Antropologia cristiana: Del Concilio Vaticano II a Juan Pablo II.* Madrid: Palabra, 1996.
Lozano, Sergio. *La interpersonalidad en Karol Wojtyla.* Valencia: Edicep, 2016.
Lubac, Henri de. *The Drama of Atheist Humanism.* Translated by Edith M. Riley, Anne Englund Nash, and Mark Sebanc. London: Sheed & Ward, 1949.
Macmurray, John. *Freedom in the Modern World.* London: Faber, 1932.

——. *Interpreting the Universe*. London: Faber, 1933.

——. *Reason and Emotion*. London: Faber, 1935.

——. *The Boundaries of Science: A Study in the Philosophy of Psychology*. London: Faber, 1939.

——. *The Conditions of Freedom*. London: Faber, 1949.

——. *The Self as Agent*. London: Faber, 1957.

——. *Persons in Relation*. London: Faber, 1961.

——. *Selected Philosophical Writings*. Edited by Esther McIntosh. Exeter, UK: Imprint Academic, 2004.

Mander, W. J., and Alan Sell, eds. *Dictionary of Nineteenth Century British Philosophers*. Bristol, UK: Thoemmes Press, 2002.

Marcel, Gabriel. *Du réfus à l'invocation*. Paris: Gallimard, 1940. Re-issued as *Essai de philosophie concrète* (Paris: Gallimard, 1999). Translated by Robert Rosthal as *Creative Fidelity* (New York: Fordham University Press, 2002).

——. *Men Against Humanity*. Translated by G. S. Fraser. London: Harvill Press, 1952.

——. *Homo Viator*. Translated by Emma Craufurd. London: Harper, 1962.

——. *Dos discursos y un prólogo autobiográfico*. Barcelona: Herder, 1967.

——. *Être et avoir I (1928–1933)*. Translated by Katherine Farrer as *Being and Having: An Existentialist Diary* (New York: Harper & Row, 1965).

——. "Concrete Approaches to Investigating the Ontological Mystery." In Marcel, *Gabriel Marcel's Perspectives on the Broken World*, translated by Katharine Rose Hanley (Chicago: Marquette University Press, 1998), 172–209. Originally published as *Positions et approches concrètes du Mystère ontologique* (Paris: J. Vrin, 1949).

Mardas, Nancy, Agnes B. Curry, and George F. Mclean, eds. *Karol Wojtyła's Philosophical Legacy*. Washington, D.C.: Council for Research in Values and Philosophy, 2008.

Marías, Julián. *Introducción a la filosofía*. Madrid: Revista de Occidente, 1967. Translated by Kenneth S. Reid and Edward Sarmiento as *Reason and Life: The Introduction to Philosophy* (New Haven, Conn.: Yale University Press, 1956).

——. *Antropología metafísica*. Madrid: Alianza, 1970. Translated by Frances M. López-Morillas as *Metaphysical Anthropology: The Empirical Structure of Human Life* (University Park, Pa.: Pennsylvania State University Press, 1971).

———. *La felicidad humana*. Madrid: Alianza, 1994.

———. *Persona*. Madrid: Alianza, 1997.

———. *Mapa del mundo personal*. Madrid: Alianza, 2006.

———. *Una vida presente: Memorias*. Madrid: Páginas de Espuma, 2008.

Maritain, Jacques. *La philosophie bergsonienne*. Paris: Rivière, 1914.

———. *Trois réformateurs: Luther, Descartes, Rousseau*. 1925. Translated as *Three Reformers: Luther, Descartes, Rousseau* (New York: Charles Scribner's Sons, 1929).

———. *Primauté du spirituel*. Paris: Plon, 1927. Translated by J. F. Scanlan as *The Things That Are Not Caesar's* (London: Sheed & Ward, 1932).

———. *Sept leçons sur l'être*. Paris: Pierre Téqui, 1933. Translated as *A Preface to Metaphysics: Seven Lectures on Being* (New York: Sheed and Ward, 1939).

———. *Humanisme intégral*. 1936. Translated by Joseph Evans as "Integral Humanism: Temporal and Spiritual Problems of a New Christendom," in *The Collected Works of Jacques Maritain*, vol. 11, *Integral Humanism, Freedom in the Modern World, and A Letter on Independence*, translated by Otto Bird, Joseph Evans, and Richard O'Sullivan (Notre Dame, Ind.: University of Notre Dame Press, 1996), 141–345.

———. *The Rights of Man and the Natural Law*. Translated by Doris C. Anson. New York, Charles Scribner's Sons, 1943.

———. *Christianity and Democracy*. Translated by Doris C. Anson. London, Centenary Press, 1945.

———. *Court traité de l'existence et de l'existant*. Paris: Hartmann, 1947. Translated by Lewis Galantière and Gerald B. Phelan as *Existence and the Existent* (New York: Pantheon Books, 1948).

———. *Man and the State*. Chicago: University of Chicago Press, 1951.

———. *Neuf leçons sur les notions premières de la philosophie morale*. Paris: Pierre Téqui, 1951. Translated by Cornelia N. Borgerhoff as *An Introduction to Basic Problems of Moral Philosophy* (Albany, N.Y.: Magi Books, 1990).

———. *Reflections on America*. New York: Scribner, 1958.

———. *Le Paysan de la Garonne*. Paris: Desclée de Brouwer, 1966. Translated by Micheal Cuddihy and Elizabeth Hughes as *The Peasant of the Garonne: An Old Layman Questions Himself about the Present Time* (New York: Holt, Rinehart, and Winston, 1968).

———. *The Person and the Common Good*. Translated by John Fitzgerald. Notre Dame, Ind.: University of Notre Dame Press, 1966.

———. *La loi naturelle ou loi non écrite: texte inédit*. Edited by Georges Brazzola. Fribourg, Suisse: Éditions universitaires, 1986. Translated by William Sweet as "Lectures on Natural Law," in *The Collected Works of Jacques Maritain*, vol. 6 (Notre Dame, Ind.: University of Notre Dame Press, forthcoming).

———. *Oeuvres complètes*, vol. 11, *Le philosophe dans la cité*. Paris: Ed. Saint-Paul, 1992.

———. *Oeuvres complètes*, vol. 12, *Carnet de notes*. Paris: Ed. Saint-Paul, 1992. Translated by Joseph W. Evans as *Notebooks* (Albany, N.Y.: Magi Books, 1984).

Maritain, Raïssa. *Les grandes amitiés*. Paris: Desclée de Brower, 1949. Translated by Julie Kernan as *We Have Been Friends Together: Memoirs* (New York: Longmans, Green and Co., 1942).

Marx, Karl, and Friedrich Engels. *The Communist Manifesto*. New York: Pocket Books, 1964.

MacIntyre, Alasdair. *Three Rival Versions of Moral Enquiry*. London: Duckworth, 1990.

———. *Edith Stein: A Philosophical Prologue*. Lanham, Md.: Rowman & Littlefield Publishers, 2006.

McCool, Gerard A. *From Unity to Pluralism: The Internal Evolution of Thomism*. New York: Fordham University Press, 1992.

McLeod, Hugh, and Ustorf, Werner, eds. *The Decline of Christendom in Western Europe (1750–2000)*. Cambridge: Cambridge University Press, 2003.

Melé, Domènec. "Integrating Personalism into Virtue-based Business Ethics: The Personalist and the Common Good Principles." *Journal of Business Ethics* 88, no. 1 (2009): 227–44.

Michel, Johann. *Paul Ricoeur, un philosophie de l'agir humain*. Paris: Cerf, 2006.

Mill, John Stuart. *On Liberty*. New Haven : Yale University Press, 2003.

Mondin, Battista. *Storia dell'Antropologia Filosofica*, vol. 2, *Da Kant ai giorni nostri*. Bologna: Edizioni Studio Domenicano, 2002.

Mounier, Emmanuel. *Manifeste au service du personnalisme*. 1936. In *Oeuvres*, vol. 1, *1931–1939*, 481–649. Paris: Éditions du Seuil, 1961. Translated by Monks of St. John's Abbey as *A Personalist Manifesto*, edited by Joseph T. Delos et al. (New York: Longman, Green, 1938).

———. *Qu'est-ce que le personnalisme?* Paris, Éditions du Seuil, 1947. Republished in *Oeuvres*, vol. 3, *1944–1950*. Paris, Éditions du Seuil, 1962. Translated by Cynthia Rowland as "What Is Personalism?" in *Be Not Afraid* (London, Rockcliff, 1951; reprinted New York: Sheed and Ward, 1962), 109–196.

———. *Introduction to the Existentialisms*. Translated by Philip Mairet. London: Methuen, 1948.

———. *Feu la Chrétienté*. Paris, Éditions du Seuil, 1950. Republished in *Oeuvres*, vol. 3, *1944–1950*. Paris, Éditions du Seuil, 1962.

———. *Personalism*. Translated by Philip Mairet. London: Routledge and Kegan Paul, 1952.

———. *L'affrontement chrétien*. In *Oeuvres*, vol. 1, *1931–1939*. Paris: Éditions du Seuil, 1961.

———. *Personnalisme et Christianisme*. In *Oeuvres*, vol. 1, *1931–1939*, 841–70. Paris: Éditions du Seuil, 1961. Translated as "Personalism and Christianity," in *Race, Nation, Person* (New York: Barnes and Noble, 1944), 323–80.

———. *Révolution personnaliste et communautaire*. In *Oeuvres*, vol 1, *1931–1939*. Paris: Éditions du Seuil, 1961.

———. *Communisme, anarchie, personnalisme*. Paris: Éditions du Seuil, 1966.

Mounier, Paulette. "Cristiani e non credenti nell'ambito del personalismo." In *Mounier trent'anni dopo. Atti del Convergo di studio dell'università cattolica*. Milan: Vita e Pensiero, 1981.

Mouroux, Jean. *Sens chrétien de l'homme*. Paris: Aubier, 1945. Translated by A. H. C. Downes as *The Meaning of Man* (London: Sheed & Ward, 1948).

Mulhall, Stephen, and Adam Swift. *Liberals and Communitarians*. Oxford: Blackwell, 1992.

Nédoncelle, Maurice. *La réciprocité des consciences*. Paris: Aubier, 1942.

———. "Prosopon et persona dans l'antiquité classique. Essai de bilan linguistic." *Revue des Sciences Religieuses* 22, no. 3–4 (1948): 277–99.

———. *De la fidélité*. Paris: Aubier Editions Montaigne, 1953.

———. *Conscience et logos: Horizons et méthodes d'une philosophie personnaliste*. Paris: Editions de l'Epi, 1961.

———. *Love and the Person*. Translated by Sr. Ruth Adelaide. New York: Sheed and Ward 1966.

———. *Persona y naturaleza humana. Estudio lógico y metafísico*. Translated by Carlos Díaz. Salamanca: Fundación Emmanuel Mounier, 2005.

Nicola, Giulia Paola di. *La reciprocità uomo-donna*. Rome: Città Nuova, 1988.

Norgaard Mortensen, Jonas. *The Common Good: An Introduction to Personalism*. Wilmington, Del.: Vernon Press, 2017.

Notthingham, William J. *Christian Faith and Secular Action: An Introduction* to the Life and Thought of Jacques Maritain. St. Louis, Mo.: The Bethany Press, 1968.

O'Malley, John B. *The Fellowship of Being: An Essay on the Concept of Person in the Philosophy of Gabriel Marcel*. The Hague: Nijhoff, 1966.

Pareyson, Luigi. "Filosofia e Verità (interview with Marisa Serra)." *Studi Cattolici* 193 (1977): 171–79.

———. *Verità e Interpretazione*. Milan: Mursia, 1982. Translated by Robert T. Valgenti as *Truth and Interpretation* (Albany, N.Y.: SUNY Press, 2013).

———. *Esistenza e persona*. Genoa: Il Melangolo, 1985.

Pavan, Antonio. *La formazione del pensiero di J. Maritain*, 2nd ed. Padova: Libreria Gregoriana Editrice, 1985.

Pearce, Joseph. *Literary Converts: Spiritual Inspiration in an Age of Unbelief*. London: Harper Collins, 1999.

Peces-Barba, Gregorio. *Persona, sociedad, estado*. Madrid: Cuadernos para el diálogo, 1972.

Pérez-Soba, Juan José. *El amor: introducción a un misterio*. Madrid: BAC, 2011.

Polanyi, Michael. *Meaning*. With Harry Prosch. Chicago: Chicago University Press, 1974.

———. *Science, Faith and Society*. London: Oxford University Press, 1946.

———. *The Logic of Liberty*. London: Routledge, 1951.

———. *Personal Knowledge: Towards a Post-Critical Philosophy*. London: Routledge, 1958.

———. *The Study of Man*. London: Routledge, 1959.

———. *The Tacit Dimension*. Doubleday: New York, 1966.

———. *Knowing and Being*. Edited by Marjorie Grene. London: Routledge, 1969.

———. *Meaning*. With Harry Prosch. Chicago: Chicago University Press, 1974.

———. *Society, Economics and Philosophy: Selected Papers by Michael Polanyi*. Edited by Richard T. Allen. Rutgers, N.J.: Transaction Publishers, 1997.

Polo, Leonardo. *Antropología transcendental*, vol. 1, *La persona humana*. Pamplona: EUNSA, 1999.

Possenti, Vittorio. *Il principio persona*. Rome: Armando Editore, 2006.

Pringle-Pattison, Andrew S. *Hegelianism and Personality*. Edinburgh: William D. Blackwood and Sons, 1887. Reprint, London: Bibliolife, 2009.

Raley, Harold. *Responsible Vision: The Philosophy of Julián Marías*. Indiana: Clear Creek, Ind.: American Hispanist, 1980.

———. *A Watch Over Mortality: The Philosophical Story of Julián Marías*. Albany, N.Y.: State University of New York Press, 1997.

Ratzinger, Joseph. *Milestones: Memoirs 1927–1997*. Translated by Erasmo Leiva-Merikakis. San Francisco: Ignatius Press, 2005.

Reimers, Adrian. *Truth about the Good: Moral Norms in the Philosophy of John Paul II*. Ave Maria, Fla.: Sapientia Press, 2011.

Ricoeur, Paul. "Une philosophie personnaliste." *Esprit* 174, no. 12 (1950): 860–87. Translated by Charles A. Kelbley as "Emmanuel Mounier: A Personalist Philosopher," in Ricoeur, *History and Truth* (Evanston, Ill.: Northwestern University Press, 1965), 133–61.

———. "Meurt le personnalisme, revient la personne." *Esprit* 73, no. 1 (1983): 113–19. Translated by Tomás Domingo Moratalla as "Muere el personalismo, vuelve la persona ...," in *Amor y justicia* (Madrid: Caparrós, 1993), 95–104.

———. *Oneself as Another*. Translated by Kathleen Blamey. Chicago: The University of Chicago Press, 1992.

———. "Self as Ipse." In *Freedom and Interpretation*, edited by Barbara Johnson, 103–19. New York: Basic Books, 1993.

———. *Figuring the Sacred: Religion, Narrative and Imagination*. Translated by David Pellauer, edited by Mark I. Wallace. Minneapolis: Fortress Press, 1995.

———. "Intellectual Autobiography." In *The Philosophy of Paul Ricoeur*, edited by L. E. Hahn, 3–53. Library of Living Philosophers 22. Chicago: Open Court Publishing Co., 1995.

Rigobello, Armando. *Il contributo filosofico di E. Mounier*. Rome: Bocca, 1955.

———. *Il personalismo*, 2nd ed. Rome: Città Nuova, 1978.

Rogers, Carl. *On Becoming a Person: A Therapist's View of Psychotherapy*. London: Constable, 1961.

———. *Dialogues*. Edited by Howard Kirschenbaum and Valerie L. Henderson. London: Constable, 1990.

Rosenzweig, Franz. *Franz Rosenzweig's "The New Thinking."* Translated by Alan Udoff and Barbara E. Galli. Syracuse, N.Y.: Syracuse University Press, 1999.

Rougemont, Denis de. *Passion and Society*, 2nd ed. Translated by Montgomery Belgion. London: Faber, 1956.

Rourke, Thomas and Rosita C. Rourke. *A Theory of Personalism*. Lanham, Md.: Lexington Books, 2005.

Santamaria, Carlos. *Jacques Maritain y la polémica del bien común*. Madrid: Asociación Católica Nacional de Propagandistas, 1955.

Sartre, Jean-Paul. *Existentialism and Humanism*. Translated by Philip Mairet. London: Methuen, 1949.

Scheler, Max. *Wesen und Formen der Sympathie*. 1913. 5th ed. Frankfurt am Main: Verlag G. Schulte-Bulmke, 1948. Translated by Peter Heath as *The Nature of Sympathy* (London: Routledge, 1954).

———. *Der Formalismus in der Ethik und die materiale Wertethik: Neuer Versuch der Grundlegung eines ethischen Personalismus, 1913–16*, 6th ed. Berlin: Franke Verlag, 1980. 1st–5th eds. published as vol. 2 of *Gesammelte Werke* (Bern, Franke Verlag 1971). Translated by Manfred S. Frings and Roger Funk as *Formalism in Ethics and Non-Formal Ethics of Values: A New Attempt Toward the Foundation of an Ethical Personalism* (Evanston, Ill.: Northwestern University Press, 1973).

———. *Problems of a Sociology of Knowledge*. Translated by Kenneth W. Stikkers. London: Routledge, 1980.

———. *Person and Self-Value: Three Essays*. Translated by Manfred S. Frings. Dordrecht: Martinus Nijhoff, 1987.

Sciacca, Michele Federico. *La filosofía dello spirito*. Turin, Italy: Societa editrice internazionale, 1951.

Seifert, Josef. "El concepto de persona en la renovación de la Teología Moral." In *El primado de la persona en la moral contemporáneo*. Pamplona: EUNSA, 1997.

———. *Erkenntnis der Vollkommenen: Wege der Vernunft zu Gott*. Bonn: Lepanto Verlag, 2010.

Sgreccia, Elio. *Personalist Bioethics: Foundations and Applications*. Translated by John A. Camillo and Michael J. Miller. Philadelphia: The National Catholic Bioethics Center, 2012. Originally published as *Manuale di bioethica*, vol. 1, *Fondamenti ed etica biomedica* (Milan: Vita e Pensiero, 2007).

Solovyov, Vladimir. *The Meaning of Love*. Translated by Thomas R. Beyer Jr. Library of Russian Philosophy. Steiner Books, 1985.

Spaemann, Robert. *Persons: The Difference between "Someone" and "Something."* Translated by Oliver O'Donovan. Oxford: Oxford University Press, 2006.

Stein, Edith. *Zum Problem der Einfühlung*. Freiburg i. Br.: Univ., 1916. Translated by Waltraut Stein as *On the Problem of Empathy* (Washington, D.C.: ICS Publications, 1989).

———. *Collected Works*, vol. 1, *Life in a Jewish Family: An Autobiography, 1891–1916*. Translated by Josephine Koeppel. Washington, D.C.: ICS Publications, 1986.

———. *Collected Works*, vol. 2, *Essays on Woman*. Translated by Freda Mary Oben. Washington, D.C.: ICS Publications, 1987.

———. *Collected Works*, vol. 9, *Finite and Eternal Being: An Attempt at an Ascent to the Meaning of Being*, trans. Kurt F. Reinhardt. Washington, D.C.: ICS Publications, 2002.

Stefanini, Luigi. *Personalismo sociale*, 2nd ed. Rome: Studium, 1979.

Szulc, Tad. *Pope John Paul II: The Biography*. London: Simon and Schuster, 2007.

Tallis, Raymond. *The Hand: A Philosophical Inquiry into Human Being*. Edinburgh: Edinburgh University Press, 2003.

———. *I Am: A Philosophical Inquiry into First Person Being*. Edinburgh: Edinburgh University Press, 2004.

———. *The Knowing Animal: A Philosophical Inquiry into Knowledge and Truth*. Edinburgh: Edinburgh University Press, 2005.

Thomas Aquinas. *Summa theologiae*. Literally translated by Fathers of the English Dominican Province as *The Summa Theologiæ of St. Thomas Aquinas*, 2nd and rev. edition (London: Burns, Oates and Washbourne, 1920). http://www.newadvent.org/summa/.

———. *Quaestiones disputatae de potentia Dei*. Translated by the English Dominican Fathers as *Disputed Questions on the Power of God* (Westminster, Md.: The Newman Press, 1952). http://dhspriory.org/thomas/QDdePotentia.htm.

———. *Scriptum super libros Sententiarum* [Commentary on the *Sentences* of Peter Lombard]. (No full English-language translation exists.)

Troisfontaines, Roger. *De l'existence à l'être: La philosophie de G. Marcel*. 2 vols. Leuven: Nauwelarts, 1968.

Trower, Philip. *Turmoil and Truth: The Historical Roots of the Modern Crisis in the Catholic Church*. Oxford: Family Press, 2003.

Tusell, Javier. *El personalismo en España*. Madrid: Fundación Humanismo y Democracia, 1985.

Van der Meer, Pieter. *Hombres y Dios*. Translated by W. de Ulupe. Buenos Aires: Desclée de Brower, 1949.

Van Rompuy, Herman. "Du personnalisme a l'action politique" [Grandes Conférences Catholiques]. *Notes et Documents* (Institut International Jacques Maritain) 34 (December 2009): 36–40.

Vatican Council II. *Gaudium et Spes*. December 7, 1965. http://www.vatican.va/archive/hist_councils/ii_vatican_council/documents/vat-ii_const_1965 1207_gaudium-et-spes_en.html.

Von Balthasar, Hans Urs. *The God Question and Modern Man*. Translated by Hilda Graef. New York: Seabury Press, 1956.

Von Hildebrand, Alice. *The Soul of a Lion: Dietrich Von Hildebrand: A Biography*. San Francisco: Ignatius Press, 2000.

Von Hildebrand, Dietrich. *Liturgy and Personality*. New York: Longmans, Green and Co., 1943.

———. *Transformation in Christ*. New York: Longmans, Green and Co., 1948.

———. *Ethics*. Chicago: Franciscan Herald Press, 1953.

———. *What Is Philosophy?* Chicago: Franciscan Herald Press, 1973.

———. *The Heart*. Chicago: Franciscan Herald Press, 1977.

———. *The Nature of Love*. South Bend, Ind.: St. Augustine's Press, 2010.

———. *Aesthetics*. Steubenville, Ohio: Hildebrand Project, 2015.

Von Reinach, Adolf. "Concerning Phenomenology." *The Personalist* 50, no. 2 (1969): 194–211. In *The Apriori Foundations of the Civil Law: Along with the Lecture "Concerning Phenomenology."* Berlin: De Gruyter, 2012.

Waldenfels, Bernhard. *Einführung in die Phänomenologie*. Munich: Fink, 1992.

Weber, Max. *The Protestant Ethic and the Spirit of Capitalism*. Translated by Talcott Parsons. New York: Scribner, 1958.

Weigel, George. *Witness to Hope: The Biography of Pope John Paul II*. New York: Harper Collins, 2001.

Werkmeister, William H. *A History of Philosophical Ideas in America*. New York: Ronald Press, 1949. Reprint Westport, Conn.: Greenwood, 1981.

Winock, Michel. *Histoire politique de la revue Esprit (1930–50)*. Paris: Editions du Seuil, 1975.

Wojtyła, Karol. *Doctrina de fide apud S. Joannem a Cruce*. STD diss. Rome: Pontifical University of St. Thomas Aquinas, 1948. Translated by Jordan Aumann as *Faith According to St. John of the Cross* (San Francisco: Ignatius Press, 1981).

———. "La experiencia religiosa de la pureza." 1953. In *El don del amor. Escritos sobre la familia*, 5th ed. Madrid: Palabra, 2006.

———. *Ocena możliwości zbudowania etyki chrześcijańskiej przy założeniach systemu Maksa Schelera* [Evaluation of the Possibilities of Building Christian Ethics on the Principles of Max Scheler's System]. Lublin: Catholic University of Lublin, 1959.

———. *The Acting Person*. Translated by Anna-Teresa Tymieniecka. Annalecta Husserliana 10. Dordrecht: D. Reidel Pub. Co, 1979.

———. *Love and Responsibility*. Translated by H. T. Willetts. San Francisco: Ignatius Press, 1981. Originally published as *Miłość i odpowiedzialność* (Krakow: Wydawnicto, Znak, 1960).

———. "The Person: Subject and Community." In Wojtyła, *Person and Community: Selected Essays*, trans. Theresa Sandok, OSM (New York: Peter Lang, 1993), 219–261. Originally published as "Osoba: Podmiot i wspólnota," *Roczniki Filozoficzne* 24, no. 2 (1976): 5–39.

———. "El personalismo tomista." In *Mi visión del hombre*, 6th ed. Translated by Pilar Ferrer. Madrid: Palabra, 2006.

Zank, Michael, and Zachary Braiterman. "Martin Buber." In *The Stanford Encyclopedia of Philosophy*, Winter 2014 edition, edited by Edward N. Zalta. http://plato.stanford.edu/archives/win2014/entries/buber/.

Zubiri, Xabier. *El hombre y Dios*. Madrid: Alianza-Fundación Xavier Zubiri, 1984.

———. *Inteligencia sentiente: Inteligencia y realidad*. Madrid: Alianza, 1984.

Zuñiga, Gloria L. "What Is Economic Personalism? A Phenomenological Analysis." *Journal of Markets & Morality* 4, no. 2 (2001): 151–75.

Zurdo, Manuel. *La verdad sobre Emmanuel Mounier: De Mounier a la teología de la violencia*. Madrid: Iris de Paz, 1969.

Index

Acosta, Miguel, 177
Adamczyk, Stanislaw, 103
Allen, Richard, ix, 163, 169, 233
Amato, Joseph, 64
Aquinas, Thomas, x, 24, 25, 27, 28–30, 32, 40, 43, 44–46, 48, 49, 105–7, 111, 120, 176, 179, 196, 199, 202, 204, 210, 224, 227
Aristotle, x, 30, 111, 124, 129, 132, 176, 202, 204, 227, 228
Augustine of Hippo, St., 120, 140, 176, 196, 216

Balboni, Paolo, 99
Barré, Jean-Luc, 39
Bartnik, Czeslaw, 55, 102, 103, 115, 117–19, 34
Basave Fernández del Vall, Agustín, 142
Beauregard, James, 208, 232
Bengtsson, Jan O., 164, 170
Bentham, Jeremy, 9
Berdyaev, Nikolai, 27, 35, 64, 66, 182, 185
Bergson, Henri-Louis, 17, 35, 36, 39, 40, 43, 56, 64, 86
Bernanos, Georges, 27, 102
Bertocci, Peter Anthony, 174
Blondel, Maurice, 17, 32, 35, 37, 64, 86

Bloy, Léon, 3, 27, 35, 37, 39, 84
Boethius, 196, 204
Bombacci, Nunzio, 32
Bonaventure, St., 138, 196
Bonhöffer, Dietrich, 32
Bosanquet, Bernard, 164
Bowne, Border Parker, 170, 171, 173, 200
Bradley, Francis H., 56, 164
Brentano, Franz, 22
Brightman, Edgar Sheffield, 174
Brizendine, Louann, 230
Brunschvicg, Léon, 86
Bubbio, Paolo D., 95, 98
Buber, Martin, 2, 12, 16, 32, 54, 60, 119, 120, 127, 129–35, 153, 160, 179, 194, 200, 209, 212, 227
Buber, Salomon, 129
Buford, Thomas O., 174, 176
Burgos, Juan Manuel, ix, x, 30, 31, 39, 47, 48, 104, 142, 150, 156, 159–61, 180, 194, 205–8, 223, 232
Busch, Thomas W., 56
Buttiglione, Rocco, 101, 103, 230

Caird, Edward, 164
Campanini, Giorgio, 100
Cañas, José Luis, 56, 156, 198, 233

255

256 Index

Carlini, Armando, 91, 92, 93
Caturelli, Alberto, 142
Chagall, Marc, 40
Chenaux, Philipe, 100
Chenu, Marie-Dominique, 32
Chévalier, Jacques, 64, 68
Claudel, Paul, 27, 40
Clerissac, Humbert, 44
Cocteau, Jean, 40
Cohen, Hermann, 128
Coleridge, Samuel T., 56, 163
Coll, Josep Maria, 191, 202
Collingwood, R. G., 165
Comín, Alfonso, 148
Conrad, Theodor, 23
Copleston, Frederick, 29
Croce, Benedetto, 91
Crosby, John F., 17, 170, 176, 177, 216
Crosby, John Henry, 177

d'Agostino, Francesco, 100
Dahl, Robert A., 52
Dali, Salvador, 43
dalla Torre, Giuseppe, 100
Danese, Attilio, 100
Dante Alligeri, 43, 137, 139
de Campoamor, Ramón, 67
de Gasperi, Alcide, 100
de Gaulle, Charles, 41
de Koninck, Charles, 54
Déléage, André, 65, 83
de Lubac, Henri, 196
Derisi, Nicolás, 142
Derrida, Jacques, 120
Descartes, René, 5, 29, 40, 46, 48, 166, 169, 208, 223
Díaz, Carlos, 19, 32, 64, 86, 136, 142, 148, 150, 159, 160, 191
di Nicola, Giulia P., 230
Doménach, Jean-Marie, 37, 65, 81
Domingo, Agustín, 34
Domingo, Tomás, 186

Domínguez, Xosé Manuel, 159, 160, 233
Donati, Pier Paolo, 100
Dostoyevsky, Fyodor, 139

Ebner, Ferdinand, 127, 128, 136, 209
Einstein, Albert, 166
Engels, Friedrich, 13
Etzioni, Amitai, 130, 232
Evans, Joseph W., 14, 39, 51

Fabre, Geneviéve, 39
Fabro, Cornelio, 20, 46
Farrer, Austin, 165, 166
Farrer, Katherine, 61
Fazio, Mariano, 27, 122, 208
Fernández Labastida, Francisco, 122
Feuerbach, Ludwig, 6, 13, 196
Fichte, Johann G., 164
Fitzgerald, John, 48, 184
Flewelling, Ralph T., 175
Francis, Pope, 140
Frankl, Viktor, 196, 206, 224, 233

Gacka, Bogumil, 170, 173
Gadamer, Hans-Georg, 96
Garrigou-Lagrange, Réginald, 48, 60, 105
Gentile, Giovanni, 91
Gerl, Hanna Barbara, 137
Gilson, Étienne, 8, 26–29, 40, 41, 61, 102
Gioberti, Vicenzo, 92
González Álvarez, Ángel, 210
Granat, Wincenty, 103, 115, 116
Green, Harold J., 127, 209
Green, Julien, 40
Gregor-Smith, Ronald, 16, 131
Grevillot, Jacques, 222
Grote, John, 163
Guardini, Romano, 15, 27, 119, 120, 126, 137–42, 146, 160, 162, 194, 221, 223, 227
Guena, Sylvain, 41
Guitton, Jean, 64, 68, 229
Guzowski, Krzysztof, 115, 116

Habermas, Jürgen, 208
Hamilton, William, 163
Hegel, George W., 1, 12, 13, 20, 21, 91, 164, 170, 172, 179, 208
Heidegger, Martin, 120, 135, 196
Hellman, John, 81
Hobbes, Thomas, 9
Hölderlin, Friedrich, 139, 140
Howison, George H., 175
Hume, David, 9, 106, 163
Husserl, Edmund, 5, 21–23, 38, 86, 123, 125, 200, 223

Ingarden, Roman, 23, 102, 125
Izard, Georges, 65, 83

Jacobi, Friedrich H., 163
Jaspers, Karl, 38, 95, 221
John the Evangelist, St., 128
John Paul II, Pope St., 18, 44, 45, 101, 103, 104, 105, 108, 115, 116, 136, 150, 177, 212, 214, 215, 228. *See also* Wojtyła, Karol

Kant, Immanuel, 1, 5, 9, 17–19, 91, 92, 106, 107, 110, 121, 163, 164, 170–72, 179, 185, 199, 208, 223
Kierkegaard, Soren, 1, 3, 5, 17, 19–21, 37, 95, 127, 139, 151, 223
King, Martin Luther, Jr., 175
Kitching, Gavin, 13
Knudson, Albert C., 174
Koyré, Alexander, 23
Krapiec, Mieczyslaw, 103
Kuhn, Thomas S., 8

Lacroix, Jean, 37, 38, 87, 160, 184, 185, 186, 191
Laín Entralgo, Pedro, 119, 142, 151–53
Landsberg, Paul, 8, 9, 16, 27, 154, 160, 212
Lavelle, Louis, 36, 88
Lazea, Dan, 95
Leclercq, Paulette. *See* Mounier, Paulette

Legaz Lacambra, Luis, 144
Leo XIII, Pope, 24, 27, 28, 44, 45
le Senne, René, 36
Lévinas, Emmanuel, 2, 57, 120, 127, 135–37, 201
Lewis, Clive S., 47, 229
Lewis, Hywel H., 165
Locke, John, 9
López Aranguren, José Luis, 149
López Quintás, Alfonso, 159, 161, 162, 230
Lorda, Juan Luis, 17, 20
Lotze, Hermann 163, 171
Lourie, Arthur, 40
Lozano, Sergio, 114

MacIntyre, Alasdair, 97, 125, 219, 232
Macmurray, John, 165–67, 227
Mansel, Henry L., 163
Marcel, Gabriel, 2, 5, 21, 27, 37, 38, 55–64, 75, 85, 87, 102, 143, 150, 154, 157, 170, 185, 194, 195, 207, 211, 212, 216, 219, 222, 223, 230
Maréchal, Joseph, 25
Marías, Julián, 109, 119, 124, 142, 145, 150, 151, 154–60, 194, 195, 204, 216, 219, 223, 230
Marion, Jean-Luc, 120
Maritain, Jacques, 2, 3, 5, 7, 8, 12, 14, 24, 27, 28, 32, 35–55, 61, 64, 67, 68, 85, 98, 99–103, 143–45, 147, 148, 154, 160, 170, 184, 191, 194, 200, 202, 209, 212, 213, 231
Maritain, Raïssa, 7, 35, 36, 42
Martius, Hedwig, 23
Marx, Karl, 13, 208
Maslow, Abraham, 196, 233
Mauriac, Francois, 27, 40
McCool, Gerald A., 25
Melchiorre, Vittorio, 92, 100
Mendizábal, Alfredo, 143
Mercier, Désiré, 25
Merleau-Ponty, Maurice, 120
Michel, Johann, 38

Mill, John Stuart, 9, 10
Miquel, Vincent, 71
Mondin, Battista, 33, 36, 87, 91, 92, 142
Montaigne, Michel de, 139
More, Thomas, 195
Mounier, Emmanuel, 2–4, 8, 9, 11, 12, 15, 19, 21, 25, 27, 30, 32, 33, 37–41, 52, 53, 55, 64–71, 73–86, 89, 95, 99, 100, 102, 119, 120, 136, 143, 144, 146–48, 150, 157, 159, 160, 170, 178–82, 184–88, 190, 192, 194, 195, 200, 201, 207, 212, 214, 217, 223, 231
Mounier, Paulette, 3, 4, 66
Mouroux, Jean, 229
Mulhall, Stephen, 232
Mussolini, Benito, 14

Nédoncelle, Maurice, 17, 32, 37, 38, 60, 85, 87–90, 119, 120, 133, 153, 160, 190, 191, 194, 207, 227, 229
Newman, John Henry, x, 17, 127, 176, 177, 222
Nietzsche, Friedrich, 6, 26
Norgaard Mortensen, Jonas, 34
Notthingham, William J., 39

O'Malley, John, 56
Ortega y Gasset, José, 120, 142, 143, 145, 151, 152, 154–56
O'Sullivan, Richard, 14, 51

Pareyson, Luigi, 95–97, 223
Pascal, Blaise, 139
Patochka, Jan, 120
Paul VI, Pope, 98
Pearce, Joseph, 27
Peces-Barba, Gregorio, 148, 149
Péguy, Charles, 27, 35, 37, 39, 76, 84, 102
Pérez-Soba, Juan José, 229
Picasso, Pablo, 43
Pieper, Joseph, 139
Pius XI, Pope, 40, 99

Plato, 132, 176
Polanyi, Michael, 165, 167–69
Polo, Leonardo, 93, 151–53, 211, 223
Popper, Karl, 8
Possenti, Vittorio, 34, 45, 100
Pringle-Pattinson, Andrew S., 164, 170

Quiles, Ismael, 142

Ratzinger, Joseph, 30, 119, 120, 208
Reimers, Adrian, 103, 177
Renouvier, Charles, 37, 185
Ricoeur, Paul, 23, 25, 38, 57, 64, 74, 120, 153, 186–91
Rigobello, Armando, 34, 64, 91, 92, 95, 100, 156
Rilke, Rainer Maria, 139, 140
Rogers, Carl, 134, 196, 233, 249
Rosenzweig, Franz, 127–30, 136, 160, 212
Rouault, Georges, 40
Rourke, Rosita C., 34
Rourke, Thomas, 34
Rourke, Vernon J., 216
Rousseau, Jean-Jacques, 40, 48
Royce, Josiah, 56

Sandel, Michel, 232
Santamaría, Carlos, 48, 54
Sapieha, Adam S., 101
Sartre, Jean-Paul, 21, 55, 120, 135, 208, 220
Satie, Erik, 40
Scheler, Max, 2, 9, 17, 19, 23, 32, 75, 86, 102, 105, 106, 108, 113, 120–23, 142, 154, 176, 194, 200, 221
Schelling, Friedrich, 56, 163
Sciacca, Michele Federico, 36
Seifert, Josef, 14, 93, 197, 199, 222
Semprún Gurrea, José María, 143, 144
Serrahima, Maurici, 143
Severini, Gino, 40
Sgreccia, Elio, 100, 232
Smith, Adam, 9

Smith, Simon, 14, 208
Solovyov, Vladimir, 229
Sorley, William R., 164
Spaemann, Robert, 223
Stefanini, Luigi, 92, 93, 94, 95, 211, 217
Stein, Edith, 5, 23–25, 27, 115, 120, 121, 124–26, 150, 160, 194, 212, 230
Stravinsky, Igor, 40
Sturzo, Luigi, 27, 143
Styzcén, Tadeusz, 106, 107
Swiezawski, Stefan, 103
Swift, Adam, 232
Szulc, Tad, 103

Taylor, Charles, 232
Thomas Aquinas, St., x, 24, 28–30, 40, 45, 111, 120, 176, 179, 196, 202, 204, 224, 227
Troisfontaines, Roger, 56
Trower, Philip, 29, 40, 55
Tusell, Javier, 147, 251

Ulrici, Hermann, 171
Unamuno, Miguel, 27, 142, 151, 158

van der Meer, Pierre, 3
von Hildebrand, Alice, 123
von Hildebrand, Dietrich, 5, 19, 24, 113, 119–24, 146, 150, 176, 177, 194, 200, 212, 225
von Reinach, Adolf, 22, 23

Wahl, Jean, 57
Waldenfels, Bernhard, 22
Walzer, Michel, 232
Watson, John, 6, 7
Weber, Max, 10
Weigel, George, 103
Winock, Michel, 65, 83
Wojtyła, Karol, x, 18, 19, 25, 47, 58, 87, 94, 101, 102, 103–15, 117, 118, 120–26, 130, 150, 157, 160, 161, 171, 176, 177, 179, 194, 201, 202, 207, 208, 212, 214, 216, 220, 223, 224, 226, 230. *See also* John Paul II
Wyszynski, Stefan 102

Zamagni, Stefano, 100
Zubiri, Xavier, 93, 142, 151–54, 194, 211, 217, 223
Zuñiga, Gloria L., 233
Zurdo, Manuel, 148

An Introduction to Personalism was designed in Meta Serif with Meta Sans and composed by Kachergis Book Design of Pittsboro, North Carolina. It was printed on 60-pound Natures Book Natural and bound by Thomson-Shore of Dexter, Michigan.

www.ingramcontent.com/pod-product-compliance
Lightning Source LLC
Chambersburg PA
CBHW051938290426
44110CB00015B/2023